THE STRAW BALE HOUSE

THE STRAW BALE HOUSE

Athena Swentzell Steen
Bill Steen
David Bainbridge
with
David Eisenberg

CHELSEA GREEN PUBLISHING COMPANY   White River Junction, Vermont

Frontispiece: Interior archways in the Hughes-Rhoades residence (see color section).

Photo and illustration credits, with page numbers:
Scott Barkdol (9 top); Mary Biggs (16); courtesy of the Burritt Museum (7; 45); Ross Burkhardt (249); Simon Butcher collection, Nebraska Historical Society (2); Thoric Cederström (16 bottom right); John Daglish (15; 97 top); David Eisenberg (5 top and middle; 11 top; 46; 66 left; 82 top; 112, 113 top left; 116; 124; 126; 245); courtesy of EOS Institute (107; 172); Mike Evans (272); courtesy of Pliny Fisk (105; 108; 114 top & middle; 118-119); Terry Henderson (16 bottom left; 93 bottom; 146; 170-71, 171 bottom); Rita Jacobian (150; 169); Judy Knox (11 bottom); Robert LaPorte (119); Terrence Moore (52, 53); courtesy of Bob Munk (109 top); Matts Myhrman (8 bottom); Brian Reeves (9 bottom); courtesy of Simonton family (4); John Swearingen (xviii); François Tanguay (164; 165; 181); Kim Thompson (14 bottom); John Valentine (8 middle); Peter Vitale (40, 42); Catherine Wanek (5 bottom; 14 top; 19; 167); Jan Wisinewski (279 perspective drawing).

Printed in the United States of America

3 4 5 6 7 8 9
95 96 97 98 99

Due to the variability of local conditions, materials, skills, site, and so forth, Chelsea Green Publishing Company and the authors assume no liability for personal injury, property damage, or loss from actions inspired by information in this book. Remember that any construction process can be dangerous. Moreover, building codes in most areas do not yet address the practice of straw bale construction, and because each new straw bale building may serve as an example and prototype for others, it is especially important that builders approach their work with due caution, care, and a sense of responsibility.

Library of Congress Cataloging-in-Publication Data:
Bainbridge, David A.
    The straw bale house / David Bainbridge, Athena Swentzell Steen,
  Bill Steen.
       p. cm. — (A real goods independent living book)
    Includes bibliographical references (p.) and index.
    ISBN 0–930031–71–7
    1. Straw bale houses—Design and construction. I. Steen, Athena
  Swentzell, 1961– . II. Steen, Bill. III. Title. IV. Series.
TH4818.S77B35 1994
693'.997—dc20   94–39518

CHELSEA GREEN PUBLISHING COMPANY
P.O. Box 428
White River Junction, Vermont 05001

This straw appears small and light, and most people do not know how really weighty it is. If people knew the true value of this straw, a human revolution could occur, which would become powerful enough to move the country and the world.

—MASANOBU FUKUOKA,
The One Straw Revolution

THE REAL GOODS INDEPENDENT LIVING BOOKS

Paul Gipe, *Wind Power for Home & Business: Renewable Energy for the 1990s and Beyond*

Michael Potts, *The Independent Home: Living Well with Power from the Sun, Wind, and Water*

Gene Logsdon, *The Contrary Farmer*

Edward Harland, *Eco-Renovation: The Ecological Home Improvement Guide*

Leandre Poisson and Gretchen Vogel Poisson, *Solar Gardening: Growing Vegetables Year-Round the American Intensive Way*

Real Goods Solar Living Sourcebook: The Complete Guide to Renewable Energy Technologies, Eighth Edition, edited by John Schaeffer

Athena Swentzell Steen, Bill Steen, and David Bainbridge, *The Straw Bale House*

Real Goods Trading Company in Ukiah, California, was founded in 1978 to make available new tools to help people live self-sufficiently and sustainably. Through seasonal catalogs, a tri-quarterly newspaper (*The Real Goods News*), the *Solar Living Sourcebook,* as well as a book catalog and retail outlets, Real Goods provides a broad range of renewable-energy and resource-efficient products for independent living.

"Knowledge is our most important product" is the Real Goods motto. To further its mission, Real Goods has joined with Chelsea Green Publishing Company to co-create and co-publish the Real Goods Independent Living Book series. The titles in this series are written by pioneering individuals who have firsthand experience in using innovative technology to live lightly on the planet. Chelsea Green books are both practical and inspirational, and they enlarge our view of what is possible as we enter the next millennium.

Ian Baldwin, Jr.
President, Chelsea Green

John Schaeffer
President, Real Goods

For all those who have wished
for a simple and comfortable home

CONTENTS

PREFACE

ATHENA SWENTZELL STEEN'S STORY

I grew up building. My mother, originally from Santa Clara Pueblo in northern New Mexico, would regularly haul my two sisters and me from our home in Santa Fe to the pueblo a half hour away, where we were expected, as part of the extended family, to participate in the continual building projects. There was always something that needed to be built: a larger bread oven, another adobe wall, or an extra room for my grandparents.

Like the rest of the pueblo, Grandma's house was constantly in flux. Walls would go up and then come down. Spaces forever shifted in order to meet changing demands. Not only the needs of the individual, family, and community had to be met, but the larger needs of nature as well. Houses, like people, were allowed to be alive. Structures were built and respected as over time they grew, flourished, and eventually died.

We would come together as a family to build. There was never a right or wrong way—we just did it however we knew how. We used whatever was close by: rocks from the wash, dirt from the side of the house, or the neighbor's melting adobe blocks. The process was not much different from making pottery and bread, and primarily involved women and children. Little ones learned as they played alongside us. Our hands coated with mud, we would let the earth take form and watch with amazement as it did. We would laugh at each other and at ourselves.

This was my mother's world. A world which taught me that the process of building and the process of being together were as important as the final product. From this way of being came a highly natural and organic aesthetic. My father, on the other hand, had his own approach to building. Thriving more on theory than in the actual doing, he would spend much more time analyzing a building on his computer than he would building it. He loved things to be simple, cheap, and easy, and, consequently, he built that way.

He was always accused of not having an aesthetic. I realize now that it wasn't a lack of an aesthetic sense, but that his was different than most. My mother could never understand how he could find breathtaking beauty in the massive power lines drolloped across the mesa, looking like "giant kachinas holding up their skirts," or in the way the highway department could slice perfectly through the middle of a hill instead of going around it. He had a way of looking beyond the principle of the thing and seeing an astonishing sense of natural order, even amidst, as my mother would call it, "the utter insensitivity of mankind." It was from these two seemingly opposed worlds that I learned to build.

In 1979, while I was in high school, we built our house on the outskirts of Santa Fe. My mother, fresh out of architecture school, was ready to build a beautiful mud home, while my father, taking a year off from teaching at a liberal arts college, wanted to build the ultimate passive solar house. I can still remember the arguments between them. Yet the house got built. With its mud floors, curved adobe walls, black water barrels, and lots of south-facing glass, it was a house I will always come back to as a model.

In the middle of winter in 1981, my first husband and I found ourselves in sudden need of shelter. We decided to build on our land on Glorieta Mesa, near Santa Fe. There was no electricity or water on the property, and being full-time students, we had very little time or money. We weren't carpenters, and working with adobe at that time of year was out of the question. We considered buying a teepee or a yurt, but after watching friends suffer through winters in such structures, we opted to look for something warmer.

In the search for something fast, easy, warm, and inexpensive, we talked to my father. As soon as he mentioned straw bales, we knew that was the answer. Enthusiastically, we began to build. Not knowing exactly what to do, we made it up as we went along, learning in the process what not to do again.

It was a cozy little one-room house. The roof rested on the bales, even though we had posts in each corner. The south side was framed with double-paned plastic panels, and 55-gallon drums for thermal mass lined the inside. Our bed was a simple loft with storage underneath. A buried tub beneath a trap door, a removable "hoola hoop" curtain, and a suspended bucket of warm water served as our shower. We burned very little wood and often had the door open during sunny winter days. We had a propane stove and refrigerator, and studied by kerosene light. The space was small but highly efficient. Quite comfortably, we lived there for five years—the last two years with babies. It was a wonderful place; however, Brian and I eventually separated, and the property and house were sold.

It was not until I received a phone call from Bill Steen, eight years later, wanting to photograph my little straw house, that I discovered that straw bales had been used historically in Nebraska as well as more recently by a handful of others.

Bill and I were soon married, and together our inspiration for working with bales grew. As we've had the opportunity to work on projects, each patio wall, guest house, wall-raising, and experimental dome has taken us ever closer to comprehending the vast potential of straw bale construction.

Now as I watch bale walls rise into highly insulated, functional space with remarkable speed, the whole process feeling more like play than work, I am reminded of my father. Watching hands of all sizes plaster the undulating walls, shaping subtle curves with layer upon layer of mud, I am reminded of my mother. Reflected in the golden walls of straw, I see their two worlds becoming one.

A.S.
Canelo, Arizona

BILL STEEN'S STORY

It seems like I have spent my life chasing those things that have stretched the limits of my imagination. The idea of building with straw bales easily fit my imagination-stretching criteria, and seemed to do the same to almost anybody I talked with. The thought of a straw bale building consistently conjured up images of insect invasions, overnight deterioration, fire, mold, rot, and total disaster.

Despite the enjoyment and entertainment provided by these conversations, and by my ongoing search for the unconventional, I now see that my greatest joy in working with straw bales has come from an unexpected source. In the beginning my thinking was confined to notions of affordability and environmentally sound housing, which of course have value; yet ultimately it has been the social and personal facets of this remarkable building system that have truly been the most rewarding.

One of the most satisfying aspects of the journey has been watching people who appear to have done very little physical work in their lives participate in a straw bale wall-raising, and leave with the belief that they too could build a house of their own. Granted, there is more to building a house than assembling a pile of bales, but it has been an amazing experience to watch people push past the limits they had set for themselves, and end up believing that building a quality house is something within their reach. At a time when modern construction has developed into a highly complex and specialized field in which most people don't dare participate, this change is significant. It is particularly exciting to see women and children become actively involved.

Group wall-raisings, which evoke the community spirit associated with Amish and old-fashioned barn-raisings, bring a social dimension to house building, and on a practical side, make it possible to raise the walls of a moderate-sized house in one or two days.

This social dimension extends to the sharing of information and techniques relevant to improving bale building. To date no one has tried, with visions of huge personal profits, to exploit or patent their "secret straw bale techniques."

Straw bale building has become as much a process of building communities as a highly efficient and sensible way of building affordable and environmentally sound buildings. People seem to change fundamentally when they gain the added security that comes from knowing they are capable of providing their own shelter. When a community of people possess that confidence and come together to help create one another's homes, it necessarily makes the world a better place to live.

It is this facet of straw bale building that has given me the greatest satisfaction and simultaneously the greatest hope. The process of building with bales includes the possibility of making a profound change in the fabric of human societies around the world. In fact, this vision is not exclusively a matter of straw bales; the questions we are trying to pose in this book are basic: how do we build, and how does that process occur in relation to the community and to the life around us? Straw bales happen to be a material that has inspired many to look at the process of building in a different light.

For me, this book is not merely about finding the best way to build with straw bales, but is more broadly about setting aside our conventional preconceptions as to how things ought to be done—and about how much more can be accomplished when people come together.

By far the most satisfying aspect of this book, much like the spirit of a wall-raising, is the way the results represent a highly collaborative effort in its most concentrated form. The fact that we were all able to come together and make it happen has made this a tremendously rewarding experience, and it has been fascinating once again to see how building with straw bales also builds relationships among people and relationships of people to the place they live and the materials they use.

B.S.
Canelo, Arizona

DAVID BAINBRIDGE'S STORY

Under the tutelage of an old master, Tod Neubauer, one of the great solar pioneers of the 1940s and 1950s, I started working on energy-efficient housing in the early 1970s at Jon Hammond's innovative design firm, Living Systems. Jon was one of the first to recognize the enormous potential of straw bale building in California. Our work included providing data and workshops for the city of Davis, California, where we developed a climatically oriented building code.

My work continued at Mike and Judy Corbett's Village Homes Development, where more than two hundred contemporary homes, many designed by John Hofacre, demonstrated how effective simple passive solar designs can be (see the book *Village Homes Solar House Designs*, listed in the appendix). The energy-efficient virtues of these otherwise normal looking houses have made this subdivision one of the favored (and now most expensive) places to live in Davis.

My explorations with solar buildings continued while investigating the benefits of super-insulation, which had first been recognized in Canada and Alaska. I traveled widely to talk with builders and owners of super-insulated homes, and discovered that the major problem with most of these houses was the extra complexity and the high cost of building double stud walls with spacers, trusses, and other features in order to gain an insulation factor of R-40–60. Even with these high initial costs, the life-cycle costs of super-insulated homes are much lower, and the additional comfort and energy savings can be worth the expense. And yet, in a society that ignores life-cycle costs, and in an era when few people can afford a house of any kind, these up-front costs can be prohibitive.

I was so frustrated by this problem that I gradually eased out of solar design and returned to my roots in ecological planning and development. Still I remained interested in "affordable housing," and kept up with innovations in the use of alternative building materials. I maintained a small file on straw bale construction, and while working on a sustainable agriculture research project I was introduced to the growing problem of straw disposal. I was shocked to learn that straw burning by farmers created more pollution (specifically, carbon monoxide) than all of the electric power generating facilities in California!

It was then that all the pieces clicked into place. Why not use this time-proven building material to provide low-cost, highly insulated buildings. With this realization I began a more determined search for information on straw bale building, with the help of friends in the U.S. and Canada. The wealth of documentation was just waiting to be discovered, from a virtually unknown Canadian technical study to extensive information on the many existing straw bale buildings in the United States.

I published a couple of articles on bale building in 1986, and began talking about the subject to various public audiences. So began my straw bale adventure, which has continued to the present with the publication of this book. I hope that we have succeeded in communicating some of what has inspired us.

D.B.
La Jolla, California

DAVID EISENBERG'S STORY

The early stages of my work in straw bale construction have been similar to putting in a new garden. Much of the initial effort has been like preparing the soil, with considerable satisfaction coming from the hard work and a promise of the harvest to come. From the beginning the learning, sharing, new places, and warmth from working with friends have compelled and more than sustained me. Recently, on more tangible levels, there have been small harvests and rapidly growing possibilities.

Over the past three years the door to straw bale construction has been more open in remote rural areas, and less open in urban areas where building codes are more strictly enforced. While the situation is changing quickly, much work needs to be done to swing this door wide open for all those who need affordable, durable, safe, healthy, and of course, beautiful housing.

I have chosen to focus my efforts on trying to open that door for everyone. In many ways, research and testing is the key. How the research and testing are conducted will affect how the building codes are written, and that will determine how accessible and affordable this way of building will be. We have created a Bale Research Advisory Network (BRAN—to keep us loose in the straw bale movement), to coordinate and maximize the effectiveness of this work. We also plan to create a comprehensive straw bale database and publish and distribute research and test results, serving as a hub for sharing technical information.

I am keenly aware of the need to move past building codes that ultimately force people to give up the right to create their own shelter in their own way, that often preclude building in a sustainable manner, and that take away the responsiblity we all have for our actions and decisions.

I have personal interest in the development of alternative building codes, so far limited to low-density, rural, owner-built buildings in a few places around the country. These alternative codes are usually structured to inspect for basic health and safety issues—to be sure that the building won't fall down on anyone, that wiring is safe (especially if connected to the power grid), and that wastewater systems will not pollute the local water supplies. Beyond that, people are allowed to build whatever they want. Alternative codes result from broad-based grassroots support and have, thus far, not been developed in any urban settings that I am aware of. Those who long for the freedom to build from their heart might choose to help in this effort.

I don't claim to be an expert in alternative codes, only someone seeking a path to a more natural way of building. Over the years I have built a number of innovative and complex structures from a wide variety of materials, but I have never seen anything with the potential benefits of straw bale construction. This potential is probably greatest in the less developed parts of the world, because of the enormous need for decent shelter and because of the way straw bale building easily adapts to vernacular building styles and simple materials. This is an exciting new realm, filled with possibility.

D.E.
Tucson, Arizona

ACKNOWLEDGMENTS

Creating this book required the gathering of an enormous amount of information from many wonderful people whose generous contributions of time, experience, photographs, hard work, and beautiful creations have been invaluable. Our most appreciative thanks to you all.

A little extra thanks to:

Paul Weiner, who has an invisible but significant presence in many pages of this book.

Steve and Nena MacDonald of Gila, New Mexico, for their pioneering spirit, which has inspired countless people.

Tony Perry, for his help in gaining access to the extensive world of straw bale building that has arisen in northern New Mexico.

Steve Kemble and Carol Escott for their steady and often quiet contributions to straw bale building.

Matts Myhrman and Judy Knox, whose work together has helped pioneer the rediscovery of plastered straw bale building.

The Out on Bale and Last Straw staffs, who work with such dedication behind the scenes.

Catherine Wanek for her generosity and devotion to a worthy cause.

Ken Haggard and Polly Cooper for their encouragement and support.

Pat Eisenberg for her graciousness and enduring patience.

Rina and Ralph Swentzell, who continually bring a wider scope and broader dimension to this work.

Four young children: Arin, Micah, Benito, and Arjuna (Oso), for patiently hearing day after day, "Not now, we have to work on the book."

And those at Chelsea Green Publishing Company for the trust and confidence extended to us.

INTRODUCTION

THE IDEA OF BUILDING ANYTHING OUT OF STRAW can seem laughable, but traditional cultures throughout the world have long recognized the value of straw, grasses, and reeds as building materials, and have used them effectively in combination with earth and timber to create shelter for thousands of years. Once the development of modern baling equipment in the late 1800s made it possible to compress straw and hay into bales, it wasn't long before pioneers in the Sand Hills of west Nebraska started using bales of meadow hay like giant building blocks, to build everything from churches to houses. The pioneers' motivation to build with bales came from a shortage of locally available building materials, but baled hay proved to be equal if not superior to the standard building materials of the time. This book is about how the traditions of building with baled materials have continued into our present time and are now beginning to spread the world over.

Straw bales are made from the leftover stems of harvested grain, while hay bales typically consist of finer-stemmed grasses baled green with the seed heads. Both have been and can be used for building, but because hay is valued as animal feed, it is commonly much more expensive than straw. Baled hay and straw have many positive attributes that recommend them as excellent building materials and yet they have definite limitations which need to be respected. As long as they are protected from moisture and are not used in ways which overlook their structural characteristics, they can be used to create structures that are durable, safe, and will last indefinitely. They are super energy efficient, environmentally safe, simple to work with and can be used both inexpensively and aesthetically. As illustrated in the many photographs in this book, bale homes can be traditional or innovative, big or small, light and spacious or cozy and intimate.

In the early 1980s, a handful of inspired owner-builders began combining their enthusiasm, foolishness, and building experience with bales of straw, simple tools, and plaster, and took the first steps down a road that in a relatively short time led bale construction to be widely recognized as a sensible and viable building technique.

It was an entertaining, sometimes tiring journey, enlivened by many wonderful and fascinating people along the way. Countless bale-home builders, workshop participants, readers, critics, friends, and family members made rapid progress possible, their enthusiasm often fueled by the possibility and promise that bale construction might help alleviate the desperate global need for adequate and affordable housing.

The majority of people around the world live in houses that are poorly constructed and uncomfortable much of the year. Maintaining adequate comfort levels in those structures often results in high and unaffordable utility bills, and damaging environmental practices such as over-cutting of timber.

Building with baled materials could dramatically improve housing conditions in a variety of climates and conditions. Anywhere wheat, barley, oats, rice, or other straws are available, bale building can make economic and environmental sense. Wherever the goal is to provide ecologically sound, sustainable structures that are inexpensive to build and maintain, that are energy efficient and compatible with renewable energy sources, and that can be owner-built to further reduce costs, bale buildings can be an ideal solution.

Bale building is still very much in its infancy, however, and evolving on a daily basis. It is evident from both historic and recent examples that it is possible to build a durable bale structure, but much remains to be learned about how baled materials behave in different conditions and climates, as well as in combination with other materials. To date, bales have largely been used with construction methods that were designed for other building materials. Designs that take advantage of the unique characteristics of bales have only begun to be explored.

This book will help facilitate the process of developing bale building strategies for a multitude of conditions and purposes by sharing the building experiences of a diverse collection of owner-builders, architects, contractors, and Nebraska pioneers. It is written for people who have never heard of bale building as well as those who are preparing to break ground, so to speak, on their own straw bale homes or buildings. Besides the numerous beautiful photographs, this book includes practical information about the benefits of building with bales, common concerns, how to build with bales, building options, environmental design issues, and other uses for bales.

THE STRAW BALE HOUSE

CHAPTER 1

A BRIEF HISTORY

AS LONG AS HUMAN BEINGS have been creating shelter, straw and grasses have been used in conjunction with a variety of building methods to provide safe, dependable, and comfortable housing in many climates and environments. Walls made from tied bundles of long lengths of straw, stacked in mud mortar, have been constructed for centuries throughout Asia and Europe. Another ancient method, also employed in Asia and Europe, used compacted loose straw coated with a clay slip for walls. Those methods and materials remain in use today, their use declining only where modern construction methods, materials, and codes have become commonplace.

Stationary "two-horsepower" baler.

In the United States, a new era of building with straw and grasses began in the late 1800s with the development of the stationary horse and the steam-powered baler, which made it possible to compress hay and straw into string- or wire-tied rectangular units called bales. It took only a slight stretch of the imagination for early homesteaders in the timber-poor region of the Great Plains of North America to think of using bales as oversized bricks. It was in the Sand Hills of Nebraska, a land that yielded magnificent stands of meadow hay, that the first bale buildings were constructed.

The reasons vary as to why many pioneers chose to build with baled straw or hay. Some seem to have simply been intrigued by the method, while others found building with bales easier than building with sod. Some families decided to replace their original small sod houses with larger bale houses. It was also noted that using baled meadow grasses seemed much more efficient than stripping a large section of productive meadow land for sod.

In some cases, families were in immediate need of housing, and bales were looked upon as the quickest way of getting a roof overhead. Many of those structures were first viewed as temporary, but when it was discovered that they were both durable and comfortable in the extremes of the Nebraska winter and summer, they were soon plastered and adopted as permanent housing.

According to bale-building researcher Roger Welsch, the oldest docu-

3

Simonton House, Purdum, Nebraska, 1908.

Facing page Top: Fawn Lake Ranch Headquarters and bunkhouse, near Hyannis Nebraska, 1900–1914. Middle: Burke homestead, Alliance Nebraska, 1903. Bottom: Martin-Monhart house, Arthur, Nebraska, 1925.

mented building was a one-room schoolhouse built near Bayard, Nebraska, in 1886 or 1887. In 1902, William K. Fowler, who was Nebraska state superintendent of schools around the turn of the century, reported:

> *Some five or six years ago in district No. 5 of Scotts Bluff county there was erected a temple of learning, the walls of which were baled straw, the floor was the primitive mother earth and the roof above presented a face of the earth to the heavens. This roof was made of poles laid across from side to side and covered with sod. The building was sixteen feet long, twelve feet wide, and seven feet high. There was a window in each side and a door in one end. The bales of straw were laid in mud instead of mortar, and with some half bales the joints were broken the way that bricks are laid....(Welsch, "Baled Hay")*

In 1903 the Burke homestead was built near Alliance, Nebraska, and was occupied by Marie Burke and her husband and children and later by others, until 1956 when it was abandoned. The exterior walls were left unplastered for the first ten years. Even though the building has not been maintained, it has withstood ninety years of wide swings in temperature and blizzard winds, and still stands in relatively good but deteriorating condition.

Some of the other oldest bale buildings are the headquarters and bunkhouse at the Fawn Lake Ranch near Hyannis, Nebraska. The two hay-bale structures were built sometime between the turn of the century and 1914. Both are still in use, and according to owner Mike Milligan, recent repair work on the walls confirmed that the bales remain in excellent condition. The bales for both buildings were made with a stationary baler and were hand tied. The house had an addition built in the 1950s. When the walls were opened up for the addition, some of the bales were set to one side by a corral. Horses on the other side reached over the fence and ate the bales that were around fifty years old.

In 1921, Warren Withee, who had only one arm, built a 1,000-square-foot home near Alsen-Fawnlville, South Dakota, using mortared hay bales in the walls. In addition to meadow hay, some of the bales that were used were made of flax. The building, which is still in good condition, is currently being used for storage. It is the only known bale structure built during this early time period that is not in Nebraska.

The Martin-Monhart house of Arthur, Nebraska, was built in 1925. Originally plastered with mud, it was re-stuccoed with cement by new owners in 1930. The house is not currently occupied but remains a family museum and is open to the public.

Also in Arthur, the Pilgrim Holiness Church was built in 1928. Bales for the church were made at a homestead outside of town using an old-fashioned stationary baler. The bales were hand tied with wire and hauled to town by mule. The dimensions of the church are 28 by 50 feet and include four additional rooms that were used as living quarters. It sustained thirty-five years of active use before being retired and converted to a museum. In 1976, the Arthur County Historical Society carried out a restoration project on the church.

One of the finest examples of historic Nebraska bale construction is the Scott house, built between 1935 and 1938 near Gordon, Nebraska, by Leonard and Tom Scott. The house is a beautifully detailed 900-square-foot structure with a basement which is reported to use bales in its walls. The bales used in the house were made from wheat straw using a stationary horse-powered baler. Lois Scott, the current resident, has lived there since she was a small child. She remembers that her mother was initially very much against building and living in a bale house, and that her parents continued arguing for over a year before construction on the house actually began. Once the house was completed, however, her mother lived there happily for twenty-five years, until her death. Lois reports that the bale house has had no noticeable problems during its lifetime and that her utility bills are estimated to be as much as 40 percent less than those of her neighbors.

Estimates vary of how many bale buildings were constructed in Nebraska between the late 1890s and the late 1930s. In 1973, Roger Welsch calculated that sixty bale structures were built in the Sand Hills area, but in more recent informal research conducted by Matts Myhrman and Judy Knox, only twenty-eight buildings were confirmed.

Before 1936, all known bale structures in the United States used the bale walls as the support for the roof ("Nebraska style"). In that year, Dr. William Henry Burritt built a two-story straw bale mansion in Huntsville, Alabama, with a post-and-beam support structure. The present house is actually the second one built on that site. The first house, which had a structure of wood and native stone and incorporated 2,200 wheat-straw bales as an in-fill material, burned the day Dr. Burritt moved in on June 6, 1936. The straw was apparently not the problem, and Dr. Burritt rebuilt the house using straw once again but replacing much of the wood with concrete and concrete-fiber-reinforced shingles. The second house was completed in 1938 and remains in good condition. One unique feature of the house is that it is built in the shape of an X, some say in order to hold a cross-grid of antennae to improve radio reception. The mansion also features large Doric columns of concrete, which were cast on site by hand.

In 1948, a general store was built in Glendo, Wyoming, using bales that were mortared like bricks (see photo on page 97). After visiting that store,

Pilgrim Holiness Church, Arthur, Nebraska, 1928. Below: Burritt Museum, Huntsville, Alabama, 1938.

Chuck Bruner and his wife Mary returned home to Douglas, Wyoming, and built a 1300-square-foot home using the same mortared-bale system. They still occupy and enjoy their home, built in 1949 (see Chuck's essay on page 245).

Bale building seemed to slow between the early 1950s and the early 1980s, possibly due to the increased availability of mass-produced construction materials that made it unnecessary for homeowners and builders to rely on locally produced building supplies.

During that period, Roger Welsch, who is also known for his series "Postcards from Nebraska" on the CBS Sunday Morning News, was conducting research on folk and vernacular architecture including sod and baled-hay construction. Roger felt that baled-hay construction was a superior method for the needs of the geography and time in pioneer Nebraska, and a dramatic example of what can be learned from the past. In 1974, Shelter Publications published a book of essays entitled *Shelter* which contained an article Roger had written called "Baled Hay." That article probably did more to initiate a revival of bale building than any other factor, and there was a resurgence of bale building in the late 1970s and early 1980s.

In 1978, Dan Huntington built a straw bale structure with a concrete post-and-beam framework near Rockport, Washington, which receives in the vicinity of 75 inches of rain a year. He applied for a permit "to put a roof" over his bales. He was issued the most basic permit available and proceeded to build the structure which he and his wife then lived in for two years while they were building their full-sized home; it is now used for storage.

Architect Jon Hammond of northern California, inspired by the Welsch article, built a straw bale, post-and-beam cottage that was featured in

Facing page
Top: Scott House, near Gordon, Nebraska, 1935–1938.
Middle: Chuck and Mary Bruner's house, Douglas, Wyoming, 1949.
Bottom: Jon Hammond's cottage, northern California, 1981.

Above
Top: Paul Neuffer's house, near Bozeman, Montana, 1981.
Bottom: Athena Swentzell Steen's and Brian Reeves's load-bearing straw bale house, near Santa Fe, New Mexico, 1981.

an article in *Fine Homebuilding* in December of 1984. That article in turn inspired a number of people, including this book's co-author Dave Bainbridge, who by 1986 was publishing articles and giving many talks on straw bale housing. In 1986, one of his articles was circulated worldwide in issue number 16 of the magazine *Agriculture, Ecosystems, and the Environment.* In 1987 he spoke at a Permaculture Design Course sponsored by the Sonoran Permaculture Association (now Permaculture Drylands). Attending that course were a number of people who later went on to build their own straw bale houses and play major roles in the development of bale building, including Sue Mullen of Gila, New Mexico, who on her way home from the course discovered neighbors Steve and Nena MacDonald building a straw bale house almost in her backyard. The MacDonalds had drawn their inspiration from the *Fine Home Building* article. Their $7.50-a-square-foot home has inspired people all over the world—(and disappointed a few who were not able to build as cheaply).

In early 1988, a newsletter summarizing the 1987 Permaculture Design Course included an article on straw bale housing by Dave Bainbridge. The article influenced numerous people, including Matts Myhrman, who went on to found a straw bale information and education service called Out on Bale (un)Ltd., in Tucson, Arizona. In 1989, a straw bale workshop in Oracle, Arizona, brought together Dave Bainbridge, Bill Steen, Matts Myhrman, and Pliny Fisk of the Center for Maximum Potential Building Systems in Austin, Texas, to brainstorm on the best methods for bale building. It was a small but significant step in the modern revival of straw bale building.

The early 1990s saw a dramatic increase in newspaper articles, television coverage, and con-

Top: Sue Mullen's house,
Gila, New Mexico, 1988.
Bottom: Steve and Nena
MacDonald's house, Gila,
New Mexico, 1987.

struction workshops focused on straw bale building, as well as the first code approvals for a limited number of non-load-bearing straw bale buildings. The first permitted straw bale house was also the first insured, bank-financed, straw bale house. Built in 1991 in Tesuque, New Mexico, by Virginia Carabelli, who served as her own contractor, this Santa Fe–style house marked the beginning of a new era for straw bale homes.

Following Carabelli's permit, the Construction Industries Division (CID) of the state of New Mexico issued ten experimental permits in 1991 for non-load-bearing straw bale structures. Around the same time, also in Santa Fe, Tony Perry was instrumental in organizing the Straw Bale Construction Association (SBCA) to bring together professionals interested in designing and building with straw bales. Perry, president of the association, together with vice president Burke Denman, secretary Beverley Spears, and treasurer Danny Buck, worked hard to get straw bale construction into New Mexico's building codes. The SBCA successfully sponsored a Small Scale Fire Test and a Transverse Load Test.

The testing and work with building officials in New Mexico followed similar efforts in Tucson, Arizona. Matts Myhrman and Judy Knox of Out on Bale began teaching straw bale workshops and supervising wall raisings around the United States and abroad. Their experiences led to the creation of the informative straw bale newsletter, "The Last Straw," which is published on a quarterly basis (see appendix). Working closely with local officials, together with David Eisenberg, they also helped coordinate a structural wall testing program which was conducted by graduate engineering student Ghailene Bou-Ali at the University of Arizona as his master's thesis in structural engineering.

By 1993 straw bale buildings were going up faster than anyone could track. The first Straw Bale Building Conference, "Roots and Revival," took place in Arthur, Nebraska, in September, 1993. It was attended by fifty architects, builders, designers, and enthusiasts. The conference included tours of the local historic straw bale buildings and sessions on straw bale building. On the final day of the conference, members of the Codes, Research and Testing working group drafted a proposal to create a National Straw Bale Research Advisory Network in order to facilitate communication between key regional representatives of straw bale construction and to ensure that efficient, non-duplicative testing would be conducted with common research directives, regional perspectives, and the best use of engineering resources.

Above: Virginia Carabelli's house, near Tesuque, New Mexico, 1991. The first permitted straw bale house. Right: David Bainbridge, Bill Steen, and Pliny Fisk.

*Matts Myhrman and
Judy Knox at the straw
bale wall-raising.*

In October of 1993, Judy Knox and Matts Myhrman began construction on Mom's Place in Tucson, the first load-bearing straw bale house anywhere to be granted a building permit. The small guest house, built for Matts's mother, was issued the permit under Sections 105 and 107 of the Uniform Building Code (UBC). These sections allow building officials to approve materials and methods of construction not specifically covered by the code. The second load-bearing permit was issued in the spring of 1994 to the Tree of Life Rejuvenation Center in Patagonia, Arizona, for a building designed by Paul Weiner of Tucson.

The spring of 1994 also saw the Construction Industries Division of the state of New Mexico issue an additional twenty permits for bale in-fill structures. As this book is being published, prescriptive standards are imminent for the states of Arizona and New Mexico. While awaiting the completion of its prescriptive straw bale standards, the state of New Mexico announced it would issue an unlimited number of experimental permits due to high public demand.

THE INTERNATIONAL SCENE

In the early 1980s, straw bale structures began to make an appearance around Quebec, Canada. François Tanguay was inspired to build a roof system out of straw after reading Roger Welsch's article, "Baled Hay." François decided that as long as he was building a straw roof, he might as well build the walls out of straw. In 1981, he built a post-and-beam straw bale in-fill house southeast of Quebec, near the United States border.

In 1982, the Canada Mortgage and Housing Corporation provided funding through its Housing Technology Incentives program to demonstrate the practical applications of a straw bale and mortar system as a load-bearing wall for use in residential construction. Louis Gagné of Hull, Quebec, developed a wall system called the mortared-bale matrix system (see page 96) for use in the program, in which a sample wall consisting of bales stacked in columns with mortared joints was tested by independent consultants in accordance with recognized procedures for thermal resistance, load bearing, moisture penetration, and fire endurance. The results of the testing indicated that the sample mortared-bale matrix wall met or exceeded residential construction requirements in the areas tested.

After completion of the testing, Louis went on to build himself a house at La Peche and two other houses which were financed by private individuals, using the mortared-bale matrix system. The Canada Mortgage and Housing Corporation provided funding for Louis to be involved in the construction of the houses and prepare a report documenting the work. One house was built in Chelsea, the other in La Peche. Both houses had two stories and basements.

In the mid 1980s, François Tanguay and Michel Bergeron were doing further work with straw bale structures in Quebec. In addition to straw bale wall systems, Michel was focusing his work on developing a concrete slab that used embedded straw bales and required no steel reinforcement. Together with a woman partner named Clode Deguise, François and Michel formed a non-profit group in Quebec named ArchiBio (from Architecture Bioclimatique), which is dedicated to researching materials and techniques appropriate to eco-logical housing. A significant part of their work has focused on straw bale building, to which they have made unique contributions such as living roofs made from bales and Michel's straw bale slabs. Their work also focuses on

Facing page top: Tree of Life Rejuvenation Center, Patagonia, Arizona, 1994. The second permitted load-bearing straw bale structure.

composting toilets (that work), solar design, and stackwall buildings. They have published four books (in French) on those subjects. Archi-Bio is very active in Canada and France and has been involved in nearly a hundred projects, consulting, and workshops involving straw bale construction.

François's work has also extended to France, where in 1985, 1987, and 1989 he gave numerous lectures and taught workshops on straw bale building. The first building that resulted from his work was constructed at La Chassagne in 1986–87 and was patterned after the mortared-bale matrix system.

About fourteen buildings, houses, workshops, and farm buildings have been built in France since 1986 using post-and-beam timber-style structures with bale in-fill, or mortared bales. Most have been plastered without the use of wire mesh. The first known straw bale house in France was built in 1979 by Le CUN, a group that promotes nonviolent conflict resolution, at Larzac in the south of France. It has been suggested that this building was influenced by Roger Welsch's article on baled buildings, which was translated into French.

One of the more creative French buildings was designed by architect Jean Luc Thomas and built by owner Thierry Dronet in combination with a workshop led by François Tanguay (see the color section).

A beautiful two-story home, the Guillarmin residence in Seine et Marne was also designed by Jean Luc Thomas. It was built in 1989 and incorporates walls built of a straw bale mortar matrix.

In 1989, a 6,000-square-foot stable for thoroughbred horses was built near Paris. The structure is a post-and-beam straw bale in-fill with a flat roof, designed by Jean Charles Fabre and built by François Tanguay. It is said that the horses fell in love with the building and their dispositions and

temperaments changed remarkably for the better after moving into their new quarters.

The French straw bale effort is currently being coordinated by John Daglish, an architect who, in addition to straw bale construction, is focusing his work on bau-biologie and permaculture (see appendix).

In Canada, Kim Thompson of Ship Harbor, Nova Scotia, held a workshop in 1993 to build a two-story straw bale house. Armed with the *Straw Bale Construction Primer* by Steve MacDonald, a group of friends, and support from the Cooperation Agreement on Sustainable Economic Development, participants constructed a building using load-bearing walls, seven bales high on the first story and three on the second, with a cathedral ceiling. The building sits on a wooden platform supported by large telephone poles that are sunk 4 feet into the ground. Straw bales were used to insulate between the floor joists. The National Research Council of Canada is conducting a year of on-site testing and monitoring of the walls for temperature and moisture, as well as in-lab testing for compression and loads.

Above: Thierry Dronet's workshop/stables, Vosges, France 1987.
Left: Kim Thompson's house, Ship Harbor, Nova Scotia, 1993.
Right: Guillarmin residence, Seine et Marne, France, 1989.

*Above: Puebla house,
Mexico, 1994.
Left: Women working,
Aves de Castillo, Mexico,
1993.*

Mary Biggs of Coronation, in Alberta, Canada, also built a load-bearing straw bale house in 1993, in conjunction with architects Helen and Jorg Ostrowski of Calgary. Her house was possibly the first one to be pinned with bamboo stakes instead of rebar. It is 2,000 square feet and was built for a cost of approximately $75 a square foot. The house also incorporates rammed-earth interior walls.

The structures built by Kim Thompson and Mary Biggs are significant in that they are load-bearing buildings constructed in areas that are subject to heavy snow loads and relatively high humidity. Bales will compress under a heavy load of snow, and yet they tend to return to their original size and dimension as the snow melts and the load is removed.

Facing page top: Mary Biggs's house, Coronation, Alberta, Canada, 1993.

In the early 1990s, straw bale buildings began appearing in Mexico. The first known structure was an agricultural building built on a pig farm in the southern part of the state of Sonora, outside Ciudad Obregon by Jose Rubio Artee (see photo on page 241). In 1993, also in Sonora, Elizabeth Nuzom built a thatched straw bale studio (see photo on page 150).

In 1993, Save the Children invited the Farmer to Farmer Program of the University of Arizona to the Aves de Castillo neighborhood in Ciudad Obregon. Like many small Mexican neighborhoods and communities, Aves de Castillo lacked adequate electricity, drinking water, transportation, sewage treatment, and housing. It is surrounded on three sides by a broad agricultural region, where wheat and soybeans are grown. Following the harvest, farmers burn the fields to get rid of the waste straw, surrounding the community in great clouds of smoke for about a month every spring. During those times Aves del Castillo residents suffer respiratory problems and eye irritation.

The people of the community are poor and generally cannot afford the materials to build effective shelter. Most current homes are built with whatever is available—usually a combination of corrugated tin and asphalt board, old lumber, cardboard, or anything that can help keep the extreme summer heat and winter cold at bay. The staggering heat represents a health problem for the young and old as well as creating pervasive discomfort.

In conjunction with a neighborhood women's group called Mujeres Activas de Aves de Castillo, Thoric Cederström, Dan Dorsey, and other representatives of the Farmer to Farmer program conducted a five-day straw bale workshop to build a small load-bearing, shed-roofed building as a meeting headquarters for the women's group. The building was primarily constructed by more than one hundred women who participated in the event, and is called La Casa Ecologia de Aves de Castillo.

At the same time, the group held a workshop to develop specific objectives for improving the quality of life of the community and to develop a long-term sustainable lifestyle. The objectives included providing low-cost shelter, reducing pollution, providing energy-efficient housing, encouraging use of local skills and developing new skills, and developing a market use for baled straw.

The workshop was successful enough to attract the attention of the state of Sonora, which agreed to finance an additional fifteen straw bale houses during 1994–95. The first of these, a two-bedroom private residence, has already been built by two brothers who reduced costs by using a concrete roof in place of wood and cardboard boxes of straw between the ceiling beams for insulation.

This project has brought together people from both sides of the Mexican-American border, combining limited resources of government and nongovernment organizations, a technical training institute, community members, and private enterprise. Anyone wishing to help or be a part of this project can contact the Farmer to Farmer Program at the University of Arizona.

The Farmer to Farmer Program also co-sponsored a straw bale project in southern Mexico, along with the Projeccion Humana de Mexico, a program of the Mexican Methodist church. Projeccion Humana is dedicated to the development of appropriate technology in rural communities, under the guidance of Terry and Muriel Henderson. The building the groups constructed was designed by Mexican architect Alejandra Caballero de Gomez, and uses only traditional techniques. It is built on a traditional stone foundation, uses bamboo for the roof plate, bamboo trusses, and a tile roof. In 1994, Caballero received a MacArthur Foundation grant to teach straw bale construction to women in Mexico.

In 1994, the Ezra Taft Benson Agriculture and Food Institute based in Provo, Utah, initiated a straw bale project in humid Guatemala. The first buildings will consist of a training complex with offices, a conference center, and apartments at the institute's experimental farm.

Other straw bale efforts are underway in Europe. In the early 1990s, Tapani Marjamaa built the first straw bale structure in Finland without any knowledge of such buildings being constructed elsewhere. He continues his work leading testing and research efforts for a national code for straw bale buildings (see appendix).

American Scott Pittman and Australian Permaculture founder Bill Mollison led a straw bale workshop on the Myak collective farm in the Ural mountains near Chelyabinsk, Russia, in 1994. They were the first foreigners

First Russian straw bale house, Ural Mountains near Chelyabinsk, 1994.

to ever visit the rural collective. The house they built had a timber-frame structure and was crafted on site with hand tools, using bale in-fill for the walls.

Straw bale buildings are going up in other places around the world and in almost every region in the United States. The future of straw bale building is now being written.

CHAPTER 2

BENEFITS OF STRAW BALE CONSTRUCTION

ALL THINGS CONSIDERED, straw bales literally stack up as a remarkable building material. They are produced from a waste product that can be sustainably grown in a short period of time, are biodegradable, and can help alleviate multiple environmental problems with their use. They are easy to modify, flexible enough to be used in a variety of ways, solid and substantial, durable over time, and easy to maintain. In addition, they require only inexpensive uncomplicated tools and unspecialized labor, and are easily acquired and affordable in most locations around the world.

Modern building materials, in contrast, tend to be difficult to work with, inflexible, require specialized tools and labor, can be expensive, possess little aesthetic character, are often toxic, and generate significant amounts of pollution and waste as they are produced, maintained, and demolished.

An additional benefit of straw bale buildings not traditionally measured when evaluating building materials is the high level of social interaction and community participation that occurs in this process. People who might otherwise be excluded from the building process become directly and enthusiastically involved.

When straw bales are combined with other materials of similar characteristics, it becomes possible to create buildings that are affordable in all respects, natural in character, and beautiful.

Sunroom of the Hughes and Rhoades Residence, Santa Fe, New Mexico.

BEAUTY AND COMFORT

The thickness and subtle curves of straw bale walls have a special character and beauty. Combined with their high insulation value and breathability, these walls create an overall feeling of comfort not found in the thin flat walls often produced from modern materials. Straw bale walls are similar in appearance to old thick stone and adobe walls, reminiscent of European country cottages,

Mediterranean villas, and Southwestern adobes. Yet, at the same time, they have an intangible quality all their own.

Sometimes people's personal lives can most easily be read in the walls of their buildings, such as where a deep and softened entryway graciously welcomes one in, where a detailed niche displays precious belongings, where intimate nooks with built-in seats invite quiet repose, or where beautifully beveled window edges frame a treasured view. The thickness of straw bale walls and their ability to be easily modified make it easy to change bale walls according to the needs and creativity of its inhabitants.

The mass and dimensions of straw bale walls can induce physical and psychological feelings of well-being. When combined with a soft adobe or gypsum plaster, the flowing surfaces are not only a pleasure to look at and to touch, but instill a soft sound quality to each room.

When finished with natural plasters and paints, straw bale walls can breathe, resulting in indoor air that feels fresh, invigorating, and clean compared to the low-oxygen, stale, toxic air common to most homes. The high insulation value of bales also helps create a very stable environment which is easy to cool and heat and provides far superior living conditions to that of most modern housing.

In the Great Plains, baled homes were preferred because they were extremely quiet and could seal out the howling of the Northers, winds that can torment a person's mind on the open plains. In the city, bale houses could provide a much needed haven in a noisy and chaotic world. Perhaps it is within these silent, sculpted walls, which impart a sense of timeless peace, that a new and better vision of shelter resides.

EASE OF CONSTRUCTION

Building walls from straw is much less labor intensive than using other materials such as concrete block, brick, adobe, or stone, and requires considerably less skill. Bale building is forgiving, encourages individual creativity, and leads to final structures that are climatically adapted and energy efficient.

Many people would have a great deal of fear and anxiety about building a home with more conventional materials. The complexity, skill required, time involved, and cost can seem prohibitive and daunting. Building with straw bales relaxes the whole construction process and allows inexperienced and unskilled people the opportunity to become directly involved in creating their own homes.

Above: Wall-raising at first Out On Bale/Canelo Project straw bale workshop, Canelo, Arizona, 1990.
Below: Women working together at straw bale wall-raising.

It has been demonstrated in the United States that the basic methods of straw bale construction can be learned in a two-day workshop. One of the great beauties of this system is that everyone can participate in building a home, including women, children, and others who have been disenfranchised from the building process. This coming together of people to help each other build often generates a great deal of excitement. Group wall-raisings facilitate community-based projects that might not otherwise happen.

After the original Tree of Life Nursery in southern California burned down, the owners received a broad outpouring of community support offering to help them put up a new building. In response to that enthusiasm, owners Mike Evans and Jeff Bohm decided to construct their new building out of straw bales because it would afford community members the greatest opportunity to participate. The event was conducted much in the spirit of an old-time barn raising, and the food, music, and work were so delightful that Mike and Jeff have decided to host an annual wall raising whether they need a building or not.

Tree of Life Nursery wall-raising.
Inset: Mike Evans and Jeff Bohm, owners of Tree of Life Nursery.

ENERGY EFFICIENCY

Insulation is rated by R-value, the resistance to heat flow. The R-value of wood is 1 per inch, brick is 0.2, fiberglass batts are 3.0. The higher the R-value the better the insulation. Straw bale buildings are thermally efficient and energy conserving, with R-values significantly better than conventional construction, depending on the type of straw and the wall thickness. Research by Joe McCabe at the University of Arizona found that the R-value for both wheat and rice bales was about R-2.4 per inch with the grain, and R-3 per inch across the grain, which would give a three-string bale laid flat (23 inches wide) an R-value of R-54.7, and laid on edge (16 inches wide) an R-value of R-49.5. For two-string bales laid flat (18 inches wide), the R-value would be R-42.8, and for a two-string bale on edge (14 inches wide), it would be R-32.1. That is two to three times better than the wall system of most well-insulated homes, and often five to ten times better than older houses. Additionally, the mass gained from the plaster of the bale wall can help increase the thermal performance of the wall system.

Straw bale walls can provide greatly improved comfort and dramatic energy savings compared to more expensive conventional building systems, as they allow smaller heating or cooling systems to be installed than in conventional homes because of the increased insulation. Bale building is of special value in severe environments where energy is expensive.

To get the most benefit from the highly efficient walls of a bale building, the building should include a well-insulated attic or roof (straw can be used in many cases), good perimeter foundation insulation, insulated windows and doors, proper sealing to minimize drafts, and optimal ventilation achieved either by plastering and coloring the walls with a breathable finish or by using an air-to-air heat exchanger to efficiently bring in fresh air. The high insulation and mass of bale walls will make it possible to keep the windows open much of the year, providing cleaner air inside.

The traditional designs of many homes optimize solar gain for heating and climate resources for cooling, but are hampered by the lack of insulation. Traditional Chinese rural homes, for example, are oriented with the long axis running east-west and most of the windows on the south side, an ideal configuration for solar heating and natural cooling. Unfortunately, the poor thermal properties of the brick walls reduce many of the advantages of this excellent design. Straw bale building could enable rural home builders to achieve thermal comfort without costly fuel consumption.

The excellent insulation value of straw bales also makes passive cooling systems, such as the cool pool or down draft cooling towers, more practical and efficient for homeowners in very hot, arid areas. It may also make the installation of extra cooling systems unnecessary. In her straw bale house near Huachuca City, Arizona, Mary Diamond installed a cooling tower. It was included in the design of the building because it was calculated that a well-insulated home in the area where she lives would require the extra cooling. The house was built before the cooling tower was completed and moved into during the hot summer months. It was discovered that the straw bale house remained sufficiently cool without any help from the tower, and therefore the cooling tower was never finished. The house's photovoltaic electrical system makes it even more energy efficient.

The savings from reduced utility bills and not having to purchase expensive heating and cooling equipment can help offset the cost of buying more efficient appliances, like a heat exchanger (for severe climates) and a photovoltaic electric system.

Mary Diamond's load-bearing, solar powered straw bale guest house, near Huachuca City, Arizona.

ENVIRONMENTAL BENEFITS

Straw bale construction can provide benefits in regions where straw has become an unwanted waste product. The slow rate at which straw deteriorates creates disposal problems for farmers because unlike nitrogen-rich hay, straw cannot be used for animal fodder, and the stems are too long to be thoroughly tilled in. In California, for example, almost a million tons of rice straw are burned each fall, and the fires cast a pall of smoke over the Sacramento Valley for several weeks. Annual straw burning in California produces more carbon monoxide and particulate than all of the electric-power-generating plants in the state combined. This air pollution has prompted the state's Air Resources Board to initiate the process of banning this burning.

Straw burning near Ciudad Obregon, Sonora, Mexico.

ANNUAL CARBON MONOXIDE PRODUCTION FROM POWER PLANTS AND STRAW BURNING (IN TONS)

	TONS BURNED	TONS CO
Rice straw	1 million	56,000
Wheat straw	97,000	5,000
Power plants		25,000

Source: *California Agricultural Magazine,* Vol. 45, no. 4 (July–August 1991)

A million tons of grass are burned each year in the Willamette Valley of Oregon, creating visual pollution and health hazards. In 1988, a chain-reaction highway accident that was caused by smoke from field burning resulted in seven deaths and thirty-seven injuries. The Oregon Department of Environmental Quality has stated that this smoke is "carcinogenic . . . containing tiny particles that irritate the lungs." Rice straw may be even worse because of its high silica content and particle size. Here, also, the state government has begun to crack down on burning, and straw disposal is becoming a problem. The Department of Environmental Quality is funding research into alternatives but has yet to come up with an economically viable use for straw.

Large quantities of straw are burned in other areas as well. Close to two hundred million tons of waste straw are produced in the United States every year. Increasing amounts of straw are also burned in Europe and Mexico. The use of straw for domestic fuel has been reduced in eastern China, where extensive reforestation has enabled farmers to begin using wood instead. That could make straw available for bale buildings.

Straw bale construction could be useful in the effort to control global warming and atmospheric deterioration. A large reduction in the amount of straw burned would cut back the production of carbon monoxide and nitrous oxides by many thousands of tons per year. The removal of rice straw from the wet fields for use in bale buildings would substantially reduce methane emissions from microbial decomposition, the second major cause of global warming. Not all straw needs to be disposed of, for if left in alternating swaths or strips on the contour of the land, straw can provide erosion control in fields. Waste straw, however, for which disposal is a problem, could be baled and used in buildings.

There could be a significant decline in the devastation of timber areas if homes were built from straw bales instead of the lumber-consumptive construction methods so prevalent today. In many developing countries, the cutting of firewood for heating is as devastating to forests as woodcutting for the buildings themselves. Energy-efficient bale buildings could lessen this impact as well. The plaster-stucco construction often used with bale buildings could also reduce the need for maintenance and the use of paints and solvents that adversely affect the atmosphere and human health.

According to Matts Myhrman of Out on Bale: "If all the straw left in the United States after the harvest of major grains was baled instead of burned, five million 2,000-square-foot houses could be built every year."

Jujube trees intercropped with wheat, China.

SUSTAINABILITY

In contrast to the timber used for wood framing, straw can be grown in less than a year in a completely sustainable production system. Without developing an elaborate definition, the term *sustainable* here refers to a system that conceivably could be perpetuated forever. If large crops of straw are removed from a field every year, the use of soil amendments, intercropping, or crop rotations may be required to maintain soil health and fertility. If perennial straw crops are used, however, the need for such measures will be reduced, as will erosion and runoff.

Straw can be successfully intercropped with other valuable crops, thereby increasing the yield and productivity of the same piece of land. Certain fruit and other useful trees are good candidates. In China, wheat is successfully intercropped with highly valued fruit-producing jujube trees. The sustainable yield of a piece of land is enhanced when each element in the system provides multiple benefits and uses and when the relationship between those elements is beneficial.

The conversion of straw into a sustainable renewable resource to be used as a dominant building material could be especially beneficial in areas like the steppes of Russia and the plains of northern China, where the climate is severe and timber is scarce, but straw is plentiful.

Straw bale construction would also be ideal for many desert areas where winter wheats are grown along riparian belts and river valleys. The soils that make good adobe or earth blocks are often the same soils that are used for cultivation. Using those soils to make bricks, as is happening in Egypt, where agricultural land is at a premium, is clearly not a sustainable practice. Desert areas are also traditionally timber poor.

In timber-poor areas where roof framing materials are needed, assorted poles and bamboo could be quickly and sustainably grown in combination with straw. In areas where straw is not available, it can be grown specifically for buildings. Some economists estimate that half of the land now farmed in Europe will become available as farm subsidies are eliminated. A similar situation may develop in the United States. These lands could be used to grow special building straw while still maintaining the rural vistas that everyone enjoys.

Straw can also be grown on saline or low-quality land. Tall wheat-grass (Aelongatum), for example, is long-stemmed and durable, and productive in soils with high water tables, high salinity, and alkalinity.

The prospect of sustainability for any given product or system is increased if the energy required to manufacture or operate it is kept to a minimum. When straw is evaluated for sustainability as a building material, it rates very high. It bypasses much of the energy and waste needed to produce industrial building materials. For example, the production of one ton of straw requires 112,500 BTUs , in comparison to 5,800,000 BTUs for concrete. According to calculations performed by Richard Hoffmeister at Taliesin West, the Frank Lloyd Wright school of architecture in Scottsdale, Arizona, straw bale walls are at least thirty times less energy intensive than a wood-frame wall with equivalent fiberglass insulation. This reduction can significantly help mini-mize the environmental and financial impact of construction. Ideally, a sus-tainable straw-growing operation would seek to grow straw as close as pos-sible to building sites to minimize the energy requirements of transporting it.

Another aspect of straw's sustainability is the material's remarkable dura-bility:

> *My grandfather had a hay bale barn, roughly 40' by 60', that existed until I was an adolescent. That's when it was destroyed and by that time it was about fifty years old. A tornado came through and picked it up and moved it—actually took the building and twisted it roughly ninety degrees and moved it about forty feet. Strangely, it stayed intact, unlike all the wood buildings. The barn had clapboard on the outside and was protected on the inside from the cows by stucco. When it was finally destroyed, the cows were very excited about the straw. They thought that was the best straw they had ever had. They clipped off fences to get to it. That straw was from a sweetgrass that's now extinct.*
>
> —ED SANDERS, former Nebraska resident

STRUCTURAL TESTING

In the mid 1980s, the Canada Mortgage and Housing Corporation was the first to sponsor tests of the strength of plastered straw bale construction using a mortared bale-wall system. Even though that wall system is very different from most building methods currently being used, those tests were a signifi-cant first step. Walls in those tests had mortar in the joints between the bales as well as plaster on both sides. A 12-foot-long, 8-foot-high wall did not fail when loaded with 18,000 pounds of compressive load and 719 pounds of transverse force. The structural consultants felt the mortared bale-wall system would be adequate for the following loads:

Live loads due to use and occupancy	45 lbs./ft.^{2}
Snow loads	60 lbs./ft.^{2}
Wind loads	16 lbs./ft.^{2}
Dead loads	48 lbs./ft.^{2}

Initial tests conducted by Ghailene Bou-Ali at the University of Arizona as part of his master's thesis in civil engineering showed that pinned, unplastered, three-string bale walls were strong and withstood lateral and vertical loads well. The first part of his study measured the compressive strength of unconfined individual bales, producing impressive results when three-string bales were tested laid flat (23 inches wide by 46 inches long). The hydraulic press used for the testing sensed a change in the resistance of the bales at about 72,600 pounds per bale, or 10,000 pounds per square foot. That was considered the failure point, although none of the bale strings broke. Deflection of the bales at the point of failure was 50 percent of the original height, and the bales recovered most of their initial height after the load was removed. The ability of a material to perform this way is known as elastic deformation, or simply, the ability to handle a short-term load and recover without permanent deformation. Design strategies to eliminate or distribute point loads, give adequate roof support for snow loads, and accommodate movement are important.

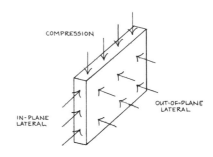

Compressive and lateral forces.

The results from testing three-string bales laid on edge (16 inches wide) were less impressive. The bales demonstrated considerably less strength in this position. Laid on edge, the bales failed at 13,850 pounds, or 2,770 pounds per square foot (with the middle strings breaking). Since the strings in this position go around the bales horizontally, when pressure is applied to the bales they become barrel-shaped, which puts the middle string in tension immediately. Therefore, the testing that was done for bales on edge was really testing the strength of the string. These results seem to indicate that bales used in this position are much better suited as in-fill in non-load-bearing structures and retrofits, or in very small load-bearing structures. Used on edge, bales provide a larger wall area using the same number of bales, while taking up less floor space. They also have a higher net insulation value per inch in that orientation.

The second part of Ghailene's study, conducted on wall panels built of straw bales, also yielded impressive results. Each of three wall panels was loaded with 15,800 pounds, simulating a very large roof load. The panels, 12 feet long and 8 feet high (six courses or rows), were pinned together only with rebar. The bales were bare, with no finish material such as stucco or plaster. The vertical deflection was measured and averaged about 7 inches. That amount of deflection is far greater than that seen in any existing straw bale buildings, leading to speculation about the structural role that stucco or other wall finishes might play in handling high temporary loads, such as snow on the roof. More research and testing are planned in this area. It is worth noting that the many historic load-bearing straw bale buildings in Nebraska do not show evidence of problems from the snow loads they have endured over the years.

In the wall panel tests for out-of-plane lateral loading (a wind load simulation of one hundred miles per hour), the three unplastered panels showed a maximum deflection of 1 inch or less. The six panels used for the lateral tests were the same size as those used for the compression tests, 12 feet long by 8 feet high. They were pinned together with rebar and had two all-thread connections from anchor bolts in the floor to the roof plates on top of the walls.

In-plane lateral loading (pushing on the end of the wall) allowed an average deflection of 4 inches at the top of the wall with a loading of 2,135 pounds applied to the end of the wall. Panels in this test showed a large varia-

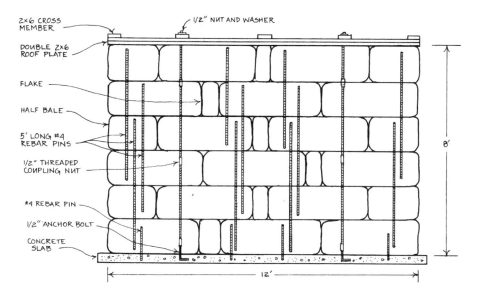

Wall test panel design.

tion in results, presumably caused by differences in the degrees of compression from the all-thread securing the roof plates. The tightest of the three, which represented a normal condition in a common straw bale wall, showed only a 2⅜-inch deflection. The addition of any type of wall finish would greatly enhance the performance of the wall panels in this direction.

Additional research and testing are needed to develop a better understanding of bale assemblies for more varied uses—in multistory structures, construction that can withstand heavy snow loads, and appliances linking bales with other materials. There seem to be no serious problems with load-bearing single-story structures (now experimentally approved in Tucson).

During construction of a load-bearing rice-straw building at the Shenoa Retreat Center in northern California in May of 1994, architect Bob Theis had a rice-straw bale wall constructed to test deflection under vertical loading. A significant feature of his test, not included in Ghailene's test, was a series of loadings in succession. That is essentially what happens in areas of heavy snows, when a structure is subjected to loads of falling snow which melt and release the loads, a pattern that repeats itself many times during the winter. Bob's test was conducted as follows.

The wall was built on a concrete foundation and measured 2 feet wide, 12 feet long, and 8 feet (six courses of bales) high. It utilized dense three-string rice-straw bales made expressly as construction material the previous October by Rick Green in Willows, California.

The wall assembly matched the detailing of the wall assembly for Shenoa Cottage, including ½-inch diameter threaded rods running up through the center of the wall's width at quarter points along its length. These rods extended through a box beam made of 2-by-8 vertical sides with ¾-inch plywood top and bottom. Each rod was straddled by two 2-by-8 cross pieces connected to the 2-by-8 sides with beam hangers installed upside-down. This high-strength connection permits the wall to be precompressed via the box beam, by tightening nuts over malleable iron washers on the threaded rods.

After completion of the test wall, the wall height was measured at the corners and the midpoints of the sides. The bolts were then cranked down as tightly as possible with a hand-held wrench, and the heights remeasured. Vertical displacement averaged 3⅞ inches.

The bolts were relaxed and a test frame constructed over the wall that distributed the weight of five stock tanks approximately 2 by 2 by 6 feet along the length of the wall. The frame suspended two tanks along each side of the wall and one tank on top. The total maximum weight of the test frame and the filled tanks was 7,640 pounds, or 636 pounds per linear foot of wall. This is

1.6 times the design load of four hundred pounds per lineal foot. The wall was loaded by filling the stock tanks with water and the deflection measured. The tanks were drained and the deflection measured again. This cycle was repeated three times until equilibrium was reached, where the deflection and recovery were approximately equal. (At equilibrium, the wall deflected an average of $7/16$ inch at a pressure of four hundred pounds per lineal foot; increasing the pressure to six hundred pounds per lineal foot increased the deflection an additional $1/8$ inch.) The final height of the wall, loaded at 600 pounds per lineal foot, averaged $3 1/2$ inches below original height after these cycles.

The initial test precompression had depressed the wall an average of $3 7/8$ inches, which demonstrated that the threaded rod and box beam assembly could precompress the wall sufficiently to test for differential settlement due to loads up to one-and-a-half-times larger than anticipated.

For the final test, requested by the Building Department, the wall and box beam were covered with mesh and cement plaster approximately $7/8$ inch thick. After allowing the stucco to cure, the wall was marked just below the box beam and a transit sighted at this level; the tanks were filled to load the wall and were left full for four days. No deflection was observed at the transit, and no cracking was observed in the stucco.

SEISMIC RESISTANCE

It appears that straw bale building will be of special value in areas where earthquakes are common. Conventional buildings of earth, adobe, or stone (eight out of ten of the world's homes) are extremely hazardous in earthquakes and costly to reinforce. In 1976, during an earthquake in China, 250,000 people were killed, a great many of them from the collapse of unreinforced masonry houses. In Chile in 1985, another earthquake seriously damaged or destroyed 28,000 adobe homes, leaving 150,000 homeless.

In contrast to those buildings, straw bales have a good width-to-height ratio and can be easily and effectively reinforced with wood, bamboo, or metal pins. The nature of the bales, their flexibility and strength, are ideal for seismic design, as long as the connections between the bale wall system and the roof and foundation are adequate. Bale walls may actually absorb much of the shock of an earthquake, instead of transferring it all to the roof as in conventionally built structures. A coating of plaster (reinforced with wire) adds to the strength of these buildings. Additional sheer bracing will help resist lateral loading along with a concrete or wood bond beam for load distribution.

Architect Bob Theis designed the first permitted load-bearing rice straw building in California, which was engineered to withstand seismic forces. The evolution of straw bale buildings in the state of California should help the development of seismic-resistant straw bale design.

AFFORDABILITY

How much does a straw bale building cost? As is the case with a great many things, it all depends. The costs of building vary by region, by climate and site within a region, by the contribution of owner-builder labor, and by codes and permit requirements. In parts of California, permits and fees can cost more than $20,000, more than a small straw bale house might cost.

A good comparison to begin with is the cost of building the same house of two different wall materials. In the words of Ted Varney, a New Mexico contractor, "I can build for someone the identical structure here in Santa Fe out of a 2-by-6 frame with R-19 walls or out of straw bales with R-42 walls for exactly the same price. The difference is that the one built out of straw will be a far superior product in terms of energy efficiency, durability, comfort, and aesthetic character."

Another way of looking at cost is to break down how money is spent in the process of building a house; ideas about this can differ widely. In a 1982 *Housing* magazine study of the construction costs of a wood-frame house built in Albuquerque, New Mexico, the exterior walls of the house represented 21 percent of the total cost of the house. Other estimates have placed exterior-wall cost as low as 10 to 15 percent. That figure represents 2-by-4 wood-frame construction; the percentage increases rapidly as one begins to consider other materials and methods, such as adobe, rammed earth, double-insulated masonry walls, and super-insulated frame construction. According to various estimates, these alternative forms of construction could cost 25 to 50 percent more than baled materials. Builder Burke Denman of Santa Fe estimated that a straw bale home he completed for approximately $95 per square foot would have cost around $130 per square foot built with adobe and two inches of blown-on polystyrene insulation to meet the local energy codes. In his opinion, "For people interested in a thick-wall adobe look with good insulation, straw bale is the least expensive way to go. You can't insulate a wood-frame home to R-40 for the price."

Another variable that influences the cost of straw bale walls is the price paid per bale. Straw grown and baled within the immediate area of the site will decrease the cost of a bale, in some cases as much as 90 percent or more. In areas where straw disposal is a problem, bales could even be free. When bales are purchased from a local farmer rather than the feed stores, the cost is again much lower. The quantity of bales bought at one time also affects the price. Bales can often be delivered directly to the site, which raises the cost per bale (about fifty cents), but is usually well worth it unless you have access to a flatbed truck. A three-string bale bought in bulk from a feed store and delivered to a rural site in southeastern Arizona was $3.50. In New Mexico, a two-string bale bought in bulk (three hundred bales) from a local feed store cost $2.75.

Overall costs can be reduced in many ways. Owner-builder sweat equity can help reduce outside labor expenditures. Tony Perry, president of the Straw Bale Association in Santa Fe and chairman of the state technical advisory council on straw bale construction, received a Phase II Small Business Innovation Research Grant, part of which will be used in 1994 to construct two prototype straw bale homes to determine how much sweat equity can be used in building them. He estimates that if the layout and excavation, concrete, electrical, and plumbing are subcontracted and a qualified supervisor is maintained on the job full time, but resident family and friends provide the rest of the labor, a 50 percent savings can be realized over conventional 2-by-6 construction. Other studies suggest that baled houses with significant owner-builder labor (again, not foundations, electrical, etc.) may cost even less than a conventional-type home with similar owner labor when various alternative materials and methods are used.

Much of what makes straw bales easily adaptable to the owner-builder is the ease with which a wall can be assembled. By following simple guidelines, a relatively unskilled person can stack a straw wall in a fraction of the time it takes to build a

wood-frame wall, not to mention the time involved in building walls with masonry and earthen materials such as adobe or rammed earth.

Additional cost savings can be realized by keeping the building simple, with few floor and roof height changes, extra corners, or special details. A simple rectangular house fits this description, and it might be designed for subsequent additions as requirements change. Using local natural materials such as mud, stone, and timber, which can often be free, can add to the savings. Recycled, salvaged materials and innovative methods such as rubble trench footings can further reduce costs. A home that draws on all these strategies may not resemble a custom high-cost dream

Above: Interior of Steve and Nena MacDonald's house.
Facing page: Children working with straw.

house, but it can provide a simple, comfortable, energy-efficient shelter with high levels of owner-builder character, creativity, and beauty.

In an attempt to further define the costs associated with bale building, Richard Hoffmeister of Taliesin West created four cost categories ranging from "very low" to "high." The "very low" category estimated costs at $5 to $20 a square foot, made possible by owner-builder labor, the use of salvaged and scavenged materials, and a pay-as-you-go arrangement. The "low" category lists costs of $20 to $50 a square foot, using the system recommended by Tony Perry, in which one pays market prices for materials, subcontracts part of the construction, and assembles the walls and does the finish work oneself. The "moderate" category defines a home that is totally contractor built for $50 to $80 a square foot, with bales typically used as in-fill and a minimum of custom features. The "high" category refers to $80 or more a square foot, and describes a house that is custom built and has a significant number of details and features.

To make a truly accurate comparison of housing costs, it is necessary to talk about life-cycle cost, or the cost of finance, utilities, and maintenance over the life of the building, which in some cases could be hundreds of years. A simple method of examining life-cycle cost would be to compare four structures with similar maintenance requirements, carrying an 80-percent loan at equivalent interest in cost, finance charges, and energy over thirty years. See the tables below for the estimated costs and savings for a 1,375-square-foot, three-bedroom, two-bath home in a moderate climate with both heating and cooling demands.

LIFE CYCLE COSTS — 30 YEARS

Estimated costs and savings for a 1,375-square-foot, 3-bedroom, 2-bath home in a moderate climate with both heating and cooling demands.

CONVENTIONAL

Construction cost	$ 82,500
Down payment (20 %)	16,500
Finance	118,800
Energy (heat and cooling)	36,000
Total life-cycle costs	171,300

STRAW BALE — CONTRACTOR-BUILT

Construction cost	$ 82,500
Down payment (20 %)	16,500
Finance	118,800
Energy (heat and cooling)	18,000
Total life-cycle costs	153,300
Savings	18,000

STRAW BALE — PARTIALLY OWNER-BUILT (WALLS, ROOFING, FINISHING) AND WITH SUPER-EFFICIENT APPLIANCES

Construction cost	$ 40,000
Down payment (20 %)	8,000
Finance	57,600
Energy (heat and cooling)	9,000
Total life-cycle costs	74,600
Savings	96,700

STRAW BALE — TOTALLY OWNER-BUILT, USING RECYCLED MATERIALS,
AND WITH SUPER-EFFICIENT APPLIANCES

Construction cost (cash)	$ 20,625
Down payment	none
Finance	zero
Energy (heat and cooling)	9,000
Total life-cycle costs	29,625
Savings	141,675

The 30-year savings are important, but a well-built straw bale home should last for more than a hundred years, with very low maintenance costs. The savings become even more impressive—a nice legacy for the family.

LIFE CYCLE COSTS–100 YEARS

	COST	SAVINGS
Conventional	527,340	—
Straw Bale—contractor-built	467,900	59,440
Straw Bale—partially owner-built	227,780	299,560
Straw Bale—owner-built (as above)	29,625	497,715

More detailed studies are needed with full accounting for life-cycle costs, including utility service and construction costs. A straw bale building would prove even more cost competitive after considering environmental impact and related costs.

CHAPTER 3

COMMON CONCERNS

FIRE SAFETY

"The straw bales/mortar structure wall has proven to be exceptionally resistant to fire. The straw bales hold enough air to provide good insulation value but because they are compacted firmly they don't hold enough air to permit combustion."

—REPORT TO THE CANADA MORTGAGE AND HOUSING CORPORATION

Interior of Carol Anthony's straw bale studio.

"The results of these tests have proven that a straw bale in-fill wall assembly is a far greater fire resistive assembly than a wood frame wall assembly using the same finishes."

—1993 REPORT TO THE CONSTRUCTION INDUSTRIES COMMISSION OF NEW MEXICO
by Manuel A. Fernandez, architect, CID, based on results of two-hour fire tests

In the mid 1980s, the National Research Council of Canada carried out fire safety tests of plastered straw bales and found them to be more resistant to fire than most conventional building materials. The mortar-encased bales passed the small-scale fire test with a maximum temperature rise of only 110 degrees F. over four hours. The plaster surface coating withstood temperatures of up to 1,850 degrees F. for two hours before a small crack developed.

In 1993, fire tests completed in the state of New Mexico showed equally positive results. Two tests were conducted, one on an unplastered straw bale wall panel and the second on a straw bale wall that had been plastered on the heated side and stuccoed on the outside face. The first test conducted on the unplastered wall section met the standard requirements of exposing the interior face of the panel to 1,000 degrees F. within five minutes and increasing to 1,550 degrees F. after thirty minutes. The temperature rise on the unheated side of the panel was 1.97 degrees F. It took thirty-four minutes for the fire to burn through the center of the test wall, not through the middle of a bale, but

Niche before and after the fire.

at a joint where bales met. When the panel burned through at the joint, the rest of the bales were only charred halfway through, about 9 inches of the 18-inch thickness of the two-string bales tested.

In the second test, furnace temperatures reached 1,942 degrees F. during a two-hour test period. Flames and hot gases did not penetrate the test wall, and the temperature rise on the unheated side of the panel was about 10 degrees F. There was some cracking of the plaster on the heated side of the panel, and where this occurred there was charring of the bales to a depth of 2 inches. The Canadian and New Mexico fire tests clearly show the exceptional fire resistance of plastered straw bales.

The older Nebraska hay-bale houses, like other rural homes, sometimes burned when they were struck by lightning or ignited by fierce-burning chimney fires. Such fires were commonly carried from the roof or ceiling down to the wall. In the days before pressurized water systems and chemical fire extinguishers, the compact and relatively airtight straw walls burned slowly but were hard to put out. A fire break or fire retardant at the top of the wall will help prevent that type of fire. Plastered bale buildings with metal roofs, metal soffits, and fire-resistant window shutters might prove to be a wise choice in areas where brush and grass fires are a major threat.

The Martin-Monhart bale house in Arthur, Nebraska, was once struck by lightning but did not burn. The only casualty was a box of tissues in the dining room. A wood-framed house wrapped with straw bales in Tucson, Arizona, still under construction and unplastered, was set on fire by an arsonist. An accelerant, possibly gas, was apparently sprayed along the wall and then set on fire. The wood burned almost completely, but the straw hardly burned at all. Because the bales were set on edge, however, all the ties burned, and the bales fell apart.

One bale-house owner left a candle burning late one afternoon in a wood-framed box that had been set into an unplastered niche in a bale wall. The candle set the wood on fire, completely burning the box, but the straw around the box did not ignite and was found charred and smoldering the next morning. The charred straw was removed from the surface of the bale, and the bale was plastered.

In the summer of 1994, in San Louis Obisbo, California, a fire storm with 300-feet-high flames completely destroyed the home of Ken Haggard and Polly Cooper, architects of the Noland straw bale house. Their home was primarily frame construction. Nothing of the house or its contents remained. The one exception was a recently constructed plastered straw bale patio seat that had absorbed a large amount of heat, but did not burn. This costly piece of research clearly demonstrates the potential value of using straw as a building material in fire-prone areas. Ken and Polly are planning to rebuild their home with straw bales.

Plastered straw bale seat after the San Luis Obispo fire.

For building-code approval in the United States, one approach is to rename a straw bale wall as a 1 to 3 inch thick wire-reinforced concrete or plaster fire wall containing straw insulation. Fire retardants may be advisable in high-risk areas if arson is a likely prospect or if straw is left exposed. The unplastered straw walls of a house constructed by the EOS Institute, an organization dedicated to the sustainable development of human environments, for the Southern California Home Show were sprayed with a clear fire retardant at the convention center's request. Other builders have plastered bale walls with a light clay mix that includes borax. In addition to being a fire retardant, borax is also a fungicide and rodent repellent. It is available from chemical supply houses and is significantly cheaper than most commercially available fire retardants. Borax will dissolve in water, but not stay in solution when it is applied unless it is mixed at the right percentage and heated to the right temperature. It is only 5 percent soluble at room temperature. Tom Luecke of Boulder, Colorado, when using borax on his straw bale studio, referred to the *Kirk Othmer Encyclopedia* for this information. He used a salamander kerosene heater placed against the side of a fifty-five-gallon drum to heat the mix. Boric acid (1 part) can be added to the Borax (2 parts) to help neutralize its highly alkaline nature and bring it to a pH of 6 to 8. This will minimize its corrosive effect.

Northeast Fireshield sells an approved non-toxic fire retardant called "Inspecta-shield Plus." Other retardants are sold regionally.

Loose straw or flakes of bales, used to stuff ceilings as insulation or as fill against wood framing, are much more vulnerable to fire than dense bales and could be treated with fire retardants.

Fire safety in a straw bale house also requires the same attention to wiring practices and codes as do conventional homes. Should a bale fire ever occur, it would be preferable to use a fire extinguisher rather than water, which could create additional moisture damage.

When a fireman in northern New Mexico was asked about straw bale fire safety, he responded with a chuckle: "No problem. We use straw bales to make smoke for our training exercises. They smolder rather than burn. We set them on fire, they smolder and make smoke, we put them out. Then we drag them outside to dry and use them again."

Interior of Burritt mansion/museum, Alabama.

HUMIDITY AND MOISTURE

It has been demonstrated that bale buildings are capable of successfully surviving humid climates, but less is known about the interaction of humid air and bales than probably any other aspect of bale building. Hopefully future research will help provide greater clarity in understanding how humidity affects bales in different climates and conditions. However, no research is needed to understand that it is critical to protect bales from direct exposure to moisture. Damage from water is by far the greatest potential hazard to a bale structure, and buildings should be detailed to provide the necessary protection. Damage by water can result in problems ranging from complete disintegration of the bales to problems with mold and mildew.

The most vulnerable parts of a straw bale wall are the top and bottom. The roof structure should go on as quickly as possible after the walls have been stacked. If there will be a delay, the tops of the walls should be covered with tarps. If moisture enters the top of the bales and penetrates to lower courses in the wall, there is a chance that the bales will begin to rot before drying out. Protecting the bottom of the bales is equally important. Bales should be adequately raised 6 to 8 inches above ground level. A moisture barrier should also be placed between the bottom of the bales and the footing to prevent moisture from wicking into the bale. It is also important to protect the lower portion of straw bale walls, which are subject to splashes or excessive driven rain, with a moisture barrier underneath the stucco.

The sides of a bale wall do not pose the same problems as the top and

bottom. Buildings left unplastered for some time or even indefinitely have showed virtually no deterioration, even when subjected to rain and snow. What seems to happen is that only the outside surface of the bale becomes wet, and it dries rapidly with the return of dryer weather. There have been problems when bale walls got wet and remained so because something was up against them, trapping the water and inhibiting the bales from drying out.

A study beginning in 1983, conducted by the Canada Housing and Mortgage Corporation, checked humidity levels at three-year intervals in the walls of a house built by Louis Gagné. The study showed that the humidity levels in bale walls remain low, despite fluctuations in humidity in the environment around the walls. Test wires installed in the walls, including the bathroom, showed an average relative humidity of 13 percent. The tests also showed that bales continued to dry out after the wall was built and plastered. The moisture content in bales is measured as a percentage of dry weight and is not the same as the relative humidity of the air, also expressed as a percentage.

The Canadian studies found that the moisture content of tested bales stayed low enough to offer good thermal resistance (the resistance of a body to the flow of heat) without the use of a vapor barrier. In the case of a straw

Reed and Mary Engel's house near Tonasket, Washington.

bale refrigerator that was built using a vapor barrier on the inside wall only, the straw deteriorated within the course of a year due to the high temperature differential and the resulting condensation that occurred between the straw bales and the barrier. There are no historical precedents of bales being used with moisture barriers, and consequently no data on how the two perform together.

A bale wall with maximum breathability may be the best insurance against potential problems with moisture. George Tsongas of Portland State University in Oregon, a noted authority on moisture in buildings, energy, and indoor air quality, believes that the concept of breathing walls is probably a good idea but should be tested in very wet climates such as the Pacific Northwest.

A number of bale buildings have been built in humid climates and have successfully endured those conditions. Examples include the 1938 bale mansion in Huntsville, Alabama, and a 1978 building near Rockport, Washington, an area reported to receive 75 inches of rain a year. Also in Washington, near Tonasket, is a house built in 1984 with no foundation and the bales sitting on plastic on the ground. The exterior has never been plastered, and there is no apparent deterioration of the bales, indicating the importance of bales being able to "breathe" and dry out.

TERMITES AND PESTS, ALLERGIES AND ODORS

One of the common worries about bale buildings is the threat of pests such as rodents and insects. However, experience in both old and new bale houses has shown that this is an unfounded concern, even with hay bales, which still have the seed heads on the grasses.

Straw bales provide fewer spaces and havens for pests than conventional wood framing. If a good coat of plaster is applied and maintained, access for even small bugs is significantly reduced. Walls left unplastered are another matter. Experience has shown that bumble bees like to nest in straw, and it seems quite likely that they would not be alone. Shelters in Nebraska that were not plastered developed some problems with fleas in the early days.

There are few termites that like straw, compared to many that like wood. The wood in the window and door frames in the Bruner house was eaten by termites, while the straw was left untouched. Precautions such as termite shields, sand barriers, specially applied vapor barriers, diatomaceous earth (insect control, not pool-filter grade), or borate can be used to provide added protection against termites in the same areas where they are a problem in conventional housing.

Clean, bright straw has very little mold or allergy potential. Asthmatics have had problems with moldy straw, which should be avoided. Once sealed in a wall, however, even the less-clean straw seems to be acceptable. The owners of just one building have come forward with a mold or mildew problem. Their post-and-beam structure has bales used as in-fill and cement stucco on both the inside and outside. The stucco was kept wet for two weeks, to aid in the curing and reduce cracking. The walls inside the house were regularly soaked, rather than misted, as were the exterior walls. This apparently led to saturation of the bales within the stucco. Soon thereafter, the walls were painted and sealed. The problem developed after some time had elapsed. Care must be taken to avoid over-wetting stucco or plaster walls to prevent getting the bales wet underneath.

BUILDING CODES

Straw bale buildings can encounter the same problems with building codes as many other ecologically sound, proven methods of construction, like rammed earth and adobe. Unless there has already been a straw bale building approved by local building officials, the process of obtaining a permit can be a lengthy and laborious process of dialogue, education, and planning, which may be shortened by liberal doses of patience, flexibility, and good communication. The whole process can take some time, but it is possible to get approval, and once that is accomplished things will be considerably easier for those who follow.

In many areas of the country the building-code process and its officials are both flexible and helpful. Pima County, Arizona, and the city of Tucson, as well as the Construction Industries Division (CID) of New Mexico have been extremely helpful and cooperative in furthering the process of bringing straw bale construction into the building codes. Both Pima County and the city of Tucson have routinely approved buildings using straw bales as in-fill in combination with a variety of structural-support systems. Both have also issued experimental permits for load-bearing straw residential structures under sections 105 and 107 of the Uniform Building Code (UBC), which allows for experimental construction using alternative methods and materials. Prescriptive standards in these areas are close to being completed and could be adopted sometime in 1995.

While waiting for the state of New Mexico to include straw bale building in the state code, the New Mexico CID initially issued a total of thirty experimental permits for bale in-fill structures before allowing an unlimited number of experimental permits due to high public demand. By mid-1994, prescriptive standards for bale in-fill structures had gone through the initial stages of approval and were on their way to being included in New Mexico's state code. Worth noting are the comments by Manuel Fernandez, who is head of the plan review and permit section of New Mexico's CID: "Straw bales are an excellent insulating material, with lots of structural integrity. I don't know why this material has never been considered for construction." One of the major obstacles to approving load-bearing straw bale building in the New Mexico code is the lack of a field test to determine the structural integrity of the bales as well as their moisture content.

The few code-related success stories, none of them quickly achieved, were the result of a continuous effort over a period of approximately four years by a group of dedicated people—notably Matts Myhrman, David Eisenberg in Tucson, and the Straw Bale Construction Association in Santa Fe. Their work should make results possible elsewhere in considerably less time.

Probably the most logical way to begin the process, especially in areas where there is no precedent of straw bale code approval, is to learn as much as possible about straw bale construction and to establish contact with some-

Mark Hawes' solar-powered straw bale home, one of the first experimental permits issued by New Mexico's Construction Industries Division.

one who has some experience building with bales. The resource list in the back of this book contains sources of straw bale information and names of individuals capable of providing assistance. Without this kind of background it may be difficult to know what construction method best suits the building being considered.

The next step is to begin discussion with local building officials. It is usually a good idea to provide officials with as much information as possible in the way of historical precedents, examples of recently constructed straw bale buildings, and results of fire and structural testing, as well as a clear, concise idea of what is to be built. You might suggest that they contact one of the public building officials in a state or locality where straw bale building permits have been issued.

The easiest permit to secure for a residential or commercial structure will be one in which the bales are used for in-fill in combination with some type of structural support such as post-and-beam construction. Approval for a building with load-bearing bale walls will usually be considerably more difficult, but as code approvals and prescriptive standards in other areas become more commonplace, the process should become easier.

Planning to build in the United States will most probably require conforming to one of three model building codes: the Uniform Building Code (UBC), the Basic Building Code (BBC), or the Standard Building Code (SBC). They are all similar, with a slightly different emphasis for use in different parts of the country. Recently, the three organizations represented by the codes have formed the Conference of American Building Officials (CABO), which has developed a National Evaluation Service for testing and certifying building materials and systems—probably the best route for obtaining national acceptance of straw bales as a building material.

The three codes are selectively applied on state, county, and city levels. State codes are usually employed only if city and county codes are not in use. The code used in a given area is most often the one that seems the most appropriate to local conditions of wind, seismic activity, and snowfall loads. Within each of the three code systems are sections concerned with the use of alternative and new materials and methods in building. These allow building officials to approve designs, methods, and materials that they think satisfactorily comply with the intent of the code. Applying for a permit under such a section may be the best approach in areas where bale building is not established. It allows the applicant to build the structure of his or her choice while providing building officials an opportunity to observe a new building process without setting a precedent.

The process of submitting plans is usually straightforward, requiring a plot plan, foundation plan, floor plan, roof framing plan, wall elevations, and any significant details. Also needed are the electrical, plumbing, and mechanical details, which can be included on the floor plan or submitted separately if necessary.

Regular consultation with the building officials while the plans are being developed can minimize delays. Time can be saved and disappointment avoided if corrections and adjustments are made along the way rather than running the risk of having plans rejected when they are finally submitted. If setbacks arise, persistence and assistance from resourceful straw bale advocates will usually bring success.

Once several buildings have been completed in an area and it is evident that they are solid, durable, and safe, it is usually easier to develop prescriptive standards for including straw bales in local codes. David Eisenberg has written an excellent article on straw bales and building codes in issue number 5 of the newsletter, *The Last Straw* (see appendix).

The way in which research and testing is conceived and carried out will affect the way codes are eventually written. This concern was the basis for a proposal to create a national straw bale research and testing advisory network, which came out of a working group at the first national conference on straw bale building held at Arthur, Nebraska, in 1993. The intent of the proposal is for this network to provide broad-based coordination and guidance for straw bale research and testing efforts, so that duplicative testing can be avoided. The full proposal for a National Straw Bale Advisory Network can be found in issue number 6 of *The Last Straw* newsletter. For more information or to volunteer, contact David Eisenberg of the Bale Research Advisory Network (see appendix).

Hopefully, the development of code standards for straw bale construction will accommodate both owner-builders and the professional design and building industry. Although the two groups are linked in this process, the needs and priorities of each are different. On the one hand, straw bale construction is a simple building system that can be used by ordinary people who may have little or no building experience. On the other hand, straw bale construction lends itself to professionals wishing to create more complex and intricate structures requiring a higher level of construction skill.

Prescriptive codes, which basically describe how a building is to be constructed, will allow owner-builders to get permits for simple structures without the need for an architect or engineer to approve the plans. This has the advantage of lowering the affordability threshold for low-income people. It

The Brophy Chapel in southeastern Arizona.

has the disadvantage of limiting how buildings can be built and making innovation more difficult. Performance codes generally require someone qualified to do calculations and approve plans. However, they increase the flexibility of design options. It is possible to write codes that will benefit both methods, but the task needs a conscious effort to be done well. That is where a coordinated research advisory network can have a major influence and facilitate a successful outcome.

It can be easy to get discouraged with the building permit process and conforming to code may be difficult. For that reason, many of the straw bale houses now in use were built either in areas where building codes had not been adopted or outside the approval process in areas where codes exist. They are in some cases referred to as outlaw houses. Many of these structures possess a sense of ingenuity, artistry, and economy that is often not allowed (or at least is sometimes discouraged) by code approval. It is also fair to say that some of these structures have features that could potentially be problematic at some point, but could have been avoided had attention been paid to relatively simple issues.

Most indigenous cultures have relied more on the integrity of their people than a formal code to dictate standards of building. While codes provide many benefits and a margin of safety to the uninformed and unsuspecting buyer, they also radically transform the process of building from one involving families and communities to a process dominated by professional labor, high costs, standardized materials, and an often unneeded level of complexity.

An interview with Randall Croxton of Croxton Associates, the firm that retrofitted an old New York City building for the new Audubon Society offices, offers an interesting perspective on building-code compliance. Croxton describes modern building standards as a minimally code-compliant approach concerned with quick delivery of a finished product, thereby necessitating the use of mass-produced materials. He says, "All the invisible systems in modern structures are cut back to the legal minimums, so when people brag that they have built a code-compliant building, what they're really saying is that they have built the worst building that the law will allow them to build." Depending on how one feels about such things, those circumstances can be either positive or negative.

Finally, if building codes were more environmentally friendly, straw bale structures would come into favor as it would instead become impossible to build an energy-wasting, hard-to-maintain conventional house.

As Steve MacDonald, a modern straw bale pioneer from Gila, New Mexico, wrote:

Nena and I, with a little help from neighbors, built our straw bale house here in rural New Mexico over seven years ago. We did it all without the benefit of code. Given a choice, I doubt if we would do it any differently today. I say this not because I think building codes are wrong minded or inappropriate—they have their place in the proper context and at the proper scale. Rather, what I am concerned about is the erosive effect they may have on adaptation and innovation in response to local needs, and on personal and local community rights and responsibilities. In our reductive efforts to codify the construction of our shelters for health and safety, perhaps we need to worry a whole lot less over hurricane clips, rebar, and bureaucratic hoop-jumping, and a whole lot more over our effects on ecological and community health and integrity, and of our right sharing of this Earth's finite resources. The code most needed is one that asks us this one seemingly simple question: How do I least harm? From the answers that emerge comes a clearer understanding of what health and safety truly means and entails.

Right: Steve MacDonald. Below: Interior, Virginia Carabelli's house.

INSURANCE AND FINANCING

Insurance and financing have been secured successfully for a number of straw bale homes. The first was Virginia Carabelli's house in Santa Fe, New Mexico, in 1991. At the time Virginia applied, there were no straw bale houses in the area or elsewhere that had been insured or financed. Although she required no bank financing for her project, she chose to pursue it in order to establish a precedent. Virginia persevered through a year of hard work and disappointment before finally being granted a permit, financing, and insurance.

Thanks to Virginia Carabelli's efforts and those of others who have followed, hopefully the process of securing financing and insurance will be easier in the near future.

In early 1994, a straw bale house under construction by Bob Munk in New Mexico was approved for financing under federal Fannie Mae guidelines, giving his mortgage much more flexibility and marketability.

If the straw bale building under construction has secured a building permit, and the owner is in a position to obtain insurance and financing for a similar structure built from other materials, then there usually isn't a problem in obtaining insurance or financing. Insurance companies will most likely be concerned with the ability of a bale structure to withstand fire. Results of the fire tests conducted in New Mexico could help alleviate their concerns.

CHAPTER 4

WORKING WITH STRAW BALES

STRAW WAS AN IMPORTANT RESOURCE in traditional communities and found its way into the construction of walls long before the arrival of modern baling equipment. Many different varieties of straw have been used historically for various aspects of building, the type often having more to do with what was being grown locally than anything else. Rice, wheat, rye, and flax straws are particularly suited for baled building; barley, oats, and many other straws also are good. Rice straw has a high silica content, which makes it very resistant to weathering, but also makes it a little harder on baling equipment than other straws. Many of these straws have also been used for thatching.

David Eisenberg holding a custom-sized bale.

Many of the early Nebraska houses, schools, and commercial buildings were built with meadow hay, but straw is preferred. Since straw is the stems left over after the grain is harvested, it is more likely to be dry and free of seeds and other matter that attracts the pests commonly drawn to hay.

Nuisance plants such as tumbleweed can also be baled when green and used to build structures. Widely detested weeds such as Johnson grass can make excellent building material. Bean vine bales may also work for in-fill buildings, and even baled waste materials such as newspapers and magazines can be used for building.

An important point to consider is that when it comes to building, bales using different types of straw may behave differently. When rice-straw bales were used for the first time in the construction of a building at the Shenoa Learning Center in northern California, it was discovered that they did not behave like other bales previously used for wall construction. The stems of the rice straw did not tend to align in the same direction, but were matted and compacted. In the words of David Eisenberg, workshop leader for the wall-raising, "They were like working with Brillo pads or steel wool." Special techniques had to be developed to allow rebar pins and threaded rods to penetrate the bales.

It is possible that straw bales for buildings could be made with halophytes (salt-loving plants) grown with sea water. However, straw with a high salt content may be hygroscopic (good at absorbing and retaining moisture), and may require special attention to waterproofing. Tests of these high-salt straws are needed to determine the best handling procedures.

In the Dakotas, it is not uncommon for plant growth in highway medians to be cut and baled—a potential source of building materials for many counties and cities.

BALING

Baling straw or hay, while not difficult, is almost an art. If you have the opportunity to choose the source of your bales or, better still, have the baling done for you, it is possible to get bales that are higher quality and more uniform. Perhaps as important as how the baling is done is how the crop and straw are harvested. For instance, straw which is harvested with rotary combines is usually shorter and more beat up. The best book on the subject is *Hay and Forage Harvesting* by the John Deere Company (see appendix). This book also provides information on straw harvesting systems and recommendations for equipment combinations.

Baling straw or hay is not difficult, but adjusting a baler can be very frustrating for a beginner. Using a baler is best learned from an expert who can teach you how to set tension and how to judge when to cut, rake, and bale.

Hay or straw can also be baled by animal-powered balers or by hand. Many of the old houses were built with animal-powered balers, which use a rotary lever to drive a screw press. Hand baling can be done with a press (plans are available; see appendix). Half bales are usually needed on most bale projects. These are most often made on site but can sometimes be ordered directly from the baler or with the help of the outlet selling the bales. Some new balers can tie bales as short as 12 inches. It should be noted that custom-size bales, though smaller, will probably cost as much as the full-length bales due to the extra time and effort required to make them.

Bales come bound with baling wire or polypropylene binder (strings). Structures have been built using both types, and there seems to be no structural difference between them, except the stringed bales can be easier to modify, requiring only a knife or scissors to cut the strings. It is easier and more reliable to retie with strings than wires. Bales tied with sisal string should be avoided since it is weak and stretches too much.

It is best to use only bales that are sufficiently compact for building. Although excessive compression reduces the insulation value, too little tension makes bales wobbly and too soft. The compression setting on a mechanical baler should be moderate to high for building bales (250–500 pounds works well on a New Holland baler). Obviously, when buying bales, the compression settings are difficult to determine unless one deals directly with the person doing the baling. A simple test, specified in the New Mexico state code for non-structural bale walls, is that the bale should possess sufficient compression to remain intact when lifted by one baling wire or string.

Bales can usually be bought or tracked down through local feed stores and equestrian centers. Farm organizations, the local free market paper, and the want ads may also help find good bales suitable for building.

Bales come in a number of sizes. Most common are the small two-string and the medium-sized three-string bales. Besides these smaller bales, there are massive rectangular and round bales that can be moved only with special equipment. These larger bales have been used for building mostly temporary animal or agricultural shelters, while the three-string and two-string bales have been used in residential and utility buildings. When baling is done for shipment over long distances, it is more likely that the bales will be made with three-string balers. Three-string bales tend to be larger and more dense, offering more stability and insulation than two-string bales, although the latter are easier to handle.

Some areas of the country maintain a good supply of straw throughout the year, while others experience shortages toward the end of the season just before the next cuttings are done. Ideally, bales should be obtained early in the design process to allow the building design to match the average size of the bales—the "bale module." At the very least, the average size of the bales available should be verified. It is very disappointing to design a building for 42-inch bales and then find out that only 46-inch bales are available. It is also wise to check on bale availability before setting wall-raising dates to avoid finding out the week before that there are no bales to be found nearby.

To determine the average size of the bales bought for use in a building project, lay ten randomly chosen bales end to end and measure the total length, then divide by ten for an average length. Do the same for height: either put bales on edge side by side or stack two piles as high as they will be stacked in the wall, and measure to determine the average. Use slightly longer measurements for the bale module to allow for differences when building. It is much easier to fill cracks than it is to make a lot of custom bales.

Producing bales in a variety of sizes for use in different applications would be of great use, particularly smaller bales, which could be better suited for interior use and allow for greater flexibility of wall design.

In an attempt to reduce the width of bales and to get each side neatly cut, Canadian Louis Gagné was able to successfully modify a baler. The plunger compacting the straw was reduced from 500mm to 350mm in width, and walls made of steel plates were added to the chamber so it would correspond to the modified plunger. Another set of knives was added on the plunger and the chamber. A small opening was punctured on the wall receiving the injected straw, in order to eliminate the cut ends of the straw.

Field tests proved the modified baler to be extremely effective. The bales produced were neatly cut, straight, and had true flat ends. Louis believed the bales to be of a quality he had not previously experienced with straw. Because of the increased uniformity, he felt that his finely cut bales would significantly reduce the amount of labor and plaster required to build a bale structure. Another significant improvement was eliminating the folding of the straw on one side of the bale, creating good plastering surfaces on both sides of the bale.

MOISTURE CONTENT

The ideal moisture content of the bales is less than 14 percent (as a percentage of dry weight), but the New Mexico standards list 20 percent as acceptable. It is the moisture content over time that is critical and should be kept below the threshold of biological activity that results in decay, generally thought to be 14 to 16 percent, by protecting the bales as the structure is built—not allowing them to get wet, and if they do get wet, making sure they dry out.

There are two main reasons to be concerned about moisture content in bales for building. The first is to ensure that the bales are not so wet that there will be a problem with rot. The second is related to calculating the density of bales. Bale density can be determined by weighing and measuring the bales and calculating the number of pounds per cubic foot. However, if the bales contain a significant amount of water, the apparent density will be higher than the actual density. Although visual inspection will usually suffice in determining whether or not a bale is sufficiently dry to be used for in-fill, for load-bearing walls a more accurate method may be required by building officials or more cautious builders and owners.

If they are needed, bale moisture meters, calibrated for straw, are available from Straw Bale Construction Management, Inc. in Santa Fe, New Mexico. It is also possible to have a materials testing lab take samples from some of the bales and put them in sealed containers, and weigh, dry, and re-weigh them to calculate the moisture content. This percentage can then be used to adjust the density determined by weighing and measuring the bales.

A tool is being devised to gauge the actual compressibility of bales in the field. Once it is developed, tested, and made available, it should eliminate the need for moisture testing except to determine that bales are sufficiently dry to be plastered or enclosed. There has been a limited amount of research to determine the equilibrium moisture content of straw at different relative humidities and temperatures.

BALE CHARACTERISTICS

TWO-STRING BALE

14 to 16 inches high
18 inches wide
35 to 40 inches long
35 to 65 pounds (dry weight)
R-value 43.2 (laid flat)
R-value 42 to 48 (laid on edge)

THREE-STRING BALE

14 to 17 inches high
23 inches wide
43 to 47 inches long
60 to 90 pounds (dry weight)
R-value 55.2 (laid flat)
R-value 42 to 51 (laid on edge)

Comparison of two-string and three-string bales.

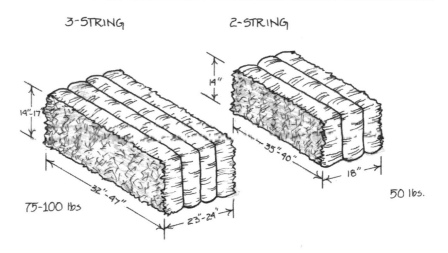

As can be seen above, bales have three different linear measures: height, width, and length. When the wider side, or the width, is laid parallel to the ground, it is commonly said that the bale has been "laid flat." When the narrower of the two sides is laid parallel to the ground, the bale has been laid "on edge."

BALE STORAGE

Bales should be kept dry, of course, before, during, and after construction. They should be stored off the ground, preferably on pallets, to keep moisture from being absorbed from the ground, and should be covered with good-quality tarps to keep off the rain. The covering should extend down each side of the stack by at least one bale, and the stack should be "crowned" on top to prevent water from standing on the tarps and possibly leaking into the middle of the stack through pinholes. The top row of bales around the perimeter of the stack should provide a small overhang so the sides of the stack are protected, even if the tarp doesn't extend all the way down.

Inexpensive rolls of plastic and tarps used by themselves are very susceptible to tearing or puncture, which makes it easy for moisture to penetrate through the bales to the middle of the stack. One method of protection is to cover the stack first with plastic sheeting to provide waterproofing, followed by a tarp. Keeping the tarps anchored securely is often difficult, especially if there are strong winds. One of the better methods is to use anything with weight such as cement blocks or old tires tied to the end of a rope and attached to the eyelets at the edges of the tarp.

Tarps should be kept at hand to cover the wall during construction, even if rain is not expected. Compact, hard, dry bales are much easier to work with and should settle very little as the roof load is applied. If bales do get wet, it would be wise to let them dry before plastering even though they will continue to dry after the plaster has been applied.

Damp or wet bales should be stored in rows rather than compact piles to speed drying and prevent possible problems with spontaneous combustion. The bales can provide enough insulation in a large cubical stack for high temperatures to develop as a result of microbial activity at the core.

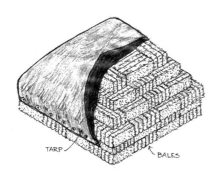

Bales stacked with crowned top.

HANDLING STRAW BALES

Straw bales are relatively easy to move around and stack. Two people working together reduce strain and speed the work. Straw bales can be abrasive, so long-sleeved shirts and pants are highly recommended, as well as dust masks, since there is often a lot of dust in bales. Gloves and hay hooks are also helpful. The secret to lifting and throwing bales is to use momentum and body weight rather than to try muscling them around. Loading a truck of bales by hand will demonstrate why most larger baling operations are now mechanized. A large wheeled dolly or wheelbarrow to haul the bales around is helpful. A small tractor with a front bucket would speed construction work on larger bale projects.

MODIFYING BALES

Full-sized bales can be modified to almost any size or shape. However, because a bale will fall apart if its ties are cut, it must be resized and tied again before the original ties are cut.

To modify bales, a bale needle and a supply of polypropylene baling twine will be needed. (In general, polypropylene twine is much easier to use for retying bales than baling wire.) A needle can be made from a piece of steel rod $5/16$ of an inch in diameter by 3 feet long. One end of the rod can be hammered flat and filed to a dull point. Drill two holes near the point, approximately $1/4$ of an inch in diameter, and remove burrs or sharp edges. The other end can be bent at a 90-degree angle to provide a handle about 6 inches long.

One of the simplest methods for modifying and retying bales was developed by Jon Ruez, builder of a number of straw bale structures in southern Arizona.

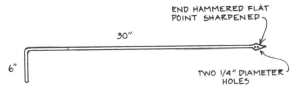

END HAMMERED FLAT
POINT SHARPENED

30"

6"

TWO 1/4" DIAMETER
HOLES

5/16" DIAMETER ROD NEEDLE

Method of using bale needle and baling twine to make two half bales.

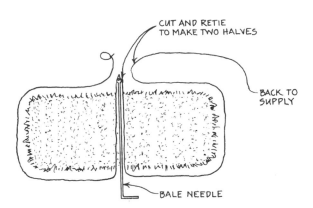

CUT AND RETIE
TO MAKE TWO HALVES

BACK TO
SUPPLY

BALE NEEDLE

- Determine what size bale is needed. Then simply mark the bale next to each of its ties at the point where it is to be divided. You will replace each of the original ties before they are cut.
- Measure the amount of twine needed for the custom-sized bale. Do this by threading the twine through the bale needle and then laying the needle across the top of the bale at the point where it is to be divided. Pull enough twine through the needle to go around the new bale, with enough left over to tie a knot at the end, and then continue pulling enough to go around the remaining section of bale.
- Insert the needle at the point where the bale is to be divided, right next to the first bale tie, and push the needle through to the opposite side of the bale, paying attention not to twist the needle as it goes through. With the twine now trailing back through the bale to the point where the needle was inserted, separate the two lengths of twine, (one going back to the supply roll and one free) keeping track of which piece of twine comes out on the left or right on the other side of the bale. This can be checked by pulling one piece back and forth through the bale to determine which side of the new bale it should wrap around. The object here is to avoid twisting the two strings, which would result in the new ties for the two modified bales being looped together like links in a chain. Then wrap them in opposite directions around the bales to the point where the needle emerged.
- Cut the twine at the needle, after checking to be sure it is long enough to go around the new bale and still allow a loop to be tied on one end, and for the other end to go through the loop and be pulled tight and tied off. Then, take the other piece of twine and repeat the process, cutting the twine from the supply roll after ensuring it is long enough to tie the loop on one end and leave enough to pull the other end through the loop, tighten it, and tie it off. Two simple half-hitch knots are usually adequate. It is important that the new ties are as tight as the original ties to maintain the degree of compaction of the bales.
- Rethread the needle and repeat the process for the remaining ties. Most bales do not have to be cut, but are easy enough to pull apart. When the last tie has been replaced, the old ties can be cut and the two new, modified bales pulled apart.

Hand modification is usually sufficient, but for large production operations a compression jig can be set up to ensure uniform size.

Early attempts at creating custom-sized bales from rice straw proved somewhat difficult. Because the stems of the straw were compressed rather than directionally aligned, the newly formed bales did not easily separate from one another when the twine was cut; each new bale tended to pull straw from the other half. Later efforts found it helpful to run a saw through the middle of the bale before dividing it.

Bales can also be cut lengthwise or notched with a chainsaw or handsaw. Extreme caution is always necessary when working with any type of chainsaw. Some builders find that small electric chainsaws (approximately 14 to 16 inches) work well. They are light and easy to work with, quiet, and don't produce a lot of noxious fumes like the gasoline versions. If a lot of cutting or trimming is to be done indoors, the electric models are a much better choice due to the reduced ventilation inside the structure. If the chainsaw is being used to straighten and level sections of wall, the saw will be laid flat against the wall section, in which case the fumes of a gas-powered saw will be continually trapped against the wall and inhaled by the operator. It should be noted that chainsaws continually clog up from cutting bales and need to be cleaned out at regular intervals. Watch out for bale ties. If one is accidentally cut, it will wrap itself thoroughly and completely around the sprocket of the chain, and the saw will have to be disassembled and the twine removed before more cutting can be done.

Check for old hay saws in antique stores, since they will cut bales more easily than a regular handsaw. A new version of the old hay saw called a "straw knife" is available from Real Goods (see appendix). Ross Burkhardt and Randy Wood developed the straw knife when it was discovered that regular hay saws, chainsaws, and handsaws dulled rapidly when cutting rice straw and did not perform satisfactorily. They experimented with

different shapes and tooth profiles before settling on an acceptable design. Their straw knife has large teeth, has sufficient bulk to push, and is straighter than the old hay saw so that it can slip underneath the strings while they are still tied and holding the bale together. It works well with all types of straw.

Mike Evans, co-owner of the Tree of Life Nursery in southern California (not to be confused with the Tree of Life Rejuvenation Center in Arizona), demonstrated during the nursery's wall-raising how a well-sharpened machete could effectively be used to trim bales. At an average cost of $15 to $25, machetes are one of the most cost-effective methods for cutting bales and are available throughout the world. As bale building finds its way into the more remote parts of the world, the machete will probably become the most common tool used for cutting bales. They are extremely quiet, provide good exercise, and can be used for a lot of other purposes. The Canelo Project (see appendix) is currently developing a fine-quality machete that can be used for bale modification.

A heavy-duty serrated kitchen knife is a highly efficient tool for smaller cuts like the ones needed for creating niches and detailing bales. It should be possible to develop a large serrated knife that could conveniently make larger cuts on bales without having to go to the size and bulk of the old hay saw.

Carol Escott and Steve Kemble report that an electric carving knife works extremely well for shaping bales on a limited basis. With extensive use, however, the knife will overheat and require a rest to cool off.

Electric grinders with a chainsaw carving disc are favored by some for cutting niches, electric outlet boxes, and channels for conduit, wiring, and plumbing. Matts Myhrman likes the

Left: Cutting a bale with a machete.
Left bottom: Grinder with a Lancelot cutting wheel
Right: Trimming bales with a weed trimmer.

"Lancelot," a 22-tooth cutting wheel that fits on the base of a 4-inch grinder (available from King Arthur Tools). This device works like a hand-operated chainsaw.

Note: Electric grinders with a tooth cutting device can be dangerous and should be operated only with a great deal of caution as well as eye protection.

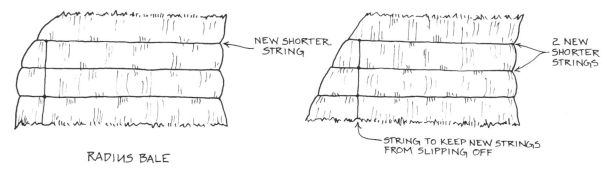

NEW SHORTER STRING

2 NEW SHORTER STRINGS

STRING TO KEEP NEW STRINGS FROM SLIPPING OFF

RADIUS BALE

Custom shaping of bales.

Left: Curving bales.
Above right: A curved bale.

Builder Ted Varney favors a Bosch 8-amp grinder with a medium wire cup brush. It too should be operated with caution and eye protection.

Weed-trimmers can be used to even out walls in preparation for plastering or for other leveling needs.

For rice straw it has been reported that a reciprocating saw equipped with a razor edge blade rather than a toothed version proved satisfactory for cutting and trimming bales. A retractable utility knife with a 3-inch blade proved useful as well.

Bales can also be modified to create an angle or wedge for use in rounded or beveled doorways and windows. For more details on modifying door and window openings, see chapter 7.

Often bales get bent through handling and will need to be straightened. Using another bale or a block to support one end of the bale, hand or knee pressure will usually suffice to make the bale straight again. The same basic technique can be used to produce curved bales for round structures.

BALE WALLS

A WIDE VARIETY OF SYSTEMS have been used to build walls out of baled materials, yet many new ones remain to be explored and refined. Each building seems to add another contribution or improvement to the field of bale building. The adaptability of bales as a building material makes it possible for them to be used with a wide variety of styles, methods, materials, and variations of individual ingenuity. Some of the methods used have been born out of necessity; the historical Nebraska houses, for example, used hay bales for load-bearing walls due to the scarcity of other building materials. In recent times some structures have used bales as in-fill with other structural combinations to meet code requirements and in cases where there has been a question of whether bales possessed sufficient structural integrity. Pliny Fisk developed the ladder trusses in his straw bale buildings (see page 111) because the state of Texas wanted a design that could withstand the force of hurricane-strength winds.

The system that is adopted for a particular building will usually be determined by a variety of factors, including codes, size, building design, costs, availability of materials, climatic and engineering considerations such as snow, wind, and seismic loads, and personal preferences. The potential for load-bearing bales to be used even more efficiently and appropriately may lie within the realm of a completely new style of building and method of construction, dictated by the bales themselves and not by the standards and aesthetics of modern construction.

To date, the known wall methods that have been developed for use with bales include:

- Load-bearing walls in which bales are stacked in a running bond like bricks and pinned together. The walls directly bear and support the weight of the roof.
- Mortared load-bearing walls in which the bales are stacked either in a

running bond or in vertical stacks with no overlaps, and mortar is used in the joints between the bales.

- Bale in-fill or bale-wrap walls in which another structural system supports and attaches the roof and the bales are either inserted as in-fill material between the columns of a structural framework, or the bale walls wrap a structural framework.
- Hybrid structures that use a combination of the above methods.
- Retrofits of existing buildings and mobile homes.
- Multiple stories
- Basements
- Light-clay straw walls (cob construction or Leichtlehm) in which a clay binder is used with large volumes of straw to form a wall in-fill material within structural framing.

LOAD-BEARING BALE WALLS AND ROOF PLATES

In load-bearing walls, straw bales bear the weight of the roof directly without any additional structural support such as wood posts or concrete columns. The bales are normally stacked like bricks in a running bond so that each bale sits over the vertical joint between the two bales beneath it. The bales are pinned together with any material that suitably reinforces the wall. A horizontal structural member or assembly (called a roof plate) that is laid on top of the bale walls is used to stabilize the walls; to bear and distribute the weight of the roof; and to provide the means connecting the roof to the foundation, enabling the structure to withstand wind and seismic forces. A masonry or concrete bond beam can be used in place of a roof plate. The walls of the structure will settle, or compress, from the weight of the roof within a short period of time. They can also be intentionally pre-compressed. Once the compression process is completed, the walls are plastered.

Load-bearing bale walls were pioneered in the Nebraska Sand Hills with the availability of baling equipment that was developed to facilitate handling, storage, and shipping of hay. Early balers, often powered by horses, produced bales that tended to be looser than the compact modern bales. Despite the fact that the Nebraska houses used those older-style bales, a number of them remain in good condition, demonstrating that load-bearing straw walls can endure the test of time.

For some structures this may be the simplest and most economical method of bale construction; however, there are several basic principles that require attention when building load-bearing bale walls. The most important point to understand is that bales are a compressible building material, in contrast to conventional structural wall materials, which do not compress. Roof loads will cause the bales to compress—the greater the load, the greater the compression. With very dense, compact bales and ordinary loads, the compression may be minimal, but even under those conditions, the roof design and door and window openings can concentrate loads in certain areas and cause problems.

If the bale walls had no openings and the roof distributed its loads relatively equally to all the walls of the building, compression would theoretically be equal in all the wall panels. In actual practice, different roof configurations and door and window designs create unequal loading of wall panels, often resulting in uneven compression of the bale walls. The resulting problems can range from minor to major depending on the amount of variation in loads and density of bales, and the design of the roof plate, doors, and windows.

For example, when the spacing of door or window openings leaves only narrow columns of bales between them, those columns can be subject to greater loading than the rest of the wall panels. This is especially true where lintels are used, because lintels take the load from over the opening and distribute it to the columns of bales on either side of the opening. Since the bales next to the openings are already carrying their normal roof load, this can more than double the loads on those bales, resulting in additional compression. If custom-sized bales next to the openings have not been retied to the same density of the other bales, more compression can result.

Small, isolated load-bearing columns of bales and very short walls without corners or returns (short, intersecting wall sections) should be avoided or used with great care for reasons similar to those stated above. It is also important not to mix load-bearing bales and non-compressible structural supports in the same wall section.

Smaller and simpler structures, and those with fewer or smaller window openings, naturally have fewer problems. Potential differences in load distribution grow as wall lengths increase and the roof structure becomes larger. Live loads, such as snow, further increase the potential differences.

A roof plate that is stiff enough in the vertical plane to resist bending or sagging while carrying the load will help significantly in evenly distributing roof loads. The more effectively the roof plate spreads the roof load without deforming, the less likely it is that differential settling will occur.

Load-bearing walls have traditionally been best suited to small structures of relatively uncomplicated design, with few windows and small window openings. Some builders think that load-bearing walls are most appropriate for use with structures under 400 square feet. Much larger load-bearing structures with large window openings have successfully been built, however, and many of the historical bale structures are about 900 to 1,000 square feet. It is possible to build even larger load-bearing structures.

The methods outlined here for building load-bearing bale walls have evolved from techniques and methods used in the early Nebraska houses and more recent efforts by a handful of people developing modern load-bearing bale wall buildings in Arizona and New Mexico. This information was concisely organized and promoted by Matts Myhrman, David Eisenberg, and Steve MacDonald. Matts's and David's work with load-bearing walls has been the primary focus of the highly successful Out On Bale straw bale workshops, and forms the basis for the prescriptive standards being developed for load-bearing bale-wall structures in Pima County, Arizona, and the city of Tucson.

It should be clearly noted, in the interest of creativity and ingenuity, that the methods presented here do not represent "the correct way" to build a load-bearing bale wall. They represent a synthesis of the best efforts used to date, and approximate a model for which code approval might be possible. The book *Build It with Bales—A Step-by-Step Guide to Straw Bale Construction,* by Steve MacDonald and Matts Myhrman, is a comprehensive how-to manual that focuses on load-bearing bale structures.

ROOF PLATE TIE-DOWNS

In load-bearing bale-wall structures it is important to connect the foundation and the roof plate. This prevents the roof from being blown off and adds structural stability for seismic forces. Several principal methods were developed during the late 1980s and early 1990s, primarily in combination with wooden roof plates. Since a particular attachment point usually needs to be included in the foundation, a method of connection must be selected before the foundation is constructed.

THREADED RODS (ALL-THREAD)

One of the most common methods of creating a continuous connection between the foundation and the roof plate is using threaded rods. These are attached to the foundation, run up through the interior of the bales and out the top, and fastened to the roof plate.

To serve as attachment points, $1/2$-inch anchor bolts are embedded in the foundation. Sections of $1/2$-inch threaded rod (all-thread) are connected to the

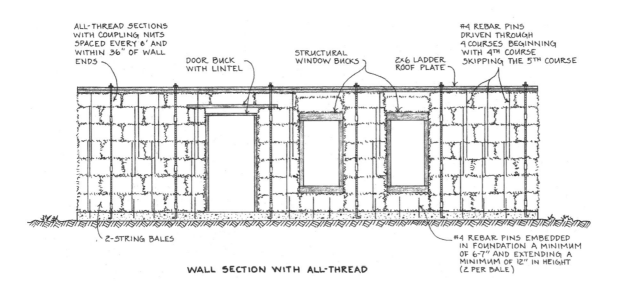

ALL-THREAD SECTIONS
WITH COUPLING NUTS
SPACED EVERY 6' AND
WITHIN 36" OF WALL
ENDS

DOOR BUCK
WITH LINTEL

STRUCTURAL
WINDOW BUCKS

2x6 LADDER
ROOF PLATE

#4 REBAR PINS
DRIVEN THROUGH
4 COURSES BEGINNING
WITH 4TH COURSE
SKIPPING THE 5TH COURSE

2-STRING BALES

#4 REBAR PINS EMBEDDED
IN FOUNDATION A MINIMUM
OF 6-7" AND EXTENDING A
MINIMUM OF 12" IN HEIGHT
(2 PER BALE)

WALL SECTION WITH ALL-THREAD

All-thread connected to anchor bolt with a coupling nut.

anchor bolts with threaded coupling nuts. The all-thread rod sections are spaced no more than 6 feet apart, with a minimum of two per wall section, and within 36 inches of the end of each wall section.

Upon completion of the Tree of Life Rejuvenation Center's load-bearing bale building in Patagonia, Arizona (see page 260), the builders observed that it would have been desirable to place all-thread within 12 inches of the corners because when the walls were pre-compressed, the corners remained higher than the rest of the wall sections.

Sections of all-thread are then connected to the original sections as the bale walls are constructed. Three-foot sections are typically used. The bales do not have to be lifted very high to be impaled on the all-thread. Once the walls are completed, the all-thread extends up through drilled holes in the roof plate, where it is anchored down with a nut and washer. Using all-thread sections to attach the foundation to the roof plate can be time consuming, primarily because of the time spent setting bales precisely over the rods so that they are correctly positioned in the wall.

Paul Weiner, architect and builder for the Tree of Life Rejuvenation Center's straw bale building, had engineering calculations done for the $1/2$-inch all-thread sections used in the load-bearing bale walls. These calculations determined that placement of all-thread every 6 feet in the wall is twenty times stronger than necessary to withstand 75 mph winds. The weakest part of the connection (the point where the all-thread connected to the wooden plate) was rated as being capable of withstanding 162 pounds of uplift, while an ability to withstand only 18 pounds was deemed sufficient to be safe in 75 mph winds. Heavy steel plate washers or malleable steel washers should be used under the nut in each all-thread location to spread the force across a larger area of wood.

Unthreaded lengths of $1/2$-inch diameter steel rod or rebar could be threaded at each end with the aid of a vise and die and used in place of all-thread. It would be less expensive (though more time consuming) and could be used in those parts of the world where all-thread is not available.

It proved very difficult to penetrate rice-straw bales with all-thread at the wall raising of the Shenoa Retreat Center. The all-thread had to be sharpened before the bales could be impaled. A device with a sharpened point called a bullet has been developed and can be screwed onto the end of a piece of all-thread for use with rice-straw bales. They are available through Real Goods (see appendix). Since rice-straw bales are different from other bales, one of the following roof-plate attachment methods may be more appropriate.

WIRE ROPE, CABLE, AND STRAPPING

Other methods for anchoring the roof plate include using wire rope, aircraft cable, or polyester strapping. These are run up the surface of the walls to the roof plate, and are attached to the foundation on each side of the wall. Experienced builders and architects can make only educated guesses as to the proper gauge and best placement of the wire ropes, cables, or strapping, although engineering calculations have recently been done for polyester cord strapping (see facing page). Most often these materials have been used at the same 6-foot intervals as all-thread sections.

There are several strategies for attaching cable to the foundation. Three-eighth-inch eyebolts can be embedded in the foundation and spaced not more than 6 feet apart, with a minimum of two eyebolts per wall section, and within 3 feet of the end of each wall. They should be embedded in the foundation a minimum of 6 inches deep, with a nut and washer threaded onto the eyebolt near the end. U-shaped conduit embedded in the foundation with

Strapping and related tools.
Top: Tensioner tool on strapping with uncrimped polyseal clip, cardboard corner protector on edge, additional polyseal clip above
Middle: Strapping with crimped polyseal clip, strapping with metal buckle to retighten strapping
Bottom: Crimping tool

banding run through it could also work, as could plastic or metal sleeves set into the upper part of the foundation.

Using strapping, wire rope, or aircraft cable saves considerable time in the stacking of a load-bearing bale wall compared to using all-thread sections. Bales in the wall can be simply stacked and pinned without having to be positioned for exact placement over the all-thread. For some, the difference in time is irrelevant. For others, the process of trying to position 80-pound bales over all-thread can be frustrating, and cable or strapping may be preferable.

When wire rope or aircraft cable is used, metal corner protectors or wire thimbles may be used at any point where the wire or cable bends around another surface such as at the roof plate or eyebolt. Turnbuckles or turning sticks can be used to tighten the wire rope or cable. Wire rope clamps attach the ends of the cable together. It should be noted that turnbuckles, eyebolts, cables, and strapping are available in different strengths, and those used must be adequate for their application.

Tom Luecke of Boulder, Colorado, who sought an alternative to using metal or steel in the walls to minimize disturbances from electro-magnetic influences, decided to use polyester cord strapping for securing the roof plate. Tom and structural engineer Jim Higerd, also of Boulder, determined that placement of strapping every 3 feet would provide sufficient strength in most applications. A report of Jim's calculations on strapping is available through

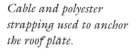

Cable and polyester strapping used to anchor the roof plate.

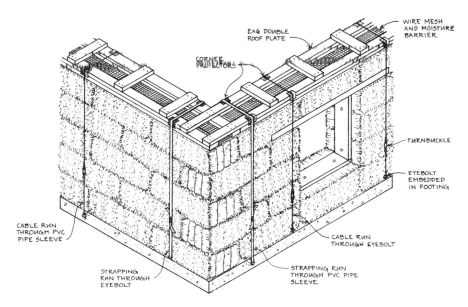

Tom (see appendix). A small building with a shed roof built by Tom in Boulder and using this placement of strapping withstood over 100-mph winds.

After evaluating different strapping tapes he has come to prefer polyester cord, rated at 1,050 pounds, which is both split and ultraviolet resistant.

Tom also uses strapping tape to precompress load-bearing bale walls. He places strapping at intervals of 2 feet around the entire perimeter of the building. To anchor the strapping to the foundation, he inserts $1/2$-inch PVC pipe into the foundation, 3 to 4 inches deep, as a sleeve for the strapping to pass through. The edges of the PVC pipe need to be rounded or softened (with a small piece of rubber, for example) so that the strapping tape is not severed. The PVC sleeves can later be filled with foam, caulking, or any suitable material to seal the holes in the foundation. One end of the strapping tape is then pushed through the sleeve, run up one side of the wall, looped over the top and down the other side, where it is fastened to the other end of the strapping. Tom prefers tightening the strapping with a tensioning tool, which allows him to precompress the walls. Where precompressing the walls isn't necessary, the strapping tape can be tightened by hand. "Tightening by hand" in this case means virtually hanging by one's full body weight on the end of the strapping. The heavier the person, the more tension can be applied. Tom has used both metal buckles, which can be retightened after settling takes place, and metal clips, called polyseals, which cannot be readjusted. Strapping tape, tools, and accessories are available through Tom, along with his expertise as a consultant about these systems.

Strapping can be run over the top of the roof plate and down each side of the wall to connecting points in the foundation. It can also be run up only one side, looped around the roof plate and back down on the same side, repeating the same method on both sides of the wall.

One possible strategy is to combine methods. All-thread could be used throughout the structure except at the corners, where strapping tape could be used. This would facilitate setting and aligning the bales in the corners, which is more difficult with all-thread.

Strapping, buckles, tools, and corner protectors are available from any supplier of packaging materials. If one cannot be found, check with Carlson Systems (see appendix).

WOOD TIE-DOWNS

Any material that will create a sufficiently strong connection between the roof and the foundation can be used as a tie-down. Various designs have incorporated small dimensional lumber to serve this purpose.

In building a storage shed, Bob Bissett of Idaho used 1-by-3s, 2 feet on center, laid flat against both sides of the bales, which were then attached to the foundation and roof plate with metal straps. Each pair of 1-by-3s was wired together through the center of each bale. The wires were tightened with a wrecking bar and attached with screws. They are connected to the roof plate and foundation with metal strap. This system has the additional benefit of providing a nailing surface for stucco wire or sheet rock, and nailing points for cabinets or shelves (see the section on Attachment Points, page 196).

Bob Cook of Tucson devised an equally clever method while building a temporary shop building. He used 1-by-2 furring strips every 2 feet on both sides of the wall to connect his footing (wooden pallets) to his wooden roof plate. The 1-by-2s were attached to the bales, which were

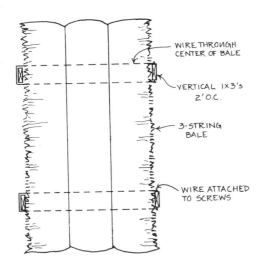

Bob Bissett's alternative to pinning.

WIRE THROUGH CENTER OF BALE

VERTICAL 1X3's 2' O.C.

3-STRING BALE

WIRE ATTACHED TO SCREWS

Bob Cook's 1-by-2 tie-down system.

stacked on edge, by slipping them between the bales and the baling strings. They provided a surface for attaching sheet rock and shelving, and acted as a minimal post-and-beam structural system to help carry the roof load.

OTHER TIE-DOWN METHODS

The stucco wire or metal lath used to cover bale walls in preparation for plaster can provide an additional tie for the roof plate. Some of the old Nebraska buildings appeared to rely primarily on stucco netting wrapped over the roof plate to help secure the roof. Embedding the stucco netting in the foundation during the pouring of the concrete is a method often used when building free-standing bale walls, to help anchor them to the foundation.

Louis Gagné, in combination with his matrix walls of straw bales and mortar, used a wood roof plate with numerous long nails or spikes driven through it, set into a bed of mortar to anchor it to the top of the bale walls. Variations of this technique could be developed either with mortar or concrete.

STACKING BALE WALLS

Laying the bales up is the most exciting part of the construction. If many people are involved in the wall raising, it helps to have someone in charge of each wall section, as well as someone to oversee the entire wall raising. It can be helpful to have plans for each wall elevation available for periodic reference. These can be taped to boards to make handling easier and to keep them from blowing away.

Door frames can be secured to the foundation and temporarily braced prior to the wall raising. Window locations can be marked on the foundation, and the window bucks or frames should be ready for installation.

*Prepared foundation,
ready for wall-raising.*

Braces can be set at each corner to guide the laying of the bales. This was common practice with the old Nebraska houses and helped keep the walls stable and aligned until the roof was in place. The density and uniformity of modern bales has reduced the need for braces, but braces can nevertheless reduce the time required to align and set corner bales. If very straight walls are desired, mason's line or nylon twine can be strung between the braces to help align the walls as they are going up, especially for long sections. Care must be taken to keep the braces plumb and properly aligned, so they should be checked regularly while the walls are going up. Adequate braces can be made out of 2-by-6s or plywood.

Use good bales that are dry, solid, and compact. Poor-quality bales will affect the structural stability of the building.

Bales laid flat (on their wide side) in load-bearing situations are usually preferable because of their increased stability. However, in smaller buildings it may be more appropriate to lay bales on edge (more common with non-load-bearing buildings) because of the savings in floor space. Three-string bales, 23 inches wide, are more stable for a load-bearing wall than two-string bales, 17 to 18 inches wide. The draft of the prescriptive standard for Tucson and Pima County Arizona specifies a width-to-height ratio of .180 or more for a load-bearing wall. For three-string bales this translates into 10 feet, 8 inches high (23"/.18=128"=10'8") and for two-string bales, 8 feet, 4 inches (18"/.18=100"=8'4"). The extra width of the three-string bale provides more stability, making it possible to construct higher walls. Keeping the ratio of unsupported wall width to wall length at least .064 is also a good idea. For a three-string bale, that converts to a maximum of 30 feet of length, for a 2-string bale, 23 feet. But-

Bales laid at corner.

tressing and anchoring the bale wall to interior walls are options that can increase the length allowable.

The first course of bales is impaled on vertical rebar pins or stakes that have been cast in the foundation. If all-thread is used to connect the roof plate, anchor bolts with connected all-thread sections will be interspersed with the rebar. The rebar is embedded in the foundation a minimum depth of 6 inches and spaced not more than 2 feet apart and within 1 foot of any corners. They are placed along the centerline of the wall, and extend at least 12 inches in height. Anchor bolts (if applicable) replace rebar where necessary.

Laying the bales beginning at the corners and door frames, then working toward the center of the walls, ensures that any gaps that must be filled with modified bales will be in the middle of the wall section. Small bales are best kept away from corners and door openings; door frames are more solid when they are firmly up against full or half bales. At corners, it is better to set the bales a little to the inside of the foundation edge than to have them overlap it. It is easier to correct corner irregularities with a little additional plaster than by trying to modify protruding bales.

Half bales as well as custom-sized bales can be made on site as needed. Gaps of less than 6 inches between the bales can be filled with untied "flakes" or stuffed with loose straw. It is better to stuff lightly, since overstuffing can knock the corners out of alignment.

Top: *Custom-sized bale.*
Bottom: *Rebar bale staple at corner.*

Staples that are 18 inches long with two 6-inch legs, made of #3 or #4 rebar and formed into a U-shape, are normally used to connect corner bales at each course. These are placed so that the two ends of each staple are driven into two adjacent bales. Staples can be used anywhere else bales need to be joined together, such as over door and window frames. In a house built in Alberta, Canada, $1/4$-inch plywood angles of 90 degrees, pinned to the bales with bamboo, were used in place of corner rebar staples. Jorg and Helen Ostrowski, architects of the project, later suggested using horizontally driven 3- to 4-foot bamboo pins in alternate directions at the corners in place of the plywood.

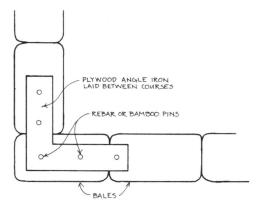

Plywood angles at corner.

When bales must be impaled on rebar or all-thread, it is easier to keep them aligned if the location of the penetration is marked on the bottom of the bale. It helps to have someone hold the all-thread straight and help guide the bale, keeping it level as it is lowered. It is often possible to align the bales by eye, a method aided greatly by a third person in the right place to see the alignment. Lifting the bale and realigning it more than once is quite common. Even with those precautions, the wall alignment should be checked regularly. A good 4-foot (or longer) level works well for this

Guiding a bale down over all-thread.

purpose. A shorter level can be attached to a longer, straight 2-by-4 as well.

Once the first course of bales has been laid, the second and subsequent courses of bales are staggered in a running bond, with each bale overlapping the two bales beneath. This overlap should not be less than 12 inches.

It is quite easy for first-time bale layers to be overcome by what is sometimes referred to as "bale frenzy," the desire to progress very quickly. The extra time it takes to be careful and accurate is worth the effort, although irregularities in the walls can often be pounded into shape later with whatever is handy on the site: a sledge hammer, a 2-by-4, or a foot, knee, or shoulder.

On the other hand, some builders have abandoned the straight-wall approach, either by choice or from their discovery once the wall has gone up. Purposely throwing the bales out of alignment can produce some interesting and pleasing results, as in the case of the Brophy Chapel in Elgin, Arizona.

WINDOWS AND DOORS

Window frame locations must be predetermined so that the frames can be set in place as the walls go up. Openings made in load-bearing bale walls for doors, windows, or other purposes should be positioned a minimum of one full bale length from any corner to avoid disrupting the structural integrity of the wall section.

Wall and roof loads above openings in a wall section need support. One way this can be done is with structural door and window frames capable of transferring loads to the bales below. Lintels, beams, or a roof plate spanning the opening are other possibilities. Use only solid and well-compressed bales in combination with these openings.

Facing page
Top: "Fine-tuning" a wall
with a sledge hammer.
Bottom: Irregular corner
of Brophy Chapel.

Right: Several courses of
bales with window frames.

Structural door and window frames, which extend to the floor, will not compress like the rest of the load-bearing wall. A space needs to be left over these structures for anticipated settling. (See Chapter 6 for details on frame construction, placement, and support.)

PINNING THE BALES

Pinning secures bales in the wall to one another and reinforces the wall. It is the most common method of strengthening a bale wall. Pinning the bales adds stability to the walls during the construction process. Before the roof plate goes on, the bale walls can be quite unstable, especially those higher than seven courses. The pins also add structural integrity during seismic events or high winds.

Rebar Pins

Rebar is the most common material for pinning. The first course of bales is anchored or pinned by the rebar and all-thread (if used) set in the foundation; subsequent courses are pinned to the lower courses with two rebar pins through each bale.

The method used for the structural tests conducted in Arizona and now commonly used elsewhere provides excellent wall stability. It uses 5-foot lengths of #4 rebar or an acceptable equivalent (for bales 16 inches high), with pinning starting at the fourth course and penetrating down through all four courses of bales. Each course thereafter is also pinned with two 5-foot pins in each bale until the top course is completed.

An alternate method of pinning is to start at the fourth course and pin every other course, always pinning the top course. So, in the case of a wall seven bales high, rebar pins would be driven on the 4th, 6th, and 7th courses. The rebar pins should be located to avoid the space between the bales, to avoid severing twine or wire ties, and to approximate the layout of the rebar pins in the foundation. Rebar pins should also be placed within 1 foot of all corners and door openings. It can be helpful to have a rebar cutting tool on site during the wall-raising. They can usually be rented or borrowed.

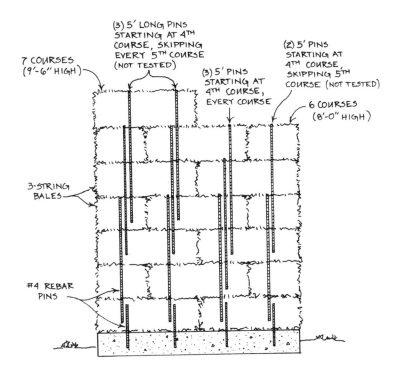

7 COURSES
(9'-6" HIGH)

(3) 5' LONG PINS
STARTING AT 4TH
COURSE, SKIPPING
EVERY 5TH COURSE
(NOT TESTED)

(3) 5' PINS
STARTING AT
4TH COURSE,
EVERY COURSE

(2) 5' PINS
STARTING AT
4TH COURSE,
SKIPPING 5TH
COURSE (NOT TESTED)

6 COURSES
(8'-0" HIGH)

3-STRING
BALES

#4 REBAR
PINS

Various wall-pinning strategies.

A small sledge hammer or maul can be used to drive the pins. A cap that slips over the end of each pin can make hammering easier and help prevent accidents. These custom-made caps are commonly called "drivers" or "targets." One style of driver can be made by using 1 1/2-inch diameter iron bar with a 3/4-inch hole drilled in one end. A cheap alternative can be made from a 3-inch length of 3/4-inch galvanized pipe with a 3/4-inch pipe cap. This type will not last, but may be sufficient for several projects. Another type of driver has been developed that has a handle and is called a slammer. It is available through Real Goods (see appendix).

Rice straw has proven to be relatively difficult to drive pins through. At the Shenoa Retreat Center, rebar pins were inserted into the rice-straw bales by attaching a 1/2-inch electric drill on one end and drilling them into the bales, but this method may damage the chuck of the drill. Sharpening one tip of the rebar with a grinder will also improve installation in rice straw.

ALTERNATIVE PINNING MATERIALS

A variety of alternative materials can be used as pins as long as they have the necesary structural strength. Besides rebar, wooden dowels, wood stakes, bamboo, and branches have all been used. In the Nebraska houses, wood or steel wheel spokes were used for pinning the bales. Lumber can be ripped to 1-by-1 inches and sharpened at one end for stakes. A dowel pointer makes sharpening faster. Branches or saplings of sufficient strength and straightness can also be used.

Ray Yould, in Crestone, Colorado, used 2-by-4 stakes, cut into wedges about 3 feet long, to pin his bales. He drove these down through each course of bales into the course below. He also used similar, shorter wedges, driven at an angle into the

Pinning with rebar.

Examples of rebar drivers.

*Rebar cutting and
bending tool.*

vertical surfaces of the bales, to tighten up any loose areas in the walls. The resulting two-story, post-and-beam structure was very solid.

Bamboo pins

Bamboo, in many circumstances and contexts, can be a great material for pins in bale walls. It can be cheaper than rebar even when the cost of shipping is included, nicer to work with, and a particularly wise choice in areas where it grows naturally.

When purchased through commercial suppliers, bamboo usually comes in 5- to 6-foot lengths, which can be sharpened if necessary for easier penetration. Bamboo with an approximate diameter of $1/2$ inch can usually be driven through bales without having to cut and sharpen the ends, but larger-diameter bamboo may need to be sharpened. A single, angled cut on one end will often suffice. For making such cuts, a miter or chop saw works well, and so does a sharp handsaw. A skil-saw with the blade set at an angle could also be used.

Some builders have reported a tendency of sharpened bamboo to curve as it is driven; it is likely to curve in the direction of the angled point, which should be aligned perpendicular to the wall. Bamboos do vary in their strengths and characteristics, and some species will behave differently than others. Using a small-diameter bamboo or one that will drive through bales without sharpening would be simplest. A piece of 2-by-4 that has been partially drilled on a flat side can be used as a driver if necessary.

Bamboo can be purchased in bundles of 250 and 500 for reasonable prices, which, including shipping, may cost 20 to 25 percent less than 5-foot lengths of #4 rebar. A.M. Leonard sells $1/2$-inch diameter bamboo in bundles of 500 5-foot lengths and 250 6-foot lengths. For slightly higher prices, Eastern Star Trading Company sells $1/2$-inch diameter, foot-long bamboo in bundles of 500.

Bamboo can easily be grown within many local communities; a variety worth considering for bale pinning might be Simonii. Some bamboos are very invasive, and should be grown with care to prevent escapes that become exotic weeds. For a list of sources for mail-order bamboos, consult the American Bamboo Society's source list.

WEAVING BALES

Bales could conceivably be laced, tied, or woven together with wire or plastic baling twine. A bale needle could be threaded and the bales sewn together a pair at a time. It might be possible to sew an entire wall section at once; however, connecting the bales as the wall is assembled adds significantly to the strength and stability of the wall.

ROOF PLATES

The roof plate is the assembly on top of the bale wall that supports the roof structure and connects it to the walls. A strong and uniform roof plate that is simple to construct is a critical component in a load-bearing bale building and in some non-load-bearing bale buildings. The structural integrity of the building will be affected to a significant extent by the design, construction, and method of attaching the roof plate.

The load-bearing roof plate does several jobs. First, it provides a rigid structure to stabilize the top of the bale walls, helping tie the walls together and keep them straight. Second, it serves as the point of attachment for the roof. This connection is important in high winds and earthquakes. There is no significant difference between a bale building and one with a more conventional wall system in terms of the connection of the roof to the roof plate. Third, the roof plate provides a method of distributing the load from the structural members of the roof to the walls. The stiffer the design of the roof plate, the more evenly the roof loads are spread along the top of the walls. Finally, the roof plate provides the means of connection between the roof and the foundation. It serves to anchor the roof to the ground and prevent it from being blown or shaken from the building, and it keeps the whole building from being tipped over by the wind or an earthquake.

Designing and building a strong and rigid roof plate for load-bearing bale walls is a task that is still very much in process. Various types of roof plates and

various ways of attaching them have been used in conjunction with bale buildings. For the most part these have performed satisfactorily, but the search for the "better" roof plate continues.

WOODEN LADDER-STYLE PLATES

The majority of roof plates used with bale buildings have been wooden ladder-type plates made from an assortment of different materials. A common design, which has been recommended for inclusion in the prescriptive standards of Pima County, Arizona as an acceptable roof plate for load-bearing straw bale construction, uses two double 2-by-6 horizontal roof plates: one that runs along the inside edge of the top of the bale wall, and another that runs along the outside edge. The doubled 2-by-6 plates are then connected by transverse 2-by-6 crosspieces, which are placed at each all-thread location and blocked underneath to provide additional strength for the all-thread connection. Additional crosspieces can be used, spaced not more than 48 inches apart. Corner construction of these plates usually includes overlaps made of 2-by material, plywood gussets, or metal plates. The double plates are face nailed with 16d nails staggered at 16-inch-on-center, with laps and intersections face nailed with four 16d nails at each end.

Facing page: Completed load-bearing walls. Right: Roof plate with all-thread connection and metal lath and plastic to protect top of bale walls.

WOODEN LADDER-STYLE PLATE NO. 2

Another version of the ladder-style roof plate has been suggested by David Eisenberg. This method uses two vertical 2-by-6s, one on each edge of the top of the wall. They sit on and are fastened to lengths of plywood, and are connected to each other with 2-by-4 cross blocking, spaced to accommodate the threaded rod, if used, but in any case not more than 48 inches apart. This design uses less wood than other ladder-style designs, yet is stiffer vertically. The other significant advantage of this design, especially for precompressed walls, is that if the roof plate is not level after precompression, the tops of the 2-by-6s can be trimmed to create a level surface for the trusses or rafters to sit on.

When sloped rafters rest on the outside edge of the roof plate, something must be done to ensure that the load is distributed equally across the top of the wall. Where the roof slope is low, tapered shims could be cut from 2-by stock to fill the gap between the rafter and the inside edge of the plate. With steeper slopes, 2-by load equalizers can be attached from the inside edge of the roof plate to the rafters, to counteract the tendency of the roof plate to twist in response to the weight of the roof on only one edge of the wall.

There has been some concern over the use of ladder-type plates. Martin

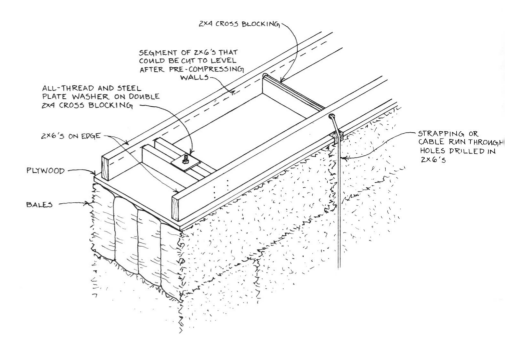

Eisenberg roof plate. This design provides a vertically and horizontally stiff roof plate, while using less lumber. It also allows for the trimming of the top of the roof plate to a level line after pre-compressing the walls.

Salter, a retired engineer, wrote to *The Last Straw* that a single roof plate, made of large-dimension 2-by lumber of adequate stiffness and placed in the middle of the wall, might function better than a ladder roof plate because the compressibility of the straw might cause an uneven load distribution on a ladder plate. In response to his suggestion, editors of the newsletter commented that double plates seemed to be working well and that the double plate provided a nailing surface for stucco netting both inside and outside at the top of the wall. It is important to keep in mind that to be safe, the roof should bear equally on both the inside and the outside of the wall, as well as in the center of the wall. Where rafters are used, the load equalizer will help.

Expanded metal lath or hardware cloth can be used under these ladder roof plates as protection from vermin. A moisture barrier also can be placed underneath the metal lath to protect the top of the wall from moisture in the event of leaks in the roof.

WOOD PLATE MADE FROM TRUSS JOISTS OR I-BEAMS

Another roof-plate system suggested by David Eisenberg, which has not yet been tried but could provide one of the strongest and most efficiently built roof plates yet developed for load-bearing bale walls to date, is one built from small truss joists or I-beams (like those used for floor joists). They are avail-

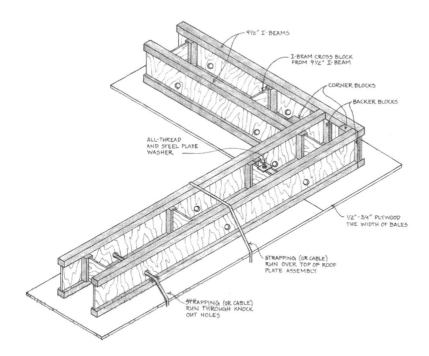

Labels on diagram:
9½" I-BEAMS
I-BEAM CROSS BLOCK FROM 9½" I-BEAM
CORNER BLOCKS
BACKER BLOCKS
ALL-THREAD AND STEEL PLATE WASHER
½" - ¾" PLYWOOD THE WIDTH OF BALES
STRAPPING (OR CABLE) RUN OVER TOP OF ROOF PLATE ASSEMBLY
STRAPPING (OR CABLE) RUN THROUGH KNOCK OUT HOLES

Wood I-beam roof plate. The width of the roof plate assembly can be varied by using larger I-beams, or plywood and 2-by lumber for the cross blocking. Cable or strapping can be run over the top of the roof plate assembly, or, in areas where wind or seismic loads are not a concern, can be run through the pre-punched knockout holes in the webs of the I-beams.

able in long sections and therefore are capable of making very stiff and full-length bond beams. They come in depths ranging from 9 1/2 to 16 inches. Parallel lengths could be run on the inside and outside edges of the top of the wall, connected with short sections of the same type of beam and sheathed with plywood on the bottom.

WOODEN BOX BEAMS

Wooden box beams or wood bond beams, as they are called by some builders, add additional strength and stability to the roof plate. A box beam developed by Bob Theis, John Swearingen, and Richard Hartwell used two parallel 2-by-8s on edge in combination with plywood sheathing top and bottom for Cottage 13 at the Shenoa Learning Center. For a three-string bale wall these would be 24 inches, so that two equal sections can be cut from one plywood sheet.

Bob's design made it possible to precompress the walls at four hundred pounds per square foot and distribute loads equally around the perimeter of the wall, especially at locations adjacent to large openings or along walls with many openings. This box beam was used for spans of as much as ten feet over window openings, and eliminated the need for the lintels and structural frames that are commonly used with many load-bearing buildings.

Another advantage of the box beam is that it acts as a horizontal beam to counteract rafter thrust for spans up to 12 feet. Studs running from the inside edge of the box plate to the rafter are used as load equalizers to offset the heavy loading of the high-slope rafters on the outside edge of the box beam. The triangular space behind the load equalizers makes a good chase to run wiring and can be easily covered with wood or plywood panels. Corners of the plywood box beams could be gussetted with plywood to make even stronger connections.

It was found that having the all-thread penetrate the center of the box beam made it difficult to level. Bob plans to run all-thread on both sides of the wall and connect them to each side of the box beam in future applications. This would make it easier to raise or lower either the inner or outer edge of the beam when necessary. Polyester strapping would also work well, since it is relatively easy to tighten or loosen.

Box beams could also be made from 2-by-6s depending on the size and design of the building. A third 2-by could be used in the middle of the box for extra support when spanning doors and windows if roof loads required it. Where all-thread sections intersect with and penetrate the box beam, two additional upright cross-pieces of 2-by material can be nailed inside the box beam, one on each side of the all-thread. These cross-braces are essential, particularly when precompressing load-bearing walls, to prevent the plywood from collapsing or breaking at the point where pressure is applied.

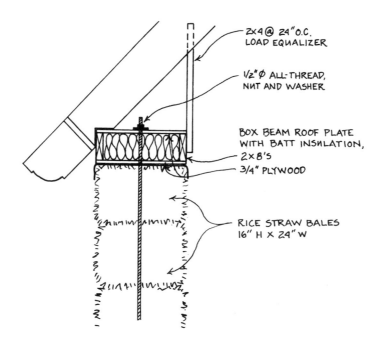

2x4 @ 24" O.C.
LOAD EQUALIZER

1/2"∅ ALL-THREAD,
NUT AND WASHER

BOX BEAM ROOF PLATE
WITH BATT INSULATION,
2x8's
3/4" PLYWOOD

RICE STRAW BALES
16" H X 24" W

Theis Box Beam roof plate.

OTHER OPTIONS

In lumber-poor areas, concrete bond beams could prove to be a practical choice in place of wood roof plates. Another alternative would be pumice-crete or other lightweight concretes, especially for seismically active areas where reducing the weight at the top of the wall is advisable.

In Alamos, Mexico, a concrete bond beam was experimentally used to retroactively remedy poor-quality bales in a load-bearing wall. The bond beam was not part of the original design. Because the upper course of bales was very irregular, a concrete bond beam was poured to provide a level surface on top of the walls. Once the walls had settled, the corners were retrofitted with concrete columns to provide additional horizontal and lateral support. A straw bale building near Puebla, Mexico, used not only bamboo trusses, but a bamboo roof plate as well.

Anything that provides a continuous connection around the perimeter of the walls and makes a good connection between the roof and the rest of the structure could be used. A metal roof plate made of angle iron and connecting metal straps could also work.

SETTLING AND PRECOMPRESSION

Once the weight of the roof and ceiling is in place, the building can be expected to settle. Typical settling seems to average from 1 to 2 inches when using compact bales and typical roof loads, and could be more. Most builders believe that the building will have done all or most of its settling within four to eight weeks. Those who don't want to wait for the building to settle naturally can precompress the walls using all-thread, strapping, or wire tie-downs to compress the bales the amount they are expected to settle. Because of the

Top: Concrete bond beam, Alamos, Sonora, Mexico.
Bottom: Bamboo roof plate, Puebla, Mexico.

*Precompressing walls at
Tree of Life Rejuvenation
Center.*

variables in load-bearing bale walls and differences in roof-plate construction,
settling and precompression can occur differentially around the perimeter of
the walls. The Tree of Life Rejuvenation Center, which has load-bearing bale
walls and all-thread connections to the roof plate, was precompressed a total of
$3\,^3/_4$ inches. In the beginning, equal amounts of pressure were applied using a
torque wrench to tighten the nuts in each all-thread connection all the way
around the perimeter of the building, but this started to produce uneven compression of the walls, evidenced by changes of elevation in the roof line and
plate. Precompression continued by tightening each connection only enough
to keep the roof plate level. This was done in conjunction with a transit. Nonetheless, a point was reached in the precompression process where certain parts
of the wall continued to compress while other sections stopped. This was also
the case with the load-bearing bale building at the Shenoa Learning Center. At
Shenoa, several sections of all-thread sheared off in the attempt to even out the

top of the wall. The precompression process started in both buildings after the completion of the roof plate and continued until the roof was completed.

After precompression was complete for the Tree of Life building, many shims were used to offset the irregularities in the roof line. A drip cap was carefully leveled on the ends of the rafters and trusses. Both Tree of Life architect Paul Weiner and Shenoa architect Bob Theis believed that a ledger or a level nailing surface could be provided on top of the plate or box beam to even out the roof line. By using the truss joist or I-beam roof plate described earlier, or an equivalent stiff roof plate, this problem might be minimized or reduced due to the vertical stiffness of the design.

It has been suggested that the uneven settling that has occurred with precompression efforts might in some part be due to the 6-foot spacing of all-thread. If a more rigid roof plate were used, one that would remain straight and uniform under pressure, the 6-foot distance might be less of a factor. The other possible, but impractical, solution would be to increase the number of all-thread sections used in each wall panel. If all-thread sections were placed every 2 feet, in place of rebar, the expense of building the load-bearing walls would increase. In addition, having to impale each bale over two all-thread sections would make the bale stacking process much more difficult. Tom Luecke suggests using polyester cord strapping every 2 feet to precompress the walls (see page 76); strapping is cheaper, easier to use, and allows short intervals between compression points. Tom has also found that he can eliminate virtually all settling by using tight bales and jumping on each course as it is laid.

It is very important to use dense, compact bales in load-bearing walls. Differences in bale compression can create uneven settling throughout wall sections and along the tops of the walls. This is especially true when attempting to precompress load-bearing walls.

Remember that modern load-bearing bale buildings, most built since 1989, are only a few years old at the time of this writing; although the majority appear to be in good condition, it is possible that problems could develop over time.

MORTARED BALE WALLS

Built in 1921, the Warren Withee house near Olsenville, South Dakota is the oldest known load-bearing mortared-bale house. Using mortar between the bales creates a wall system that is more rigid and, since the bales are separated by mortar joints, more stable. The Glendo, Wyoming, grocery store and the

Bruner house in Douglas, Wyoming, also used mortar between the bales and created durable structures that remain in good condition. This may be a good strategy to consider if bales are weak and mushy, heavy snow loads are expected, or a multistory building is planned.

It should be noted that mortared bale walls use more cement, are somewhat slower to construct, and result in walls with less insulation value than bale walls stacked without mortar.

An older version of this method, that pre-dates modern baling equipment, is the use of straw bundles in combination with mortar for walls. This method was used in China and England, and possibly elsewhere.

In the early 1980s, Louis Gagné used straw bales with mortar between the layers and plaster inside and out. This system was tested thoroughly, and the results confirmed that these mortared-bale matrix walls met residential construction requirements even with soft bales.

This matrix system isolates each bale in its own cell, surrounded by mortar above and below and stucco or plaster on the inside and outside. The mortar joints form a structural frame, and the straw bales serve as an insulating filler. Bales were placed on the foundation 1 inch apart, and the space between them was filled with a joint mortar consisting of two parts cement to one part lime blended with sand in a ratio of one to three. This mixture was thickened with straw to prevent the mortar from dripping down the sides of the bales. A similar amount of mortar was then spread on top of the bales before the next course was laid. In this system, the bales were stacked vertically in line, instead of staggered as in a running bond. A wooden top plate with protruding nails on the bottom was embedded in the final layer of mortar, and the walls were then plastered. The doors and windows were double framed with protruding nails to anchor in the mortar joints. Lintels were used over openings when it was necessary to distribute roof loads.

If reinforcing steel is incorporated in some of the mortar joints, a very strong wall system could be built. This might be done with large U-shaped pieces that would be tied to the reinforcing mesh on both sides of the wall.

IN-FILL BALE WALLS

The most common bale building method in recent times has been to use bales as an in-fill material in combination with another structural support system. This method has been used more frequently because code approval is usually simpler and people have generally felt more secure using a structural framework with bale walls. In the early phases of modern straw bale construction, it

The Guillarmin house is partially built with bales in a mortar matrix.

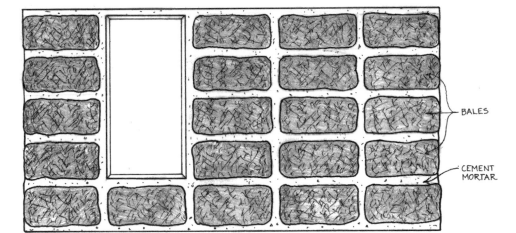

Mortared-bale-matrix wall, as built by Louis Gagné.

BALES

CEMENT MORTAR

was generally assumed that using bales as in-fill always used more lumber and was more complicated and expensive than building a load-bearing bale wall. Although that is often the case, new design strategies are being developed that, depending on the size and design of the building, can make using bales as an in-fill material in combination with a structural framework actually less expensive, easier, and less lumber consumptive than building a load-bearing bale wall.

The in-fill approach has certain advantages and in some situations will be the most appropriate style of building. It affords greater design flexibility, allowing multiple stories, greater roof spans, higher design loads, more and larger window and door openings, and the ability to easily expand the building in the future. In areas where rain or snow can be a problem, the structure and roof can be built first, the bales stored beneath, and the walls constructed while the bales remain fully protected. Bales can be used on edge, which saves on interior space and uses fewer bales. There is no need to precompress the walls or wait for them to settle as with load-bearing bale walls. Consequently, the building can be plastered as soon as the walls and roof are completed. In areas of heavy snow loads, where the bales in a load-bearing wall may compress due to the increased roof load, the in-fill approach may be a better choice.

The technique of building a bale in-fill wall is very similar to building a load-bearing bale wall. The fundamental difference is that a method for attaching a roof plate is not needed. With a bale in-fill building, the roof structure is attached to the structural framework.

Bales used with in-fill walls are normally secured to the foundation, stacked in a running bond, pinned (reinforced), and anchored to the structural frame. There have been numerous variations in accomplishing these different aspects of constructing an in-fill wall. Some are simple, and others much more extensive and complicated—like the prescriptive standards being developed for including non-load-bearing straw bale construction into New Mexico code. The New Mexico prescriptive standards are the most thorough and extensive guidelines being developed for this type of bale wall. Some builders feel that in-fill walls don't require the level of complexity that the New Mexico codes require. However, the highlights of these requirements have been included in this section, and readers can decide on their own, or in combination with other building professionals or code officials, what approach to an in-fill wall best suits their needs. New Mexico requires that the first course of straw bales be pinned to the foundation with #4 rebar, with a minimum of two pins per bale. These pins must be embedded in the foundation to a depth of not less than 7 inches and should continue vertically halfway into the second course of bales. Bales are required to be laid flat (the widest side parallel to the ground).

It is further specified that each bale be pinned with a minimum of two #4 rebar that extend vertically and completely through that bale course and halfway into the course below. Rebar must be approximately 9 inches from the bale ends and centered on the width of the bale, and continuous horizontal ladder reinforcing must be placed between courses at mid-wall height, and be fastened twice per bale to the bale twine or wire.

The in-fill panels of bales must be anchored to the adjoining structural system or support posts. New Mexico requires that anchors be placed at every horizontal joint—or in other words, in every course at each post. Metal lath has been used for this purpose, attached to the upright posts and then to the bales, using flathead spiral nails. Another method is to screw eyebolts into the posts at each course and wire the bales to them. The wires can be attached to the bale strings or to a 12-inch long rebar pin driven halfway into the center of each bale that is next to a post. Then, tie wire can be wrapped around the pin and tied to the eyebolt. The in-fill walls can also be anchored by inserting all-thread sections through the vertical posts and the bale wall. They can be attached on the side of the bale wall opposite the post with a steel nut and a large steel or plywood plate washer. These could be approximately 6 inches square and $3/16$ inch thick for steel, $1/2$ inch for plywood. The next course of bales is partially impaled on the half of the rebar pins extending up out of the bales, thereby securing the rebar.

Connecting bales to the horizontal beam or its equivalent can be done in a number of ways, but the most common method is using metal lath. The New Mexico code states that at all points where bales are butted against a dif-

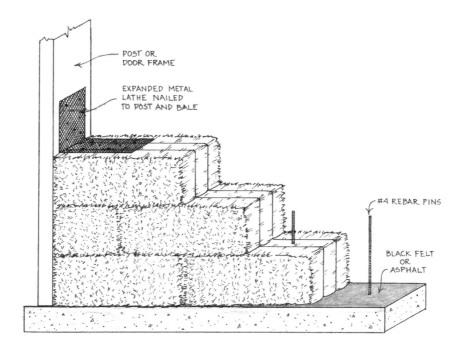

Connecting bale wall to post with expanded metal lath.

POST OR DOOR FRAME

EXPANDED METAL LATHE NAILED TO POST AND BALE

#4 REBAR PINS

BLACK FELT OR ASPHALT

ferent material (wood, concrete, steel, etc.), metal lath shall be used to cover the junction. The lath is required to extend 6 inches over the edge of the bale and be securely fastened to it. Beam connections are required, beginning not more than 12 inches from the end of each wall panel and at intervals of not more than 24 inches along the top horizontal plane of the wall panel. The top course of bales can be notched or cut to inset the beam, or they can be run up just below it and the remaining space filled with straw.

The maximum wall height allowed is 12 feet, and the maximum length of an unbuttressed in-fill panel should be no longer than 20 feet.

STRUCTURAL SYSTEMS COMMONLY USED WITH BALE IN-FILL WALLS

POST-AND-BEAM AND POLE CONSTRUCTION

Everything from conventional milled 4-by-4, 4-by-6, and 6-by-6 posts to utility posts, lodge poles, and timber bamboo have been used for structural frames in post-and-beam-type buildings. This method of construction has been used more extensively with straw bales than any other method. Any common post-and-beam structure will work, and the possibilities are almost endless. Structures can range from very basic and simple to elaborate timber frames.

Posts can be on either the exterior or the interior side of the wall, although when on the interior they can help brace the wall against the wind. Timber framing can be left exposed inside the building, while the smaller posts of simpler structures can be notched into the bales. Notching the bales can be time consuming, but in some cases the bale walls can provide the lateral bracing for the building. Larger posts will require cutting bale strings and in some cases retying. A 4-by-4 post is the largest post that can be inserted into a three-string bale without having to cut the twine or wire. If posts are to be inset, the bales must be laid flat with wires or twine on the top and bottom of the bale. When bales are laid on edge, the strings or wires are left exposed along the surface of the wall, making it almost impossible to inset the posts. Notching tools include small chainsaws, electric grinders with wire cup brushes or a cutting wheel called a Lancelot, serrated knives, hay saws, and well-sharpened machetes.

One disadvantage of post-and-beam construction is that there is a change in the plastering surface from bales to wood and then back to bales again at each post. These wood transitions require the use of expanded metal lath and black felt paper to reduce the likelihood and severity of cracking.

Facing page
Top left: Post inset into bale wall.
Top right: Exposed post.
Bottom left: Simpson post connector.
Bottom right: Bale notched to receive post.

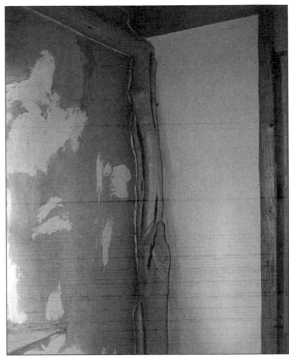

Another inset option, designed by architect Bill Cook of Sonoita, Arizona, involves setting the corner posts approximately in the middle of the bales on the exterior of the wall and leaving them exposed. In this way the plaster surface ends at each side of the posts. Posts could also be left totally exposed on the outside of the bales without being inset.

Box columns or panels that are the thickness of the wall are also sometimes used. These consist of a structural frame with plywood sheathing. For a more detailed description see the following section, on modified post-and-beam.

Bales can be very tightly fit into a post-and-beam structure. Ken and Diana Dougan of Ft. Thomas, Arizona, built a very solid and finely detailed post-and-beam bale in-fill structure without pinning the majority of bales in the walls. They determined that due to a combination of factors, including the short distances between supporting posts, numerous window and door frames, the tight fit of the bales between all the wood framing members, and the added stability provided by 17-gauge stucco wire securely tied to the bales, pinning the bales would be completely unnecessary. The bales in the first course, however, were impaled over rebar pins embedded in the foundation.

Treated posts and poles have either been set into gravel-filled holes in the ground with concrete pads at the bottom or set into holes that were then filled with concrete (see *Practical Pole Building Construction* by Leigh Seddon, 1985, Williamson Publishing). Untreated posts and poles are most often connected to the footing or piers with Simpson-type post base connectors. The option chosen depends upon the type and design of the building, codes, and builder preference.

Requirements for diagonal bracing may vary. The bales provide some diagonal bracing and lat-

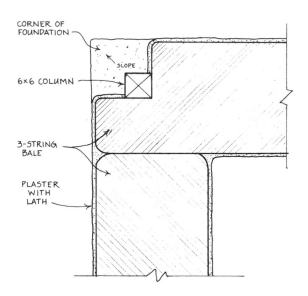

eral support when the posts or columns are inset into them or between them. That support is flexible and could be superior to other, more rigid connections during seismic activity. How much additional bracing is required will summarily depend upon local building officials.

MODIFIED POST-AND-BEAM

This system can be one of the most efficient methods of building a bale structure in terms of cost, materials, and labor. It differs from a traditional post-and-beam structure in that the window and door bucks are constructed as structural supports and distributed throughout the perimeter of the building. Posts are used only at the corners and at locations lacking window and door openings. Box columns the width of the bale wall are used as the vertical sides of the bucks and extend from the foundation to the beam. These box col-

Facing page
Top: Bill Cook's exposed corner post.
Bottom: Bill Cook's exposed corner post.

Below left: Box column.
Below right: Box column assembly.

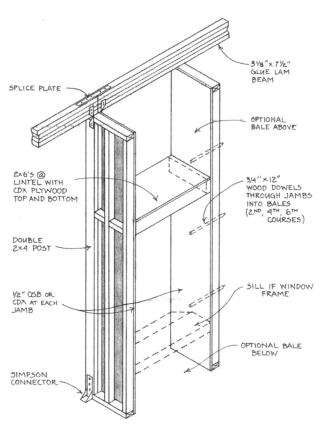

Modified post-and-beam structure.

umns consist of a structural frame of 2-by lumber sheathed with plywood or Oriented Strand Board (OSB). The edge of the box column that supports the beam needs to be stronger than the rest of the frame. This will depend on roof loads and the beam used; doubled 2-by-4s could be sufficient. The beam to be used in combination with the box columns and posts needs to be sized to accommodate the roof loads over the longest spans.

The modified post-and-beam design was conceptualized by architect Bill Cook and was first used on the Angelo and Carol Filigenzi residence in

Patagonia, Arizona. Shortly thereafter it was adopted by architect-builder Paul Weiner and used on the Pam Tillman residence in Tucson. It forms the basis for a comparison with load-bearing bale structures outlined on page 260.

Where there are insufficient windows and doors to provide structural supports, such locations can be developed with box columns that also serve as inset shelving and closes in the shell of the building. Using box columns also eliminates the need for notching the bales to insert the posts, in that these box columns are the same width as the wall.

Depending on how this structure is designed and what components are used, it can be very competitive with a load-bearing bale building in every respect, and possibly more efficient.

TRUSS WALLS

George Swanson, architect and director of CADD systems in Fairfield, Iowa, used a premanufactured "whole-house" truss system in the construction of a residence in Iowa. This truss system can be faster and cheaper to build than many other structural systems. The trusses are made from 2-by-4s and include the walls, eaves, roof, and second story if needed. In the Iowa project, the trusses were set 36 inches apart, assembled flat on the ground and tilted into place with a block and tackle. Two-string straw bales were then stacked to the roof between the wall trusses. (The bales were initially compressed a small amount, inserted between the trusses, and allowed to expand for a snug fit. This may not be possible with compact and solid bales; another system of bale attachment to the trusses may be necessary.)

One advantage this system has, even though it is somewhat lumber intensive, is that it uses only smaller dimensioned lumber, compared to most

Pliny Fisk's ladder-truss wall system.

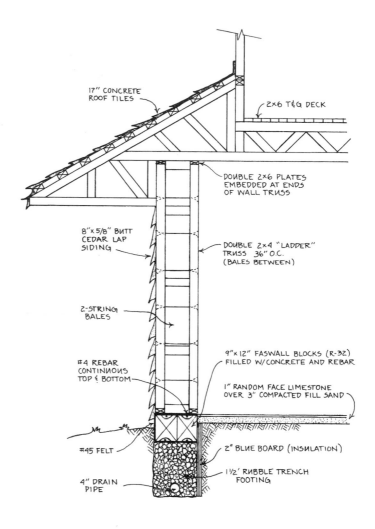

George Swanson's 2-by-4 "Whole house truss system."

17" CONCRETE ROOF TILES

2×6 T&G DECK

DOUBLE 2×6 PLATES EMBEDDED AT ENDS OF WALL TRUSS

8"×5/8" BUTT CEDAR LAP SIDING

DOUBLE 2×4 "LADDER" TRUSS 36" O.C. (BALES BETWEEN)

2-STRING BALES

9"×12" FASWALL BLOCKS (R-32) FILLED W/CONCRETE AND REBAR

#4 REBAR CONTINUOUS TOP & BOTTOM

1" RANDOM FACE LIMESTONE OVER 3" COMPACTED FILL SAND

#45 FELT

2" BLUE BOARD (INSULATION)

4" DRAIN PIPE

1 1/2' RUBBLE TRENCH FOOTING

post and beam options. George is exploring the possibility of using new experimental studs and I-beams manufactured from OSB and, when available, will use them exclusively in his trusses.

METAL FRAME

Up to now metal frames have rarely been considered for use in combination with bale construction. Of the few that we know of, one is a metal-frame house, built on a farm in southeastern Arizona using old irrigation pipe welded together. The EOS Institute's demonstration Straw Bale Eco-House at the Southern California Home and Garden Show, combined metal framing and roofing with bales. The metal framers and bale builders found it was a surprisingly good match.

Pliny Fisk also used a folded metal lightweight truss and metal roof in combination with bales for a model farm he developed for the Texas Department of Agriculture.

Tony Perry believes that it could be less expensive and less labor intensive to build bale structures using a premanufactured metal frame system. The uprights would be small enough to be set into small notches in the joints between the bales, providing a continuous and unbroken plastering surface on the bale walls. Perry plans to build two prototype houses in the Santa Fe area to determine whether or not his assumptions are valid.

Proponents of natural building methods have expressed concern that the metal structures would be undesirable because of the electromagnetic disturbance they cause. In addition, some people have questioned the sustainability of using large quantities of metal in houses, though the use of recycled steel might reduce that concern.

There are two basic options when considering a steel structure in combination with bale in-fill. Almost all modern steel calculations are based on a standard product called A36 structural steel with which all connections must be welded or bolted. Most building codes require that a "certified" welder, one with an industry license, do the welding. Bolted connections require that the steel be presized and prepunched for bolts at the supplier's yard. There is

EOS Institute's Straw Bale Demonstration Eco-House, Anaheim, California, 1993.

Pliny Fisk's metal truss system at Laredo, Texas Experimental Farm.

little room for error when using steel, and with a bale building, where precise measurements are not the norm, complications can arise.

The other option is galvanized light-gauge steel framing. It is easier to use than the heavier structural steel and is used in much the same way as wood framing. It is available in a variety of sizes and can be field cut to size with a metal cutting saw and field assembled with sheet metal screws. Roof trusses can be ordered preassembled like wood trusses. Manufacturers can supply sizing and fastening specifications.

Steel framing need not be used throughout the house. It can provide all the required struc-

tural framework, it can be used in combination with wood framing, or it can be used to roof a load-bearing bale building. As of mid–1994 none of these options had been explored.

CEMENT BLOCK OR CONCRETE COLUMNS

Cement block and concrete have probably not been used more frequently for structural support in bale buildings because lumber has been widely available in the United States, where most bale structures have been built. Either material can be an effective alternative in timber-poor areas, however, and offer a relatively uncomplicated and inexpensive system even in places where wood framing materials are plentiful.

The Bob Munk house near Santa Fe (see the color section), used single columns of grouted, reinforced concrete block in combination with a bond beam. The bond beam was 8 inches wide by 10 inches deep. Architect Beverley Spears commented that the bond beam was made narrower than the bales in an attempt to save on the amount of concrete and steel reinforcing, and as a result the forms had to be set on top of the bales. This created some difficulty because the straight edges of the wooden forms did not align well with the irregular surface on top of the bales. Consequently, during the pour, the concrete tended to seep out from under the forms.

Burke Denman, of Denman and Associates in Santa Fe, is a builder-designer who favors using concrete bond beams with some bale buildings. He would pour a thinner bond beam, approximately 4 to 5 inches high, 14 inches wide, and with 2 inches of foam insulation inside and out. With this approach, 10- to 12-inch plywood forms could extend down the sides of the bale walls and prevent the concrete from spilling.

Ted Varney used another approach on a bale building for Tony Perry. TJIs or truss joists were used to form the bond beam with a plywood bottom. Once the concrete was poured the TJIs and the plywood were left in place as part of the final structure. The plywood on the bottom kept the concrete from seeping out the bottom of the form.

In seismic areas, holes could be periodically augured into the bales and filled with reinforced concrete as part of the bond beam. This would reduce the possibility of lateral shifting of the beam during an earthquake. Leaving the vertical rebar exposed several inches above the top of the bales could also provide a good lateral connection for a concrete bond beam. Continuing the reinforcing wire mesh over the wall top and into the bond beam will also make a very strong connection.

Katherine Wells's home in northern New Mexico, structurally designed by Ted Varney, used larger cement-block columns to accommodate longer spans than in the Munk house, and laminated beams made up of three 2-by-10s. A small

Bob Munk's concrete block columns and concrete bond beam.

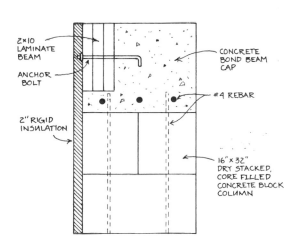

Ted Varney's dry-stacked concrete block column with concrete bond beam cap.

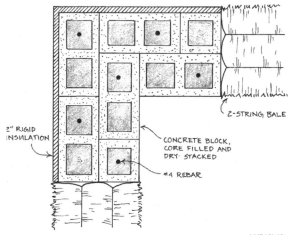

Ted Varney's dry-stacked concrete block corner columns.

concrete cap was poured on top of each of the columns, incorporating an attachment point for the wood beam. The blocks were dry stacked several courses at a time and then grouted solid. In that particular situation, three columns were used along the front of the rectangular house and three in the back. The corner columns were L-shaped, measuring 32 inches on each outside face, and 16 inches in width. The central columns were 16 by 32 inches. This is one of the simplest supporting structures we have come across. The 16- inch width allowed for an exterior application of 2 inches of rigid foam insulation, making the total width of the columns 18 inches to match the width of the two-wire bales being used.

Katherine Wells and partner Lloyd Dennis built a studio using a complex structure of concrete columns in the middle of the bale walls. They did not choose to repeat this technique on their next bale structure, but nevertheless it worked effectively. Holes were made in the bales with a powered post-hole auger. Sections of PVC pipe placed in the holes were then filled with reinforced concrete.

ALTERNATIVE PRESSED WOOD OR FOAM-INSULATED BLOCK

Faswall blocks, insulated hollow-core blocks made from 88 percent wood chips and low-toxicity cement, appear to be an excellent possibility for supporting columns. To date, they have not been used as supporting columns in bale building. They have numerous advantages over concrete block in that they are lighter (one quarter the weight), can be cut with handsaws or carbide-tipped power saws, can be nailed, screwed, and bolted, have an insulation value of 1.75 per inch, are easy to work with, and require no stucco netting. And, unlike concrete, Faswall blocks breathe. They are a rather remarkable commercially manufactured building material used widely in Europe but just appearing in the United States. They are SBC code approved as well. They come in two widths, 9 and 12 inches, and three different lengths, 12, 24, and 36 inches. These various sizes allow them to be easily incorporated with both two-wire and three-wire bales. Their initial cost is higher than concrete block, but given their energy and labor saving qualities, net cost should be competitive.

Used as structural columns, they could be used in combination with Faswall block grade beams and stem walls, as well as Faswall block bond beams. This is definitely a material worth exploring for use in bale buildings. It has recently been used in a grade beam application in one straw bale building in Iowa (see the appendix for supplier).

One potential application for Faswall blocks could be in the modified

Faswall block.

post-and-beam system described earlier in the chapter. They could be used in place of the plywood sheathed box columns at door and window openings, and anywhere structural supports are necessary. Window and door frames could be attached directly to them. Using Faswall blocks would eliminate the need for any lumber in the wall section.

HYBRID WALL SYSTEMS

Hybrid designs that borrow from both load-bearing and in-fill bale-wall approaches help open the door for structural and design possibilities based on the characteristics of the bales rather than other construction materials. They represent an attempt to look through different eyes and resolve some of the inherent problems with load-bearing bale walls while reducing the quantity of lumber required for bale in-fill approaches.

Hybrid bale structures have begun to explore the realm of using very thin structural columns by relying upon the stability of the bale wall to act as a brace. Normally, in stand-alone structures, columns such as wood posts have to be thick enough to brace themselves against buckling. However, small-diameter poles or bamboo, as well as 1-by or 2-by lumber can be used to absorb vertical roof loads when they are braced against the interior and exterior surfaces of the bale walls as pilasters. This means not only a more efficient use of materials, but, depending on the design, a potential reduction of other problems such as differential settling and the need for a stiff roof plate, as well.

One hybrid design using a modified ladder truss was developed by Pliny Fisk from the Center for Maximum Potential Building Systems in Austin, Texas. The walls are constructed by stacking the bales in columns rather than a staggered running bond. Vertical or upright 1-by-4s are placed on both the inside and the outside surfaces of the bale walls directly opposite one another. Additional 1-by-4s are placed horizontally like ladder steps between every other bale course and attached to the vertical 1-by-4s, forming the ladder truss. The vertical 1-by-4s are attached to 2-by-4s that have been mounted on top of the foundation and connect directly to the roof trusses without a roof plate, unless the truss spans are significantly long. With three-wire bales the ladder trusses are spaced at approximately 4-foot intervals along each wall section. The 1-by-4s are able to absorb the roof loads because they are braced against the bales. Further reinforcement could be added at each ladder step connection if needed, and trusses could be made from wider pieces of plywood if additional strength is needed.

The spaces between the trusses are convenient locations for expanding rooms and installing new windows and doors. Trusses also provide convenient attachment points throughout the bale walls. They can be used for attaching stucco wire, siding, sheetrock, shelves, and cabinets.

This system has advantages for both light commercial use and residential construction. The trusses allow for greater wall height, as well as for the possibility of second stories.

Bob Cook and his partner Friederike Almstedt constructed a workshop on their site in southern Arizona using a unique hybrid design. Because of their need for immediate space, Bob and Friederike did not have time to go through a long and laborious building process. They needed their workshop space quickly assembled with a minimal amount of effort and expense. They began by clearing a place for the building by hand and excavating approximately 4 inches of dirt from where the building was to stand. The excavated area was then filled with gravel.

The entire gravel-filled area was next covered with wooden pallets placed side-by-side over 6-mil plastic. The pallets were held together with 2-by-4s running around the perimeter and screwed to the edges of the pallets, and plywood sheeting nailed to the top. The plywood provided the floor for the workshop and a place to stack the straw bales safely, protecting them from ground moisture. Three 2-by-4s, laid flat, were fastened to the floor around the perimeter of the building, to provide a raised sill for the bale walls to be stacked on.

The straw bales were then stacked on edge so that their strings would be exposed on the exterior and interior surfaces of the walls. The bale walls were then pinned with rebar. A large window was framed into the south wall for direct solar gain during the winter months, along with a tiny west window for good sunsets. Dual glazing was pro-

Bob Cook's modified box beam roof plate.

vided by doubling up single-pane windows and using a removable interior stop in case of problems with moisture or leaking.

A simple modified box beam was used around the top perimeter of the bale wall and was constructed using plywood on the bottom with 2-by-4s on the outside and inside edges of the wall. Three 2-by-4s spanned the opening for the south window.

Next, two 1-by-2-inch furring strips were slipped between the baling wire and the straw on two-foot centers, and attached to both the roof plate and the floor. The furring strips anchored the roof securely to the building, provided structural support for the roof, and provided a surface for nailing. Sheetrock was nailed to the furring strips for the interior surface of the walls, while black celotex was used on the exterior of the building. Once these were in place, the building was easily plastered with a minimum of material. The result was a simple, elegant, easy-to-build straw bale workspace.

Another hybrid approach involves using load-bearing bale walls and bale in-fill walls in the same structure. For example, the south wall, which can

Bob Cook's finished building

Top: Bob Cook's roof plate with third 2-by-4 spanning window opening.
Above: Furring strip "columns."

potentially contain a lot of glazing, could be frame or post-and-beam construction, while the north wall could be load-bearing straw bale construction. The one rule to remember when combining methods is to avoid, at all costs, mixing structural posts or columns with load-bearing bales in the same wall or load-bearing plane. Load-bearing walls may settle, but in-fill walls will not. Attempting to mix the two in a wall will most likely result in cracked stucco and buckled roofs from differential settling unless very careful detailing is provided to accommodate the inevitable changes.

RETROFITS

One of the most potentially exciting areas of straw bale construction is retrofitting old thermally inefficient structures. Cinder block, cement, metal, wood-frame and adobe structures are ideal candidates for bale retrofits, as are mobile homes and old barns. The high insulation value of the bales can bring those structures from thermal horrors to super performers. Much of the abysmal housing built for low-income people in urban areas and on military bases could benefit from bale retrofits.

Depending on the structure, bales can be used on either the exterior or the interior of the building. In general, a new foundation is added outside the existing walls and then a straw bale wall is put up and fastened to the existing structure. The eaves often have to be extended to provide roof cover for the new wall.

Interior retrofits with bale walls incorporating reinforced columns and beams may be very effective in reducing seismic risk of older unreinforced buildings with limited insulation, such as commercial brick buildings.

The Center for Maximum Potential Building Systems helped develop a retrofit bale upgrade for an old 1,800-square-foot farm building in Amarillo, Texas, belonging to Hunter Ingols and Mary Emeny. The project has come to be known as the "The Great Texas Retrofit." Old pallets were used to fabricate a half-ladder truss system for attaching the bale walls to the exterior of the old building. The horizontal steps or cross runners in the ladder were placed between every two courses of bales in the wall and then attached to the existing walls of the building. Once the bales were in place, a vertical piece of lumber was attached on the outside of the bales to the steps, completing the half-ladder truss.

The straw for the bales was grown regionally and sustainably, using wastewater as the sole nutrient and water source. For food production and heating, a greenhouse was added containing a water-trickled mass wall built from local site rock for heating and humidity in the winter and evaporative cooling in the summer. Vent chimneys were also incorporated in the structure.

Karen's Wine Country Cafe in Elgin, Arizona, occupies an old building that once served as the local post office and community general store. This popular little restaurant, owned by Karen and

Harold Callaghan, draws capacity crowds from distant urban areas on a weekly basis, and has been featured in *The New York Times*. The restaurant space was created as part of a larger project that included a 300-foot section of straw bale wall designed to enclose a plaza area from the road for wine festivals and other public events. The retrofit was done by Athena and Bill Steen along with local builder and friend Reed Schmidlin in 1991, and was the first straw bale patio wall to be built. A Southwest-style post-and-beam structure was added to the front of the old building. Bale walls were in-filled between the posts in combination with doors that were used for windows, swinging open to provide ventilation. The retrofit in this case was more for creating atmosphere and usable space than for energy efficiency. For a nominal expense, a magnificent seating area was created, changing a dull, lifeless building into a restaurant with character and charm.

Mobile homes are excellent candidates for a bale retrofit. A number of such retrofits have been done using post-and-beam structures with insulated roofs constructed around the mobile home. Bales are then stacked and pinned and used as in-fill. Bale additions can be added to mobile homes to increase space.

*Facing page
Top: Half-ladder truss.
Middle: Bales being inserted into half-ladder truss.
Bottom: Finished building, "The great Texas Retrofit."*

Karen's Wine Country Cafe.

JoAn Churchman's two-story bale in-fill house in northern New Mexico.

MULTIPLE STORIES

Numerous advantages to building a two-story structure are worth considering in designing a home. Since the two-story structure uses the same amount of roof structure as a one-story, while almost doubling the amount of available living space, it can be more cost-effective than other designs. In most cases the same foundation can be used as well.

Several two-story structures have been built using bales. The earliest to be completed, according to our records, was the Burritt Mansion built in Huntsville, Alabama, in 1936 (see page 6). The mansion is a bale in-fill structure using post-and-beam construction. Some years later, a two-story office building was built in Nebraska, also using bale in-fill. Louis Gagné has constructed several two-story homes in Quebec using his mortared-bale matrix system, and other two-story homes have been built in France.

Some historic bale buildings have at least partial second stories. The Martin-Monhart house in Arthur, Nebraska, has an upstairs, which bears on the exterior structural bale walls and on framed interior walls as well. The Pilgrims Holiness Church, also in Arthur, uses a similar approach with minister's quarters in the back of the building being two stories.

In 1993–94 JoAn Churchman built a two-story, in-fill, post-and-beam bale house in northern New Mexico. The bale walls are 12 feet high, with 9-foot ceilings downstairs. The upper story is three bales high with a cathedral ceiling to gain the necessary height. The roof is steep to achieve good head-room upstairs without increasing wall height, and JoAn used dormers to further increase headroom. JoAn is part of an alliance of people called Genius Loci, an organization that includes architect Jan Wisniewski and that is involved in the designing and building of alternative structures in northern New Mexico (see appendix). As an offshoot of the work done on JoAn's home, members have developed an affordable prototype for a small two-story straw home that could be adapted and built to accommodate regional variations in climate (see page 259).

Also in 1993–94, Kim Thompson of Nova Scotia built a load-bearing two-story structure that was partially funded by the Cooperation Agreement on Sustainable Economic Development. Steve MacDonald's construction manual, *A Straw Bale Primer,* was the guiding force for a group of friends armed with common sense, good will, and lots of energy. Kim's structure used a similar approach to that of JoAn Churchman, with seven bales on the first story, and three on the second in combination with a cathedral ceiling. Her structure rests on old utility poles that are set 4 feet deep in the ground to get below the frost line. Bales were also used between the wooden floor joists for insulation.

The National Research and Resource Council of Canada committed to do one year of testing, beginning in the spring of 1994. They will monitor temperature and moisture in the building and conduct some in-lab tests of compression and loads. Considering that Kim Thompson's home is a two-story load-bearing bale-wall structure in an area subject to heavy snow loads, the test results should be very useful to those who are interested in multiple-story buildings, as well as those who would like to know more about the performance of load-bearing bale buildings with snow loads.

Kim has produced a twenty-three-minute video entitled *Straw Bale Construction,* which documents the construction process of her two-story load-bearing straw bale home (see appendix).

BASEMENTS

According to written accounts, the Scott house, built between 1935 and 1938 near Gordon, Nebraska, incorporated straw bales in the basement walls. Louis Gagné also used straw bales in basement walls in the early 1980s. In his buildings, the bales were used in conjunction with a matrix of mortar. They were covered with three coats of plaster and a coating of tar. A good drainage system was installed around the footing. Louis's basements were built in clay soils, where ground movements are most hazardous, and despite the fact that the basements aren't heated during the winter, nothing has moved or cracked. Louis reported that the temperatures in the basements have remained very stable even during the coldest part of the winter.

STRAW-CLAY CONSTRUCTION

Walls that use a mix of clay and straw deserve mention in this book even though they do not use baled straw. It is one of the oldest straw-construction techniques known. Straw-clay construction is reported to have its roots in Europe as early as the twelfth century, although examples can be found throughout other parts of the world, including the Orient. Some five-hundred-year-old straw-clay buildings are still occupied. This style of building is currently enjoying a renaissance in Europe.

In the early 1990s, Doug Lewis of Bamboo Hardwoods, based in Seattle, Washington, built a straw-clay building in Vietnam. The house was built using a structural framework of timber bamboo and clay-coated straw for the walls. Most straw-clay buildings use a timber-frame structure and incorporate a mix of loose straw coated with a clay slip or binder to form walls up to 2 feet thick between the upright posts of the building. Pliny Fisk has developed a lightweight framework for use in combination with straw-clay construction. It uses the same ladder-truss assembly that he uses with straw bale structures, and, since it uses small-dimensional lumber, it is more lumber efficient than the timber-frame approach.

Traditionally the wet mix was puddled by hand a layer at a time and called cob construction. It was also placed in the wall section with the aid of a simple wooden slip form that attached to the upright supporting posts of the timber-frame structure, an application that was generally known as "lightweight straw-clay." In the house Doug Lewis built, split bamboo used as lath was woven horizontally and vertically and attached to the bamboo structural frame as a form for the straw-clay. The mix is typically prepared in a trough or pit where 15-inch straw lengths are combined with a fine clay slurry or slip. The straw is tossed with rakes and other means until all of it is coated, and a color approximating that of the original clay is attained. The mix is allowed to sit twelve hours before it is used. The straw-clay mix creates a unique, breathable combination of high insulation with thermal mass.

Above: Exterior of the Zucker house, built using straw/clay construction. Right: Adjusting slip-form on straw-clay wall.

This method of construction requires minimum skill and uses only the simplest tools. It relies on simpler technology than bale building in that baling machines are not required for the straw. It uses locally available materials and requires little processing. Even expansive clays, those that cannot be used for other un-fired earth/masonry structures, work well. The straw-clay mix is very moldable and, once dry, can even be cut with a handsaw.

Straw-clay walls have passed the most stringent European fire codes because not only does the clay char, thus establishing a silica-based protective fire coating, but fire actually bakes the clay, preventing the straw from receiving more oxygen.

One of the most fascinating aspects of this approach is that any leftover seeds contained in the straw tend to sprout when wet. The sprouts help cure the wall through water transpiration to the air and, when dried out, become built-in reinforcement and a natural stucco netting.

One disadvantage to this system when compared to bale construction is that the walls are more labor intensive to build; if there is a labor cost, these walls will be more expensive. Another drawback is that straw-clay walls can take a long time to dry, especially in humid climates—sometimes as much as a year. Once dry, the walls are traditionally coated with a lime or earth plaster.

Pliny Fisk has built several straw-clay buildings, as has Robert LaPorte of Fairfield, Iowa. Robert leads workshops and offers an excellent and concise manual on straw-clay building techniques called *Mooseprint—A Holistic Home Building Guide,* and he is currently working on a more detailed book on the subject (see appendix).

CHAPTER 6

WINDOWS AND DOORS

DOOR AND WINDOW OPENINGS play a large part in defining the character of a bale wall. The thick bale walls create a transition zone, which can be developed in a variety of ways, between the building's interior and the outdoors; these openings can express themselves as social spaces, seating, alcoves, display areas, or intimate passageways, in contrast to the doors and windows of conventional buildings, which are usually nothing more than openings in a wall. Windows and doors require different treatment with load-bearing bale walls than do structures with bale in-fill walls. In load-bearing walls, combined live and dead loads from the roof bear directly on the wall sections, which include the window and door frames. With in-fill structures, all roof loads are absorbed by whatever bearing structure is used and only the wall loads above the window or door are carried by the buck, a rough window or door frame.

Bill and Nancy Cook's straw bale guest house, Sonoita, Arizona.

IN LOAD-BEARING BALE WALLS

The main design issue connected with windows and doors in a load-bearing bale-wall building is to determine the most effective way of absorbing the combined loads from the roof structure through the walls to the foundation. There are a number of ways of dealing with this challenge, and each has advantages and disadvantages. The early Nebraska structures used wood lintels over windows and doors. Wall sections usually contained few window openings, which were generally small with short spans for the headers. This approach appears to have been effective because it caused minimal disruption to the bale wall. When a wall is made entirely of compact bales, it will compress relatively evenly under roof loads if there are no openings in it. When openings for windows and doors are added, the amount of settling becomes potentially different at any or all of these locations. The tendency toward uneven settlement increases as the number and width of such openings increase. The

121

Nebraska builders probably found that it made good sense to minimize the potential problems by using few windows and keeping them narrow.

To allow more light into a room, narrow windows can be made taller. The distance that light penetrates into a space is determined more by the height of a window than by its width. So vertically oriented windows do a better job of illuminating a room than horizontally oriented ones. Wider openings are possible, but certain design factors have to be taken into consideration.

Modern bale buildings have dealt with door and window openings by using rigid roof plates, metal lintels, or structural frames. The least often used approach, but potentially the easiest and most efficient, would be to use a rigid roof plate capable of spanning large openings, thereby eliminating the need for lintels or cumbersome structural frames. Without having to absorb roof loads, window and door buck designs for load-bearing walls can be greatly simplified. The box beam roof plate developed by Bob Theis (see Roof Plates in Load-Bearing Walls, page 91) is capable of spanning 10 feet. Another design which could possibly achieve the same result is the I-beam roof plate (page 91).

Ladder-type steel lintel.

LINTELS

The most common approach to door and window openings in load-bearing bale walls has been to use a steel-ladder-type lintel, originally suggested by David Bainbridge, to span the opening. Wood types can also be used. Many of the first load-bearing structures built in recent years utilized a type of angle iron lintel, also suggested by David. When lintels are used, the combined dead and live roof loads from directly above the windows and doors are distributed through the lintel onto the bales on either side of the opening. Those loads are in addition to the normal loads already carried by those bales, so they will carry significantly more than the other bales in the wall, and problems may develop. Because bales compress, the difference in load on the bales under the end of the lintels, compared to other bales in the wall, may result in differential settling, causing the roof plate to dip or the wall finish system to crack. Live loads of snow, wind, etc., could further aggravate the potential problems.

To help reduce this tendency, it would be wise to avoid using lintels for significant spans. The concentration of point loads where they bear on the bales increases as the span increases. The lintel should be twice as long as the opening is wide, extending a minimum of 2 feet on either side of the opening. Lintels should be strong enough to ensure that they will not sag, yet not be unnecessarily heavy. One architect-designed metal lintel was made of such heavy metal and had so little bearing area that it caused bale failure by itself.

Also, avoid using lintels in walls with bales of varying degrees of compaction or compression, which increases the possibility of differential settling.

Most metal lintels have been made from angle iron $3/16$- or $1/4$-inch thick by 2 or $2\,1/2$ inches, with cross straps welded approximately every 1 to 2 feet. The last cross strap on both ends of the lintel can be drilled to have a piece of rebar welded in the center of the strap, extending above and below, for pinning the lintel in place. If the lintel rests on half bales at the side of a window opening, a rebar staple or two can be used to more securely fasten the half bales to the rest of the wall. The lintel should extend at least halfway onto the bales on both sides of the opening.

Window and door bucks used beneath lintels should be sized to allow for the compression that will occur in the load-bearing walls on either side of the opening. Otherwise, the lintel would exert pressure directly on the rigid buck, possibly deforming it and creating problems of differential settings in the wall.

Another option is to place the wooden window bucks in their openings after settling or precompression is complete. The window bucks can then be installed and correctly fitted to the size of the opening. One disadvantage of this method is that it is more difficult to keep the bales even around the window opening. Instead of having solid bales placed against a solid buck, one

Rough-sawn window buck the width of bales.

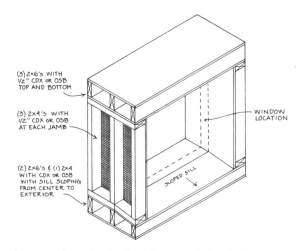

(3) 2×6'S WITH
1/2" CDX OR OSB
TOP AND BOTTOM

(3) 2×4'S WITH
1/2" CDX OR OSB
AT EACH JAMB

(2) 2×6'S & (1) 2×4
WITH CDX OR OSB
WITH SILL SLOPING
FROM CENTER TO
EXTERIOR

WINDOW
LOCATION

SLOPED SILL

Structural window buck with optional sloped sill.

must trim bales and fill with loose straw where the buck does not fit. The Nebraska builders often waited until the building settled before installing door and window frames. Rough-sawn bucks of 2-by-6s or 2-by-8s are most commonly used with lintels.

Attempts to resolve the problem of uneven loading with lintels led to the development of structural window bucks that float in the wall and essentially replace the bales that would have been in the wall where the buck has been placed. With the structural buck, the combined loads from above the frame are transferred through the buck to the bales below the frame. This type of buck should be built to match the compressed height of the bales it replaces, and be rigid enough to transfer the loads without being distorted. Otherwise, the bales in the one or two courses below are being asked to compress an amount equal to that of a wall which may be seven or eight courses of bales high. These bucks can also be constructed so that they bear directly on the foundation.

The most widely used structural window buck is one built with a box beam header of plywood-sheathed 2-by-6s which is supported by two vertical box columns of plywood-sheathed 2-by-4s. These columns sit on a box beam built to match the header. When the buck bears on bales below it and does not extend to the foundation, it is important to make the bottom of the buck as stiff as the top (header) so they can both transmit their loads without distortion. Instead of building that same strength into the bottom of the frame, the vertical columns or sides can also bear directly on the foundation. The area between the bottom of the window and the foundation can then be filled in with bales.

For most small-to-moderate spans, 2-by-6s appear to be adequate for use in the header and the bottom of the buck. The vertical 2-by-4s in the box columns are normally placed on edge or parallel to the wall section, to provide greater resistance to racking of the door frame. Both the header and column portions of the frame are sheathed in plywood. These frames are usually the same thickness of a bale wall, about 24 inches in a load-bearing wall of three-string bales.

When beveled window and door openings are desired with full-depth bucks, it is necessary to bevel the frame itself. One approach is to angle the vertical columns and bevel the bales to either side of the opening. Another variation would be making the frame larger than the door or window and framing the bevel with wood.

Structural bucks as narrow as 12 inches have also been used. Since they are narrower than the bales in the wall, they either need to be centered in the wall or securely fastened to the foundation to resist the unbalanced loads exerted on them from above. Because they do not extend the width of the wall, beveled openings can be created by modifying the bales instead of creating the bevel through with the wood frame of the buck.

Rough sawn bucks are often used for openings of 2 feet or less, instead of the larger structural bucks because of the smaller span and reduced loads.

Window bucks need some type of temporary bracing to keep them aligned during the construction process. Load-bearing bale walls are in a continual state of flux as the walls are stacked, and it is easy for the bucks to get thrown out of alignment. Builders have used everything from sheets of plywood and OSB board, completely covering the opening, to diagonal and corner braces.

Structural door bucks are constructed like structural window bucks, and bear directly on the

Structural window buck with temporary bracing.

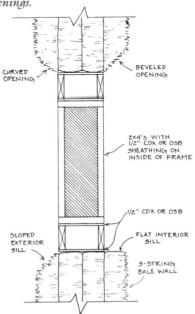

Twelve-inch structural window buck (side view) with shaped openings.

foundation. As with window bucks, it has been common to use bucks that are the same width as the bale wall. Where door or window bucks bear directly on the foundation, anchor bolts are used to attach them. It is best to anchor the bucks in place and brace them to remain plumb before the bale walls are erected.

Both window and door bucks are commonly mounted to the bale wall with $5/8$-inch by 12-inch-long wooden dowels driven through holes drilled in all four sides of the wood frame. In order to maintain the moisture protection afforded by a moisture barrier under the window, the bottom of the window buck is usually not pinned to the bales below it. Expanded metal lath between the bale and the frame is also usually used to further reinforce this connection point for the stucco and plaster finish. If there is no bale on top, the frame can be attached directly to the roof plate once all settling has occurred. Additional diagonal bracing can be run from the bucks to the roof plate or the foundation when more support is necessary.

If door and window bucks bear directly on the foundation, allowance must be made for compression above the frame. (If the frame extended all the way to the roof plate, the walls to either side would settle and the frame would not.) Another option is to attach the window frame to the roof plate and allow room for settling beneath the sill.

Because of the potential for the roof plate to bow or sag over the structural door bucks during precompression of load-bearing walls, Paul Weiner developed an adjustable shim to use in the space left for settling above the buck. Diagonally ripped 2-by-4s are placed between the frame and the bale above and are gradually pulled apart and removed as the walls settle. These adjustable shims create space above the door frame for the roof plate and any bales (if there are any) to settle onto

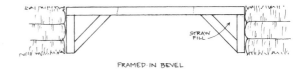

FRAMED-IN BEVEL

BALES AND FRAME BEVELLED

*Facing page
Top: Beveled window buck.
Bottom: Framed-in beveled window opening. Beveled bales and buck.*

*Above left: Structural door frame.
Top right: Wooden dowel driven to secure buck to bales.
Bottom right: Adjustable shim above door frame to help regulate settling.*

the frame without causing any unevenness in the roof plate. This approach requires some guesswork as to how much settling will occur, and therefore how much space needs to be left above the frame for the adjustable shims. If there is space remaining after the settling has finished, it can be permanently shimmed and framed. It is better to provide a little extra room than not enough. If there is no bale between the roof plate and the frame and the span is relatively small, the space can be left open so that the plate can settle freely and then be permanently framed.

In load-bearing bale walls, windows and doors should generally not be positioned near corners to maintain the structural integrity of the building. Ideally, full bales should be used at all corners of structural walls. Multiple window designs that attempt to use small pillars of shortened bales between windows should probably be avoided, as such walls do not have great strength.

BALE IN-FILL WALLS

Window and door bucks used in bale in-fill walls do not present the same challenges and complications that frames in load-bearing bale walls do. The main design issue is essentially one of deciding how to attach and secure the frame within the bale-wall section.

Probably the simplest method that can be used, primarily with small windows, is simply to set a rough-sawn buck made of 2-by-8s into the wall and secure it with wooden dowels driven through the sides of the buck into the adjoining bales. It need only be capable of supporting the weight of the bales above it, not the roof.

If the buck needs more anchorage, lengths of plywood could be attached to the top and bottom of the buck to extend between the courses of adjacent bales.

Large door and window bucks can also be attached to the structural posts. These frames can be simple and uncomplicated in that they rely upon the posts for stability and support.

Another option is to use the structural bearing supports for door and window bucks, as in the modified post-and-beam system described under Bale In-Fill Walls (see chapter 5). Not only does this improve the efficiency of the design, it also creates solidly mounted doors and windows.

GENERAL GUIDELINES

Precautions need to be taken when the combined window and door openings in a wall exceed 60 percent of the total wall surface, because the strength of the bale wall may be greatly reduced both in its ability to resist wind, seismic action, and vertical loads from the roof. The concentration of roof loads on small sections of load-bearing bale walls increases the likelihood of differential settling.

Beam or header loads are related to the square of the span, not simply the length. An 8-foot header needs four times the strength of a 4-foot header, not just twice as much. A good rule of thumb is to keep window and door headers less than 8 feet. If ever in doubt, it is a good idea to overdesign a header or get some engineering advice. A header problem can produce troublesome side effects, such as windows and doors that won't open, or broken windows.

If large window openings are wanted, like those used in south walls with solar designs, it may make more sense to use wood framing for that wall, and use the bales as in-fill or super-insulate with conventional materials. Caution must be exercised when combining frame walls with load-bearing bale walls to accommodate the difference in compressibility.

The bales directly below windows are particularly vulnerable to moisture from condensation and rain and snow. A moisture barrier can be placed on top of the bales directly below those openings. Some builders favor placing the windows to the outside edge of the exterior surface of the bale wall to guard against moisture damage. However, a well-sealed or tiled sill with adequate slope should provide sufficient protection against moisture. Concrete sills have been poured in place and used inside and outside.

Windows and doors can be set anywhere from the outside edge of the wall to the inside edge. However, both the type of buck and the method of attachment may limit the options. If doors are mounted to the outside edge of the wall, it should be noted that they will only open to a 90-degree angle unless the interior of the wall is beveled so that it can open more fully.

Architect Bill Cook and his son Bob have both built beautiful structures that use windows set to the inside of the bale wall. Their deeply inset windows are not only attractive but functional as well. This detail, when used with a flat roof, creates the overhang and shading needed for windows in the south wall

Below left: Wood framed south wall at Seeds of Change organic seed farm.
Below right: Tiled window sill of Steve Kemble and Carol Escott.

with solar designs. The top side of the opening can be beveled if additional solar gain is desired.

A compromise is possible, of course; windows can also be placed in the middle of a bale wall, so that they are equidistant from the outside and inside edges of the wall.

Beveled openings are most easily created with wood framing. A wooden frame with a box-beam header can be made 4 to 6 inches wider than the window or door. A sheet of plywood can be cut and sized to create the bevel.

The ease with which bales can be modified and shaped allows for a wide variety of window opening shapes.

With bale walls, wide interior window sills or ledges are created when the window is located to the outside edge. Nor only does this feature add to the "thick-walled" look, but it often creates a valuable and usable space for placing decorative objects like flower pots. When large enough, they can be used as natural window seats. The sill or ledge can also be expanded into the room slightly to make the seat even wider by adding to the base beneath the window.

Another option when the window frame extends all the way to the floor is to frame-in a seat underneath the window. Matts Myhrman used this technique in developing a window seat in his building "Mom's Place." A framed-in seat like this can also include a removable top for storage beneath.

When creating beveled or rounded openings, bales can be modified by shortening two successive strings on a three-string bale or one on a two-string bale (refer to the section on Modifying Bales in chapter 4, page 61). The second of the two strings on a three-string bale needs to be shortened more than the first to create the angle required. The larger the increment between the two, the greater the angle. The strings on the beveled section of bale need to be restrained from slipping off the shorter side of the bale. The easiest way to do this is to tie the strings to each other on one side of the bale, wrap the string around the bale, and tie the strings on the other side. It is also possible to shorten only one string on a three-string bale and round only the corner.

Once the bales have been retied, expanded metal lath can be wrapped around the bales from the window frame to help create the shape desired and add strength to the opening. Rounded openings can be formed the same way using expanded metal lath. Some builders feel that stucco netting is sufficient for this purpose and that metal lath is not necessary. Less of a wedge needs to be formed on the end of the bale; some builders shorten only one bale string which accents the rounded corner.

The thickness of a bale wall also makes it very easy to create alcoves. A wide window could be flanked with closets on the interior wall to develop a

Facing page
Top left: Window set to the outside in Kate Brown's pottery studio.
Top right: Bill Cook's window set to the inside.
Bottom left: Rounded window opening with transom vent above, Steve and Carol's guest house.
Bottom right: Window seat in Hughes-Rhodes house.

Above: Cross-shaped window in Brophy Chapel.
Right: Window openings, Hughes-Rhodes house.

small usable alcove, which illuminates the larger room without having to develop additional corners on the exterior of the building

Wherever half bales are used around door bucks, full bales could be substituted by turning them 90 degrees to the opening and creating a molded frame around the opening, or a stepped wall down to the ground which could also be developed as seating.

CHAPTER 7

FOUNDATIONS

Curved foundation using bales as forms.

THE FOUNDATION OF A BUILDING provides a rigid, unified base for the structure to sit on. This base needs to be strong enough to support the weight of the building, its contents and occupants, and any other loads that may be imposed on it (like snow, wind, and seismic loads) without moving, buckling or breaking.

Foundation design is always dependent on local conditions and the specifics of the building to be supported. Local factors that affect the design include such things as the load-bearing capacity of the soil, soil type, depth of frost line and water table, slope and drainage, high wind loads, and seismic conditions. Special requirements imposed by the design of the building, and sometimes the materials used, may also affect the design of the foundation.

Conventional foundations often consist of two parts, a footing and a stem wall. The footing supports the weight of the wall at a point below grade (ground level) and distributes that load evenly to the ground underneath it. The depth of the footing is determined by how deep the ground freezes in the winter, how deep it is to solid ground below grade, and several other factors having to do with the specific design of the building. Many of the same factors also determine the width of the footing.

The stem wall sits on the footing and rises above grade, usually 6 inches or more, to protect the walls and floor against water and moisture damage. It also transfers the weight of the walls to the footing below.

In many cases the footing and stem wall are not separate assemblies; concrete foundations, for example, are often formed and poured in one step. When concrete slabs are used for the floor and are poured on compacted soil directly on the ground (slab-on-grade), it is standard practice to combine the foundation with the floor slab in a monolithic pour. This is accomplished by digging deeper around the perimeter of the slab and creating a thickened slab under the exterior walls, which acts as the foundation.

Due to the extra width of bale walls, foundations for a bale building can require more than twice the material needed for a 2-by-6 wood frame building. Because of this increase in cost and material, strategies such as rubble trench foundations with concrete-grade beams are becoming increasingly popular with bale builders. They are cheaper and use significantly less concrete. Code approval may take extra effort, but the Uniform Building Code states that any system is acceptable as long as it can "support safely the loads imposed." Building officials are often not familiar with alternative foundation systems, and some discussion and/or an architect's or structural engineer's stamp of approval may be required.

The foundation should be insulated, especially in areas with extreme weather conditions. Insulating the foundation helps take full advantage of bale walls. Uninsulated foundations can be responsible for as much as 17 percent of the total heat loss of a building. One easy approach is to use underground-rated perimeter insulation. Extending insulation out horizontally can be effective. In areas where that type of insulation is not available, bales can be used on the inside of the foundation and underneath the floor of the building. See straw-formed floors in the floor section, page 179.

FOUNDATION DETAILS FOR BALE STRUCTURES

Regardless of what type of foundation is used with a bale wall, there are several areas that require special detailing. Foundations must be sized to accommodate the width and loads of the bale walls. The foundation should be high enough to protect the bottom of the wall from moisture. In most cases, 6 inches above grade is an acceptable minimum height. Good drainage should also be provided around the foundation to carry water away from the walls.

A provision for pinning the first course of bales is usually included as part of the foundation. The most common method has been placing vertical #4 rebar pins, embedded in the foundation to a minimum depth of 6 to 7 inches and extending a minimum of 12 inches in height. New Mexico prescriptive standards stipulate that the tops of the rebar pins should extend halfway into the second course of bales and be spaced at intervals that allow the placement of two pins per bale. They should be placed within 12 inches of any opening or corner for three-wire bales, and within 9 inches for two-wire bales. They are set in the foundation to be centered on the width of the bale. These rebar pins usually are L-shaped at the bottom so that they are better anchored and resist being pulled out.

*Foundation prepared for
bale wall with rebar pins,
asphalt moisture-proofing,
and perimeter insulation.*

With load-bearing structures, attachment points are normally provided in the foundation to anchor the roof plate to the footing. Three-eighth-inch diameter eyebolts, $1/2$-inch anchor bolts, or sleeves are typically used. The location of these points depends on what system is employed; further details can be found in the section on constructing a load-bearing wall in chapter 5. If wood is to be used as a connecting material for the roof plate, a 2-by piece of lumber could be attached to both sides of the foundation as an attachment point, or metal connectors or straps could be used.

The top of the foundation is normally sealed to protect the bottom of the bales from moisture. Typically they are sealed with plastic, asphalt emulsion, roofing felt, concrete sealer such as Thoroseal or Drylock, or galvanized metal flashing to prevent moisture from moving up into the bales from the foundation. Drylock is used to seal ferrocement water tanks and cisterns, and is labeled nontoxic. The New Mexico code states that a moisture barrier should be run vertically between the foundation wall and the perimeter insulation, extend horizontally under the straw bale, and then double back to the outside edge of the foundation. This approach is an attempt to combine moisture protection with an insect barrier, which is provided by the doubled-back plastic.

In some cases, builders have wrapped plastic or felt roofing paper over both the inside and the outside surfaces of the bales on the bottom course so the waterproofing extends down and overlaps the point where the bottom of the bale meets the footing. The idea is that water moving down the interior surface of the stucco due to condensation or leaks would move past the bottom of the first course of bales and exit through the exterior plaster via evaporation.

Although no evidence has been found to indicate that termites pose a threat to straw bale walls, termites can come up through the bales and damage wooden door and window frames, roof framing, and other wood components of a house. Termite prevention strategies can be effectively employed while constructing the foundation. One simple and effective strategy for curbing termites is to stop the stucco at the top of the foundation so that any tubes created by subterranean termites would be visible. Insulating the foundation without creating a path for termites can be a challenge, however. Sheet metal termite shields can be used between the foundation and the first course of bales. If the metal extends over the top of the foundation insulation and then turns down, the termites would have to build visible tubes over the metal flashing. Three inches of silica sand placed beneath and on both sides of the foundation is another prevention measure that has been used. A certain grade of diatomaceous earth, used under the foundation and the concrete slab, is also said to stop termites. Conventional poisoning of the soil to prevent ter-

Foundation plan for straw bale structure.

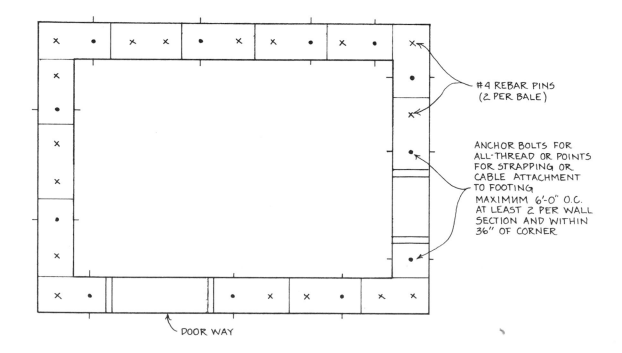

#4 REBAR PINS
(2 PER BALE)

ANCHOR BOLTS FOR
ALL-THREAD OR POINTS
FOR STRAPPING OR
CABLE ATTACHMENT
TO FOOTING
MAXIMUM 6'-0" O.C.
AT LEAST 2 PER WALL
SECTION AND WITHIN
36" OF CORNER

DOOR WAY

PROFILES OF BALE HOUSES

The collection of houses in this section
demonstrates the potential inherent in
this wonderful building material. The
buildings portrayed here could work in
a variety of settings and climates. As a
whole, they represent a cross section of
bale-wall systems that are adaptable
almost anywhere and can be modified
to match different styles.

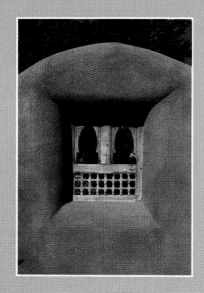

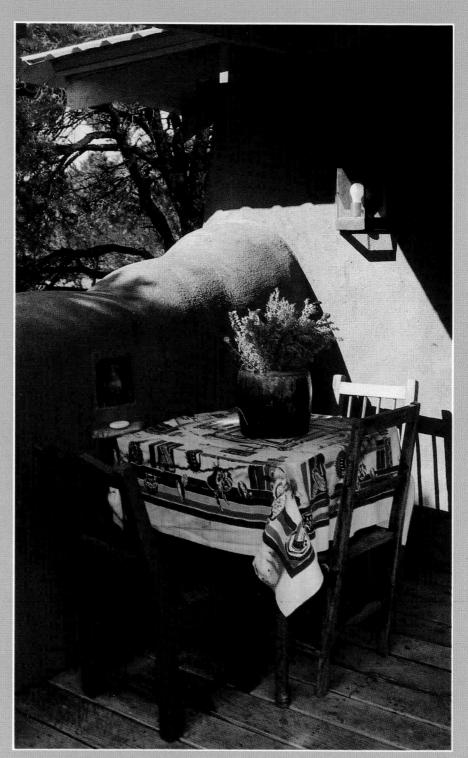

CAROL ANTHONY'S STRAW BALE CLOISTER

Artist Carol Anthony describes her New Mexico load-bearing straw bale cloister as a frozen slice of eighteenth-century time reflecting the inner courtyards and atriums of Italian villas. The building is only 400 square feet and is surrounded by a beautiful straw bale wall that incorporates a thatched African-style, adobe granary tower in one corner.

The cloister was built by a collection of friends in their spare time, with Santa Fe builder Ted Varney doing the walls. The process was in Carol's words informal and communal, "Built with friends, great humor, tequila, a few hugs, and some delicious ratatouille."

Her one-room building has an old-fashioned warmth with its front porch, old Mexican doors and shutters, and adobe earthen floors. Plastered without stucco wire, the exterior is cement based, the interior a finely finished earthen adobe. A precious work of art.

THE KATHERINE WELLS AND LLOYD DENNIS RESIDENCE AND STUDIO

Katherine Wells and Lloyd Dennis first designed and built a straw bale studio and garage at their homesite in rural New Mexico. The owner-built studio is a Pueblo-style straw bale structure incorporating "pumice-crete" columns that extend from the foundation through the bales to a pumice-crete bond beam and parapets. Holes were augured through the bales for the poured columns. The bales used were all custom baled not to exceed fifty pounds so that they could be worked with comfortably. The building was courageously plastered on the exterior with an unstabilized adobe plaster, and has held up reasonably well considering that the building has no overhangs. The interior of the building was finished beautifully with an adobe plaster. The mix used contained local clay soil, sand, mule manure, and straw. The studio was completed at a cost of $14 a square foot.

The main residence, 1,224 square feet (outside), built a year later, was designed by Katherine and built by contractor Ted Varney of Santa Fe. It is a simple, clean, and elegant structure made more impressive by the fact that it was completed at a final cost of $56 a square foot. There are two bedrooms and one bath, in addition to one large comfortable room for living, cooking, and dining. The structure of the house utilizes three concrete-block columns along both the front and the back of the building in combination with three laminated 2-by-10s for the beam. The house is heated with solar radiant floor heat.

BILL AND NANCY COOK'S GUEST HOUSE

Architect Bill Cook and his wife, Nancy, work as a team and together built this wonderful, small (640 square feet) guest house. In addition to his practice, Bill teaches architecture at the University of Arizona and in Mexico City. The influence of contemporary Mexican architecture is evident in this structure, which was built to match the style of their rammed-earth main residence.

The structure of the house is a simple post-and-beam using TJI or I-beam joists for the flat roof. The parapets of the house are wood frame. A unique detail of this house is the deeply inset windows, which provide an overhang from the summer sun. The interior is finely detailed. The cost was $50 per square foot.

BOB MUNK RESIDENCE

Bob Munk's 3,800-square-foot house in Santa Fe was designed by architect Beverley Spears, who is also secretary of the Straw Bale Construction Association. Bob was his own general contractor. The structural system of the house used straw bales as in-fill in combination with 16-inch core-filled concrete blocks for posts and an 8- to 10-inch-wide reinforced-concrete bond beam on top of the walls. The 2-by-10 rafters were thickened later to 2-by-12 in order to accommodate two R-19 fiberglass insulation batts.

The house has two bedrooms, three baths, a studio above the main room, a garage with study above, and a kitchen with a large pantry. The great room has a beautiful, high, rough-sawn pine cathedral ceiling accented by curved collar ties and a row of south-facing skylights. Beautiful custom wrought-iron work adorns the stair railing and door hardware, crafted by Peter Joseph of Santa Fe. The entire house has adobe or earth floors that contain a mix of dried ox blood and manure. The cracks that remained after the floor dried were grouted with a lighter color clay to make the floor resemble flagstone. The floors were finished and sealed with linseed oil. Radiant floor heat was installed beneath the adobe floor.

The interior of the building was plastered with a base coat of fibered gypsum and topped with a beautiful finish coat of micaceous earth plaster, which gives a subtle sparkle to the walls. In some rooms, the earthen plaster incorporates blue corn meal. Builder Max Aragon was in charge of all the adobe finishes and floor.

The exterior of the building received cement plaster for the scratch and brown coats (see chapter 11) and a finish coat of earthen plaster. A deep-gray metal roof completes the structure, allowing it to blend nicely into the piñon- and juniper-covered hills.

According to very accurate records, the finished cost of the house ran $110 per square foot, including the custom wrought-iron work. This cost did not include any site development costs, such as purchasing the land or drilling the well.

THE JERRY RIGHTMAN AND ROBERTA SYME RESIDENCE

The beautifully finished Rightman and Syme residence was designed and built by Santa Fe builder Burke Denman, vice president of the Straw Bale Construction Association. The house is a nicely finished Santa Fe style building with a flat roof and parapets. The bale in-fill walls are built around box columns that incorporate three upright or vertical 2-by-4s sheathed in 18-inch-wide plywood then filled with insulation, and 4-by-10s are used for the beam.

Vigas, or peeled beams, are incorporated in the ceilings, and the house has brick floors throughout. An exterior bale wall encloses a south patio. The house is over 3,000 square feet and cost $95 a square foot.

THE RICHARD HUGHES AND CLARE RHOADES RESIDENCE

Built by artists-turned-builders Jerry West and Charlie Southard of Santa Fe's Blue Raven Construction Works, and designed by architect Steve Robinson, this Santa Fe house is a 3,800-square-foot, two-story Pueblo-style home with a flat roof and parapets. It was built for around $120 a square foot. The second story is frame construction only because code required it; the architect had no qualms about building the second story of bales, instead.

This is a bale in-fill house, and the posts are built from 16-inch box columns that use a 2-by-6

on each end, are sheathed in flake board and stuffed with insulation, and are connected with a 2-by-10 beam.

The interior of the house is a coordinated but changing pattern of plasters, colors, textures, and beautiful details that move through each room of the house. Passive solar design provides some of the required heating, testimony to the background of architect Robinson, author of the solar design book *The Energy Efficient Home.* The house has three bedrooms, two baths, a living room, kitchen, dining room, sunroom, and study.

Laurie Roberts and Lane McClelland's Studio

Laurie Roberts came home to San Diego County from a wall-raising workshop in San Juan Capistrano excited and ready to build a straw bale studio. Her husband Lane thought she was out of her mind but decided to let her get the idea out of her system. Skeptical up to the time of the wall-raising, he watched people who appeared barely able to walk suddenly heaving bales around, feeling like they could actually build a house. It wasn't long before he was enthusiastically combining his talents as a craftsman and woodworker with Laurie's artistry. Together they created one of the most original straw bale buildings anywhere. They even took the money they had budgeted for a new indoor kitchen (their present kitchen is outdoors) and spent it on the studio.

As is evident from the photographs, the building is round, made so by simply jumping on the bales to give them a curved shape, and cordially works its way around a nearby tree. The studio has load-bearing walls and a central pole in the middle of the building to support the roof, which is felt with a decorative thatch around the edges. The outside of the building is beautifully colored with ferric nitrate, which was used to stain the cement stucco. The ceiling is made of willow branches, the leaves sprayed with linseed oil to preserve them. The floor is soil cement colored with a diluted wash of ferric nitrate.

The studio is 450 square feet and was built for a total of $3,400, or $7.50 per square foot. A workshop was held for the wall-raising and generated net proceeds of $2,000. Consequently, the studio cost the owners $1,400 in out-of-pocket expenses.

THE THIERRY DRONET WORKSHOP
AND STABLE

This exquisite structure, located at Vosges in the southeastern part of France, is a flowing S-shaped building that combines stable, workshop, and storage space. Designed by architect Jean Luc Thomas, it was owner-built in 1987 by Thierry Dronet with the aid of a workshop led by French-Canadian François Tanguay. It uses straw bales set in a matrix of mortar for the east, west, and north walls. The south wall is built of stacked cordwood. The north bale wall is waterproofed and is bermed into the side of a hill. One of the most intriguing facets of the building is a mounded and rounded living roof. The roof was made by first covering its surface with waterproof membrane and bales of straw. A sufficient layer of decomposition was allowed to form, a thin layer of compost added, and then the entire surface was planted with living vegetation. (See "The Living Roof," page 163.)

THE TOM AND KATHY NOLAND HOUSE

The Noland House is a ranch headquarters and residence located in the Owens Valley of eastern California. It has three bedrooms, two baths, and a second story. The building is designed with a high passive heating and cooling capability and contains many innovative features dealing with resource optimization, building metabolism, and occupant health. It was collaboratively designed by the San Luis Solar Group, Kenneth Haggard and Polly Cooper, along with Pliny Fisk of the Center for Maximum Building Potential in Austin, Texas, and owner Kathy Noland. Flying M Construction built the house.

The structural framework of the building is based on rigid frame trusses constructed from $2\frac{3}{4}$-by-16 microlams with straw bale in-fill. The ceiling, any framed exterior walls, and interior walls needing acoustical barriers were insulated with Air-krete, a cementitious foam material derived mainly from the minerals in sea water. The house has a scored adobe floor throughout. It has the first composting toilet permitted in California, uses an interior "live marsh" for treating gray water, and has minimized the influences of EMFs (electromagnetic fields). The entire building was plastered without the use of reinforcing mesh, and was colored on the exterior with ferrous sulfate.

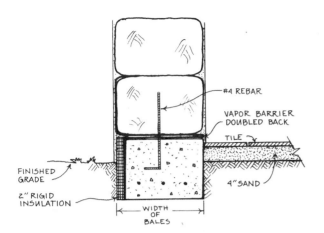

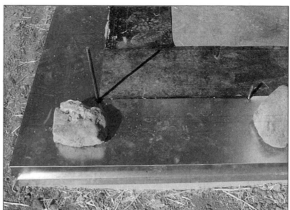

Above left: Moisture barrier as specified by the State of New Mexico. Above right: Foundation with termite shield and waterproofing.

mite infestation can be used, although there are serious questions about the health and environmental consequences of that method.

CONCRETE FOUNDATIONS

Concrete foundations have been used more extensively than any other system with straw bale construction. Concrete used in foundations needs to be reinforced because, while very strong in compression (it is hard to crush), concrete is weak in tension (easy to pull apart). Steel reinforcing bar (rebar) is the material most often used to reinforce concrete because it is very strong in tension. So, combining concrete and steel results in a very strong composite material. The size of rebar is denoted either by its diameter in fractions of an inch or by a number that represents the number of eighths of an inch in the diameter; thus #4 rebar has a diameter of $^4/_8$ inch, or $^1/_2$ inch. Rebar has a pattern of small ribs or ridges on its surface to lock it into the concrete, and the diameter does not include those ribs. So $^1/_2$-inch rebar is actually closer to $^5/_8$ inch in diameter including the ribs. Prior to the widespread availability of rebar, barbed wire, old pipe, and any other available length of steel were often used as concrete reinforcing materials.

In other parts of the world, rebar can be expensive and hard to obtain. An alternative material that is reported to have shown promise in other countries is split bamboo. It has a higher tensile strength than steel per unit weight and is certainly cheaper where it is available, but code officials in the United States will not accept this alternative until it has undergone extensive testing and been approved. Chopped fibers, mixed throughout the concrete, can also be used to reinforce it, but it is not certain to what extent these will serve as a substitute for rebar. Fiberglass reinforcing rods are also being introduced as an alternative to steel, but they are much more expensive than ordinary steel rebar.

Most builders apply 2 to 4 inches of rigid insulation to the exterior of a concrete foundation wall, some feeling that 4 inches is necessary in colder climates. The foundation should be sized so that the exterior surface of the insulation is flush with the exterior surface of the straw bale wall for ease of stucco application. In New Mexico, bales are allowed to overhang the bearing surface of the foundation by not more than 4 inches to accommodate foundation insulation. The interior surface of the foundation wall, if the bales are above the floor, should be flush with the bale wall, since no additional insulation is required inside. Masonry ripple ties (brick ties) are one convenient way to anchor insulation to the foundation. Insulation is often set into the concrete forms before the pour. It can also be attached after the foundation is poured with an adhesive suitable for attaching foam insulation to concrete. If in doubt, check with an insulation supplier, because certain products, like Liquid Nails, can eat holes through incompatible foam insulation.

Two-by-fours or smaller pressure-treated lumber is often cast into the upper inside and outside edges of the foundation to serve as nailing strips for stucco netting. If that method is used, nails or bolts should protrude from the wood into the concrete to securely hold the wood in place. Lumber such as 2-by-4s can also be secured to the top of the foundation after it has been poured at points aligning with the outside and inside edges of the bale wall. The space between them can be filled with rigid insulation or a material such as gravel. This method not only provides an attachment point for stucco netting, but also elevates the bottom course of bales above floor level as would a toed-up foundation with a monolithic pour.

Probably the most tedious aspect of pouring a concrete footing is building the form work to hold the wet concrete. A fast alternative to conventional wood forming is to use bales in place of the wooden forms. A possible drawback is that the foundation may be a little irregular in its shape, but this method has nevertheless been used satisfactorily by several builders. On the outside of the foundation, the rigid insulation, if used, can line the inside of the forms or bales. The bales can be lined with roofing felt on the inside, with stakes driven through the bales periodically to prevent movement during the pour. Wooden spacers can be inserted between the bales to maintain the proper width.

As already mentioned, in many areas it is common practice to pour a con-

*Facing page
Top: Formwork for concrete foundation.
Bottom: Formwork for monolithic pour.*

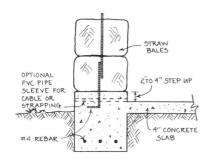

OPTIONAL
PVC PIPE
SLEEVE FOR
CABLE OR
STRAPPING

STRAW
BALES

2"TO 4" STEP UP

#4 REBAR

4" CONCRETE
SLAB

Toed-up foundation.

crete floor and foundation as a monolithic pour. In most cases the slabs average 4 inches in thickness and are sometimes insulated underneath in colder climates. A good feature to incorporate with a monolithic pour is a toed-up foundation where the stem wall is elevated above the floor slab approximately 4 inches. This slight rise in elevation protects the bottom course of bales from moisture in case of excessive rain prior to completion of the roof, and from other water-related problems inside the house, such as an overflowing bathtub or toilet.

STRAW BALE STEM WALLS

Michel Bergeron, a member of ArchiBio in Quebec, has developed a bale-insulated stem wall. He uses forms spaced extra wide to accommodate the width of the bales, and an extra couple of inches on either side. When the forms are ready, the concrete is poured a few inches deep, and then a row of bales are set into it. More concrete is then poured around and over the bales, until a couple of inches of concrete caps the entire wall. When completed, the wall looks just like an extra-wide concrete stem wall. He waterproofs the outside of the wall and uses it as a super-insulated foundation. Using a similar technique, Michel has even built a swimming pool, which cost 20 percent less than conventional construction.

RUBBLE TRENCH FOUNDATIONS

Rubble trench foundations are becoming increasingly popular with bale builders because they often can provide adequate load-bearing capacity with less concrete than a conventional foundation. A rubble trench foundation consists of a trench filled with compacted stone (usually 1 to 1 1/2-inch river rock or crushed stone), and capped with a poured, reinforced concrete grade beam. One alternative method, adapted from the floating footings sometimes used for rammed-earth buildings, is to use a mixture of gravel and sand to ensure good drainage, instead of the larger stones. In extremely cold and wet locations, however, that may not be advisable.

The grade beam is situated above the frost line, while the trench extends below it. The building's weight is distributed evenly by the grade beam and transferred to the earth by the stones that fill the trench. The rubble-filled trench is usually the same size as a conventional concrete-filled trench.

Because this type of foundation does not have concrete extending below grade, it offers less resistance to the forces of wind. Therefore, when using this method, you must be sure that the weight of the grade beam, wall system, and roof loads are sufficient to resist the tendency of the wind to tip the building over (known as overturning). This type of foundation may not be acceptable in areas of high seismic activity because of the possibility of the building moving off the footing in an earthquake.

Foundations traditionally extend below the frost line because soil expands as the water in it freezes, causing a condition called "heaving." This phenomenon can actually lift part of the building, causing the foundation to crack and fail. The traditional approach is to extend the foundation below the frost line so that the soil under the foundation will not freeze. This often results in very deep and expensive foundations. The rubble trench method replaces the concrete below grade with rock fill in a well-drained trench. Rock is much cheaper than concrete, and as long as the trench doesn't contain much standing water, it can't freeze and heave. Provision must be made to drain any water that may accumulate in the bottom of the trench, and that is typically done by sloping the bottom of the trench and placing perforated drain tile or pipe in the bottom of the trench to drain it.

This method was used extensively by Frank Lloyd Wright and has been time-tested in many of his houses. The same principle is used under highways and railroad tracks. Different climates and soils will require slightly different approaches to this type of foundation. "Treacherous soils," as Wright called them, or those with a bearing capacity of roughly less than one ton per square foot, are not suitable for this approach. Wetter climates and those with soils that drain poorly require perforated drain pipe at the bottom of the trench, while drier climates may get along without it. A drain outlet to daylight is desirable.

The bottom of the stone-filled trench must extend below the frost line, which means that it might be only 12 inches deep like one used in Tucson, or 4 feet deep like another one in Iowa, or deeper. In most cases an 8-inch high grade beam is adequate for the loads inherent in a bale wall, but different sized walls and loads may dictate different sized beams. Stem walls resting on the grade beam of poured concrete, block, or pressure-treated wood can be incorporated to support floor framing if necessary.

The trenches need to be as wide as the grade beam including the perimeter insulation, which translates into 18 inches for two-string bales and 23 inches for three-string bales. Insulation is run from the top of the foundation to the bottom of the rubble trench. Most builders use it on the exterior surface of the foundation wall, but others have placed it on the inside. Placing it on the outside provides superior insulation.

Another solution to the problem of building where the frost line is deep has recently been promoted by the National Association of Homebuilders Research Center. "Frost-protected shallow foundations" can be as shallow as 12 inches even with 48-inch-or-deeper frost lines, by relying on a horizontal insulation strategy that keeps the ground from freezing around the foundation by utilizing the heat escaping from under the house through the ground.

Rubble-filled trench foundation.

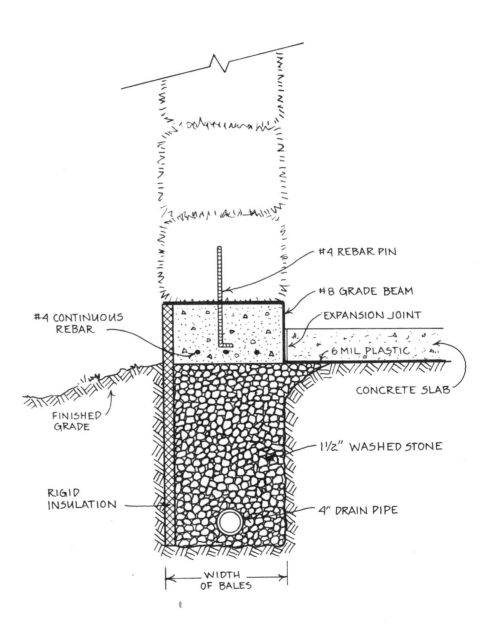

#4 REBAR PIN

#8 GRADE BEAM

EXPANSION JOINT

#4 CONTINUOUS REBAR

6 MIL PLASTIC

CONCRETE SLAB

FINISHED GRADE

1½" WASHED STONE

RIGID INSULATION

4" DRAIN PIPE

WIDTH OF BALES

The grade beam is insulated vertically, and then the insulation is sloped away from the wall, horizontally, on a sloping bed of gravel 2 to 4 feet around the perimeter of the building. The foam is then covered with at least 6 mil plastic and topped with soil. This "hot foundation" method works very well in extremely cold climates and has been used extensively in Scandinavia.

An excellent how-to article on rubble trench foundations is included in the *Fine Homebuilding* manual, "Foundations and Masonry." The frost-protected shallow foundations are described in *Popular Science*, August, 1992.

A variation of the traditional rubble trench foundation was used by George Swanson with a straw bale building in Iowa. In place of a continuous poured grade beam, he used reinforced-concrete-filled Faswall blocks on top of the stone-filled trenches. He used two rows of 9-inch-wide blocks in place of the grade beam to accommodate two-string bales; two rows of 12-inch-wide blocks could be used with three-string bales. This type of stem wall has an insulation value of about R-26.

An alternate combination for use with three-string bales would be a 9- and a 12-inch block, leaving an extra 3 inches for a rock facing on the exterior of the block. With the addition of rigid foam insulation on the inside of the blocks and the rubble trench, two 9-inch, solid grouted blocks create an R-35 plus foundation, and with two 12-inch core-filled blocks, an R-45 plus foundation.

Using Faswall blocks in place of the grade beam greatly simplifies the form work and eliminates the need for applying exterior rigid insulation. Another benefit is that plaster can be applied directly to the block. Faswall blocks can be cut with conventional saws and accept both nails and screws (see facing page for the drawing of George Swanson's Faswell block rubble trench footing).

PRESSURE-TREATED WOOD FOOTINGS

Another potentially cost-effective approach for areas where timber is in good supply is the use of pressure-treated wood in place of concrete for the footings. This type of footing can be used whenever a concrete slab is used for a floor. For use with bale walls, a trench is dug below the frost line and filled with 3/4-inch compacted gravel to grade. Two pressure treated 2-by-8s or even a 2-by-6 on top of a 2-by-8 are placed on top of the gravel trench and framed to the top of the stemwall, sheathed with PT plywood and braced well. A concrete slab is then poured, with a minimum of 4 inches of concrete covering the pressure-treated wood footing.

STONE FOUNDATIONS

Stone is probably the most traditional material for a foundation. It is an excellent choice in areas where concrete is expensive or hard to get and stone is available. Rock foundations are more labor intensive than poured concrete, but they can be very cost-effective for owner-builders. They can provide an attractive base for a bale wall and good protection from moisture.

Typically, a trench is dug below the frost line and a base of 3 to 4 inches of concrete is laid. Horizontal rebar is placed in the wet concrete and supported a minimum of 3 inches above the bottom of the trench. Stones are placed in the wet concrete and more concrete and stones are added until grade is reached. At that point, stones are set for appearance and structure in a cement mortar of 3 parts sand to 1 part Portland cement (no lime). If the exterior rock surface is not to be left exposed but is to be covered with plaster, less attention to detail is necessary. The rock foundation should extend at least 8

Stone foundation on straw bale structure near Puebla, Mexico.

inches above grade. Historically, stones were often dry stacked on a base of mortar and were sometimes mortared with mud.

If the exterior surface of the rock is to remain visible, the perimeter insulation needs to be placed on the interior surface of the rock. Rock is an extremely poor insulator, and it is a good idea to use perimeter insulation to insure maintaining the benefits of the highly insulated bale walls. An option here is to use rigid foam insulation covered by a stone veneer.

For foundation details pertinent to bale structures, refer to the section on concrete foundations (page 139).

POST OR PIER FOUNDATIONS

Bale structures can be built on raised floors resting on columns or piers. There are a great many options for supporting a bale structure on a floor raised off the ground. The few differences between bale structures and conventional buildings must be accommodated, but otherwise common practice for post or pier foundations will work. The major changes result from the extra width of bale walls, the unique methods of fastening bale walls to the foundation (rebar pins and $1/2$-inch threaded rods), and any special requirements due to waterproofing or sealing the bottom of the bale walls.

OTHER POSSIBILITIES

Any number of different foundation systems can be used in conjunction with simple bale structures. Codes can certainly be a limitation in many areas, but in others the only limitation is the scope of human ingenuity.

In cold climates, basements are often an affordable option because of the size and depth of excavation already required to get the foundation below frost line. The design of basements for bale buildings will be similar to those for conventional construction methods, except that the width of the bale walls and the unique methods of attaching the bales to the foundation must be accommodated.

Railroad ties can easily suffice as foundations for a number of different small structures, including storage sheds and greenhouses. Mobile home tie-downs, consisting of metal auger-type screws, are ideal for providing a connection to the ground for structures using railroad tie footings that are subject to significant wind loads.

In southern Arizona, Bob Cook used wooden pallets on top of 3 inches of pea gravel for a temporary shop building. The pallets were laid on heavy poly-

Soil-filled sandbags being used for wall construction.

ethylene sheeting on top of the gravel, then plywood was screwed down for the floor of the shop.

In Australia, 15 to 20-percent, asphalt-stabilized rammed earth has been used for foundations. This is an application that might be well suited to using split bamboo for reinforcement.

Sandbags filled with moist dirt, which later dry and harden like adobe bricks, could be used as a foundation. They are currently being used to build domes and vaulted rectangular rooms by Nader Khalili, an Iranian-born architect well known for his work with earthen materials and vaults and domes. In his applications, sand bags are set on a 4-inch base of sand and reinforced by using two parallel strands of barbed wire between courses of bags all the way around the perimeter of the building. Plaster is applied directly to the bags without the aid of any stucco netting. Polypropylene and burlap bags appear to be equally suitable.

For use with bale walls, a trench could be dug and filled with rubble, stone, sand, or whatever porous material is available. The depth of the trench would depend on local drainage and climatic conditions. Fill for the bags could be the dirt that has been dug from the trench. It could be stabilized if desired and treated with borate for a measure of termite protection. Two courses of bags could be used with two strands of barbed wire between them. Roof ties could be attached to them as well. Used with three-string bales, they could be laid lengthwise across the trench and the width adjusted. Long lengths of rebar could be driven through the bags into the ground and spaced as they would be in a regular foundation to provide reinforcement for the first course of bales. It is not a good practice to allow uncoated rebar to be in direct contact with the soil because of rusting and the potential migration of moisture along the length of the rebar (epoxy-coated and fiberglass rebar are other options). The bags could be capped with cement mortar and then sealed or covered with asphalt and roofing paper. This is not something which has been tried, but is being suggested as an experimental possibility.

Tires, as used in the tire-based earthship houses, are another foundation possibility. Tires can be chosen to approximate the width of the walls, filled and tamped with stabilized earth, and capped with cement mortar if desired. They have been used as a foundation for at least one bale building in northern New Mexico and two in Colorado.

For temporary structures, one of the simplest footings would be a sheet of plastic laid on the ground. Plastic could also be used to wrap the entire first course of bales, thereby preventing water from seeping between the ground cover of plastic and the bales. The ground beneath the first course could be elevated slightly to improve drainage. A strip of inexpensive interior/exterior carpet would protect the plastic membrane from sharp rocks.

CHAPTER 8

ROOFS

Palm-thatched roof on Elizabeth Nuzom's studio in Alamos, Sonora, Mexico.

MANY ROOF STYLES CAN BE USED with bale buildings. However, the method of bale-wall construction can influence the type of roof structure. Buildings using bales as in-fill in combination with a structural framework can use any type of roof. Load-bearing bale buildings are more constrained. The roof and the roof plate contribute significantly to the final stability of a load-bearing bale structure. These buildings become progressively more stable with each step of the construction process and are quite solid once the roof is in place. For that reason, one of the favorites with the early Nebraska buildings was the hip roof. It allows all four walls to be of equal height, and distributes the roof load onto all four walls. Builders of load-bearing structures typically favor simple floor plans and roofs.

Unfortunately, roof structures, as they are commonly built, still require a substantial amount of lumber and are subject to tight tolerances. It would be ideal if the roof structures of a bale building could be constructed with the same ease as a bale wall, exhibit the same relaxed tolerances, and demonstrate a similar reduction in lumber. The development of roofs with these characteristics is in many ways the new frontier of bale building.

One roof system that is a positive step in that direction, although it uses a conventional structure, is the "living roof" developed by ArchiBio of Quebec. Bales are placed on the roof of the structure, left to decompose, and overseeded with wildflowers and plants. This roof ends up being something of a cross between a turf and a thatched roof.

Discussions about alternative roofs invariably drift toward the use of bamboo, thatch, vaults, and domes. Bamboo is a very versatile material which can be quickly grown under a wide variety of circumstances. In early 1994, two straw bale buildings went up using bamboo roofs. One was constructed near Puebla, Mexico, and the other in Washington. A straw bale house with a thatched roof was constructed in southern Sonora, Mexico, during the same year. Due to code complications in the United States, it may well be that countries like Mexico, which have a good supply of indigenous building materials and people with traditional building skills, will be the first ones to make breakthroughs in construction of roofs for bale structures that generate the same level of excitement as the bale walls invariably bring to participants.

Bale vaults and domes are another possibility, but the development of successful and approved structures will require dedication, time, and research. The Canelo Project, in Canelo, Arizona, a nonprofit organization dedicated to connecting people, culture, and nature, has built experimental straw bale domes and is continuing its research. Architect Nader Khalili, who is well known for his work with earth and ceramic vaults and domes, is also experimenting with building a straw bale dome at his headquarters in Hesperia, California.

Until a creative new roof system for bale structures is developed, long horizontal spans of roofs will be most appropriately met by lumber and steel roof systems. One way builders can support the sustainable use of timber is to use it only when absolutely necessary and to choose products that do not require logging of old-growth forests. Wood trusses made from 2-by-4s and other engineered wood-fiber products that are produced from small-diameter, fast-rotation trees on forest plantations are superior to single units of large dimension lumber. The use of steel structural supports and roofs, which is common in commercial structures but relatively new for residential buildings, may also prove to be a successful alternative to lumber for bale buildings.

Vented hip roof, Kate Brown's load-bearing pottery studio, San Lorenzo, New Mexico.

A large variety of roof structures have been used in conjunction with bale buildings. Each style has its own advantages, and probably more than any other feature defines the look of the building.

Whatever roof system is used with bale structures, it is important to install gutters or something equivalent to keep water away from the walls.

THE HIP ROOF

The hip roof is one of the preferred roof designs for buildings with load-bearing bale walls and can also be used with non-load-bearing bale structures. All walls can be the same height, and the roof load is distributed onto all four walls (though not necessarily equally), unlike the gable roof, which bears weight primarily on two walls.

On longer rectangular structures with hip roofs, the central part of the roof can use trusses, usually custom made for each job and usually made with 2-by-4s. Truss manufacturers can provide either trusses or a complete hip-roof assembly. Manufactured trusses are usually cost competitive with site-built trusses if there is a local truss fabrication company.

Another advantage to the hip roof is that it is often less affected by high winds than most other roof shapes. It can be built with good-sized overhangs, which help protect the walls from weathering, and can easily be extended into porches.

If a cathedral or open-type ceiling is desired (allowing no attic space), parallel chord trusses or scissor trusses can be used for the roof framing. Parallel chord trusses are made from two parallel 2-by-4s (chords), connected by diagonally set 2-by-4s (webs), and fastened together by toothed metal connector plates or plywood gussets. The overall height of the parallel chords (depth of the truss) can be sufficient to allow substantial roof insulation. If nonparallel chords are used, the ceiling can be horizontal and the roof can slope for drainage. Scissor trusses allow similar benefits of depth of truss for insulation and a lower slope for the ceiling. They can also be used to create attic space by keeping the insulation up in the trusses.

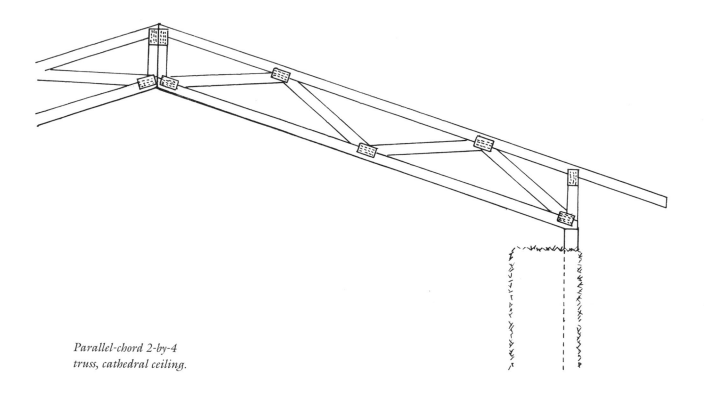

Parallel-chord 2-by-4 truss, cathedral ceiling.

THE PYRAMID ROOF

The pyramid roof is a pure hip, essentially a hip without a ridge. All four hip rafters meet at a central point at the peak of the roof. A four-sided, vented cupola can be incorporated at the peak of the roof, which is both functional and beautiful. A straw bale home in Dripping Springs, Texas, designed and built by Steve Kemble, uses this roof structure. The pyramid roof has the added advantage, over an elongated hip roof, of distributing the weight of the roof equally on each wall.

THE GABLE ROOF

Gable roofs have also been popular for modern straw bale houses. They offer the distinct advantage of allowing the incorporation of loft space and of additional solar gain when windows are placed in the south end. Like hip roofs, they are good candidates for 2-by-4 trusses. A great variety of truss designs are available for this style of roof. In most cases, the gable ends are framed in, rather than in-filled with bales. In some buildings, the bales extend up

through and between the last two rafters or trusses and are cut off to match the angle of the roof pitch. A chain saw is very effective for trimming the tops of these bales. They don't carry any load and are confined by the rafters or trusses, so if they are put in place after the roof framing is done, they can be cut using the top of the rafters as a guide, and without retying.

THE SHED ROOF

Shed roofs slope in just one direction. They are the simplest roof system to construct and are economical. This roof is a good choice for builders with limited experience. One difficulty is that they provide limited space for insulating and venting the roof when using 2-by-10 or 2-by-12 rafters. Using simple trusses or truss joists allows a deeper pocket with room for better insulation.

When the shed roof is used with load-bearing bale walls, a little extra caution should be taken in the design. The different wall heights required for the slope of the shed roof do not accommodate a continuous-perimeter roof plate, and thrust from the rafters against the lower load-bearing wall during construction could cause it to lean out. A little care and bracing, if necessary,

Top: Gable roof on Joan Chandler's house in Gila, New Mexico.
Bottom: Cutting bales with a chainsaw to match the slope of the rafters.

Shed roof, Bill and Athena Steen's guest house, Canelo, Arizona.

are usually enough to keep the walls straight. As in the case of gable end walls, the bales on the non-load-bearing sides will need to be trimmed to the roof slope if this triangular space is not framed in.

Parallel chord trusses can be used in place of large dimensional lumber for rafters. Besides being cost effective and easy to build, they are available in depths greater than a 2-by-12, and therefore allow for good roof insulation and better venting.

Truss joists or I-beams that are made from a vertical sheet of plywood sandwiched between 2-by lumber top and bottom can be used in much the same way. They come in varying depths and heights ranging from 9 1/2 inches to 16 inches. They are lightweight and easy to install. A truss joist, with a 16-inch depth, can span a distance of up to 30 feet (refer to the spec sheets for allowable loads). They offer many of the same advantages as parallel chord trusses. Care must be taken when designing load-bearing bale structures that the loads imposed by very large roof spans do not exceed the load-bearing capacity of the wall system.

Shed roofs can also be built in a way that creates attic space over a flat ceiling. There are a number of advantages to using this approach. The walls can be of equal height and use a continuous roof plate. The additional space can then be insulated and vented. Steve and Nena MacDonald's house in Gila, New Mexico, used peeled poles, or vigas, to span the distance between the walls. Steve then framed the section above to accommodate a shed roof. The remaining space between the ceiling and the roof was super-insulated and vented. Two-by-four trusses with a shed roof slope probably constitute one of the most practical and cost-effective ways to construct this type of roof.

THE CLERESTORY ROOF

Clerestory roofs are basically two shed-type roofs combined, one sloping to the back, usually at a steeper slope, and another lower one sloping to the front. These roofs have a prominent place in solar-designed buildings, and have also been used with bale buildings. They allow solar-gain heat and light to enter rooms on the north or back side of a house, which in many cases can reduce the size or need for supplementary heating systems and lighting. In

Clerestory roof at Seeds of Change Farm, Gila, New Mexico.

areas like the southwestern United States where the winter sun is strong, these types of roof structures can be very effective.

Steve Kemble has built three straw bale houses using clerestory roofs. He likes the clerestory in solar designs where the building has a lot of south-to-north depth, and feels that they are best used in conjunction with some type of structural skeleton like a post-and-beam with bales used as in-fill. His home in Bisbee used a hybrid design in which the central clerestory structure was built as a post-and-beam, while the back wall was load bearing. In retrospect, he would have built the whole structure as a post-and-beam, considering how little extra work was needed to put posts in the back wall. The 20-foot span on the rear roof section exerted a lot of thrust on the back wall and required some effort to return the wall to plumb (see photo of workshop on page 240). The clerestory can also be incorporated in a truss system to reduce thrust loads.

FLAT ROOFS AND PARAPETS

To avoid any possible confusion, flat roofs do have some slope (less than a shed roof); they are not truly flat. They have a bad reputation because they often develop leaks due to their minor slope, but most of their poor performance can be traced to the materials used in the roof structure and poor workmanship. However, they are best suited to climates with low rainfall and minimum snow loads.

Traditionally the flat roofs of Pueblo Indian and other southwestern cultures used peeled tree trunks for beams, smaller-diameter poles, or latillas, laid across their tops for the ceiling, and multiple layers of clay-based dirt. The top layer of dirt often grew grass, and in some cases, melons and squash were planted on the roof and allowed to vine down the sides of the building. These roofs were heavy, required large beams, and often leaked in extended periods of rainy weather. However, they were thermally and resource efficient, inexpensive, and provided an additional living space for a variety of purposes including summer sleeping, cooking, and food drying. A modern version of this roof used in Mexico incorporates a layer of roofing paper on top of the ceiling material before any dirt is placed on the roof. Soil cement is then used in place of plain dirt and sometimes plastered.

The modern "pueblo style" houses of New Mexico and the Southwest have flat roofs made from modern materials in imitation of that older style. A number of straw bale houses in the Santa Fe area have been built in the pueblo style, including the Hughes-Rhoades house, the Rightman-Syme

Left: Traditional Pueblo-style flat roof, Santa Clara Pueblo, northern New Mexico.
Below: Modern Pueblo-style flat roof, Catherine Well's studio, northern New Mexico.

Parapet on the Kiva at Santa Clara Pueblo, New Mexico.

house, Katherine Wells's studio, and Virginia Carabelli's house (see the color section).

Flat and shed roofs are often designed with parapets, or short vertical walls that extend above the roof line. Parapets can be on two, three or all sides of the roof. They serve as a base against which to lay flashing and roofing papers. They also serve as an anchoring point for drain spouts. Parapets range from very simple to elaborate and ornamental. Traditionally parapet style was linked to spiritual beliefs. In the pueblos, they were often used to "echo natural landscape patterns." In Arabia, they were used to connect the building to the sky.

Roof parapets, which were once adobe, have now been constructed of everything from straw bales wrapped with a moisture barrier, to frame construction, to lightweight pumice-based concrete. New Mexico's code for non-load-bearing straw bale construction allows bales to be used in parapets provided they do not exceed two courses in height. They must be pinned together vertically with rebar and have a continuous wrap with stucco netting. They also require a continuous seal to be maintained from the roof surface to the top of the parapet and down the other side, a minimum of 2 inches and a maximum of 6 inches.

A potential trouble spot for flat roofs with parapets on all sides is where roof drains, or *canales*, are used to drain water from the roofs and away from the walls. Since these roof drains go through the wall, they need to be carefully designed and built so they do not develop leaks where the drain, roof, and parapet join. One solution is to have parapets on three sides and the drainage off the roof on the fourth side

In Mexico, a modern tradition of flat roofs developed with the availability of concrete. Concrete roofs are now very common there. A number of prominent Mexican architects, notably Luis Barragan, who thought the facade of the house should be the sky, have incorporated the flat roof as a major component in their designs. In continuation of this theme, architect Bill Cook built a beautiful straw bale guest house (page 162) in a modern Mexican style with a flat roof. Rather than concrete, the roof uses pre-manufactured truss joists. He feels that trusses overcome many potential flat-roof problems resulting from the warping and twisting of large-dimension wooden joists, such as vigas. Flat roofs also allow a painted white reflective surface (good for hot climates) and are easy to work on. His roof has a slope of $1/4$ inch per foot, which he feels is the absolute minimum, and is coated with an elastomeric coating, which greatly extends the life of the roof and further protects against moisture. He framed his parapets with plywood on top of the bale wall.

Bill's son Bob built a workshop with a flat roof made from homemade 2-by-4 trusses, which were essentially parallel chords with a little slope incorporated in the upper chord. These easy and inexpensive trusses were made by Bob's partner, Friederike Almstedt. The parapets were wood framed.

Where space is limited, flat roofs can serve as invaluable living space, and

Flat roof with parapet as used on architect Bill Cook's straw bale guest house, Sonoita, Arizona.

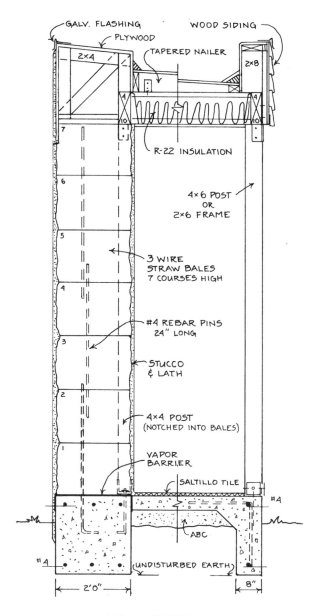

GALV. FLASHING
WOOD SIDING
PLYWOOD
TAPERED NAILER
2×4
2×8
R-22 INSULATION
4×6 POST
OR
2×6 FRAME
3 WIRE
STRAW BALES
7 COURSES HIGH
#4 REBAR PINS
24" LONG
STUCCO
& LATH
4×4 POST
(NOTCHED INTO BALES)
VAPOR
BARRIER
SALTILLO TILE
#4
ABC
#4
(UNDISTURBED EARTH)
2'0"
8"

WALL SECTION

in some cases, even space for growing and producing food. A combination of roof styles may prove advantageous on larger structures. Smaller sections of the roof, such as bedrooms, could have flat roofs used for eating or sleeping.

THE LIVING ROOF

The following was developed and described by members of the nonprofit group ArchiBio of Quebec. This roof demonstrates some very innovative thinking on the use of bales and is a very positive step in the direction of developing alternative roof systems for bale structures.

Contemporary builders usually pay a fair amount of attention to roof structuring. Some of our clients prefer prefabricated structures; others prefer more traditional framing methods like post-and-beam. We usually pay far less attention to the finishing of a roof. Materials such as asphalt shingles and aluminum sheeting are the most common choices, yet there are traditional methods that have been around for centuries that we ignore either because they are too time consuming or simply because the local codes have failed to recognize them, pushing them closer to extinction.

ArchiBio has played with the idea of alternative roofing since the mid-seventies, and since we live in a northern climate, we have had to be a little creative. Thatch roofs are more common in humid climates like those of the British Isles, northern France, and Holland. Earthen roofs are more appropriate for desertlike climates such as the Mediterranean, the southwestern part of the United States, and Australia.

After some exploration, we came up with a mix that would be a mid-point between those two extremes. We needed something that would respond to regions that have snowfalls, warm summers, and extreme temperatures. We also wanted to work with a renewable resource that could be either replaced or fixed easily and with little cost. The idea of a living roof fascinated us for its creative potential as well. Living roofs can be finished with a simple grass covering or developed into a complex garden with bulbs and wildflowers. As a matter of fact, one of the coverings we now suggest is strawberries, since they develop strong and shallow root systems that help keep the humidity level of the sod high. Just imagine an edible roof of strawberries.

We have always been involved with solar and ecological housing, so

Bales being placed for a living roof, Quebec, Canada.

we were looking for a material that would give an inertia to an already super-insulated roof. At the same time, we didn't want it to be so heavy that we would be forced into building structures that would be too complicated and beyond the reach of most owner-builders. It had to be a simple process and a relatively inexpensive one.

The living roof we finally developed weighs around 100 to 120 pounds per square foot and is subject to snow loads of the Quebec region, which vary from 40 to 60 pounds per square foot. Because of the weight of these combined loads, we increase the strength of the roof structure.

WATERPROOFING

The slope on our living roofs is usually minimal, close to flat; however, they can also have a slope up to 6 to 8 inches per foot. A waterproof membrane has to be put between the decking and the vegetation. On our first projects we tried a double thickness of agricultural-grade *polyethylene. This inexpensive material proved to be prone to puncturing and rotting. We concluded that it is not worth using for long-lasting jobs.*

We now use various polymer-based modified bitumen membranes. Materials such as montmorillonite clay (Bentonite), Volcay, PVC membranes, and Bitutene are all satisfactory; in fact, any reinforced waterproofing membrane will work. We have had success with a membrane called Armorplast (which is the least expensive on the market), made by IKO, a maker of asphalt shingles. This type of membrane is melted at the seams, creating a single membrane when the whole roof is done.

Care must be taken to make sure the roof drains and sheds moisture. The edges of the roof are finished with a side board or parapet. The membrane overlaps part way up these walls, to keep them dry. Drainage is then directed to the bottom of the slope or to the corners and then into regular gutters. These membranes have been used for many years on commercial and industrial buildings and are long lasting. We can say that they will probably stand up to their promises with a straw cover.

ROOF FINE-TUNING

The idea behind the living roof is that we use straw as a base for the compost that will eventually be formed to support the plants and flowers we will install as permanent residents. On large roofs, we simply lay the bales flat (strings on top) over the entire roof, leaving a gap of three to four feet at the edge. In that space, we use flakes of straw to taper the roof gradually to the edge. This area usually corresponds to the end of the overhang.

At this point, we walk the roof and cut all the strings so that the bales will begin to break down. We think that for the first couple of seasons, such as winter and spring, the roof should be left on its own. After a few months the straw will begin to stabilize (and shrink) and hold the minimal amount of humidity necessary for plant support. Then you can spread a couple of inches of well-aged compost or manure over the roof and sow your favorite wildflowers. You may have to water the roof for the first few weeks in order to ensure germination. Local weather will tell.

It will take at least a year before varied and robust life begins to settle in. Nature has its own terms when settling in a new habitat. But

Above: Living roof growing tomatoes on the house of Clode Deguise and Francois Tanguay, Quebec, Canada.

it's well worth the wait. A living roof is virtually care free; all it will need is an occasional weeding. Let your goat do the job.

We think that a living roof is fine for single-floor houses, for small surfaces, and, of course, on top of garden sheds, workshops, and the like. We don't think it is a good idea to install a living roof on top of a two-story building. It's usually too high to be appreciated, and it's too much out of reach for regular maintenance.

Authors' note: Wildflowers, grasses, native and other plants that can exist on local rainfall will likely provide the most suitable species for this use. Model the roof after local ecosystems or plants that have naturalized in the area. For more information on this roof, contact ArchiBio (see appendix).

Living roof on the house of Pascal Thipaux, France.

VAULTS AND DOMES

Creating vaults and domes made of bales is an intriguing possibility that seems to perpetually captivate the imaginations of those building with bales. To use bales as the actual building blocks of a vault or a dome requires overcoming several challenges. One difficulty is their bulky shape and size. Masonry vaults and domes are traditionally built from small-sized bricks, which can be adjusted incrementally to create a variety of curved shapes. Bricks or stone blocks are often beveled slightly on the ends, or else mortar is used to fill the tapered spaces between the pieces with an incompressible material. Since bales do compress, special consideration needs to be given to designs which attempt to use them structurally in these types of configurations. Caution should also be exercised because of the potential for collapse. Good exterior moisture proofing is essential, as heavy rains or snow could increase that possibility.

*Facing page
Left: Adobe Mosque at Abiquiu, New Mexico. Right: Experimental straw bale vault designed and built by Dan Smith and Bob Theis of Berkeley, California (photo by Dan Smith).*

The large, rectangular shape of bales also presents a challenge because of the size of the triangular voids that are created when the bales are laid up along an arc. These voids could be filled with clay coated loose straw or another material. Small retied beveled bales could also be mud mortared into the gaps. Experimentation will be required to determine if the structure can be adequately reinforced by pinning the bales together.

It might be possible to fill cloth or burlap bags with loose straw, coated by a thin clay slip, as is used in European Cob construction, and stack them structurally. Nader Khalili is having good success building vaults and domes out of sandbags filled with moist dirt, and variations on that theme might work even though it would be more time-consuming than stacking bales.

Experimental straw bale dome in Canelo, Arizona.

Arched door and window openings could easily be built this way.

Bill and Athena Steen, along with Athena's parents Rina and Ralph Swentzell, constructed a temporary straw bale dome in Canelo, Arizona, using the bales structurally without a supporting framework. The dome was 15 feet in diameter. The bales in the first few courses were slightly corbeled (inset) from the bales in the preceding course. In order to slowly close the dome in, the upper courses of straw bales were tilted inward by shoving flakes of straw beneath the bales on their outside edge. As the courses increased it was found that it was important to tilt the bales only slightly, otherwise it proved difficult to position them and keep them in place. In addition, the bales in the upper courses were cut and angled at the corners so that they would wedge against one another. This proved to be less satisfactory than leaving the bales in their rectangular shape, however, because the bales tended to slip out of the ring due to the lack of a compression point which the rectangular bales provided at their corners.

Since the dome was considered a temporary experiment, the bales were not pinned. Nonetheless, the structure was sturdy enough to walk on after each ring or course was complete.

Roxanne Swentzell and Joel Glanzberg from Santa Clara Pueblo also completed a straw bale dome using a similar technique.

In California, Bob Theis and Ross Burkhardt have done a number of small temporary experimental vaults using rice-straw bales as in-fill in combination with structural frames. Their research is continuing, and they plan to build a small permanent structure soon.

Domes and vaults for bale structures could be built using a double structural framework of bamboo, pipe, or flexible poles, and covered with a weatherproof skin. The space between the two layers could be filled with bags of straw or bales for insulation. Vaults might also be built using trusses with curved top chords made from bamboo or any other suitable material.

Nader Khalili's book, *Ceramic Houses,* is an excellent guide to building earthen vaults and domes. Many of the same principles would apply with straw.

THATCHED ROOFS

Thatch fastened to a rough pole or bamboo frame was undoubtedly one of the original roof systems used for human dwellings in many parts of the world. Contrary to the commonly held opinion that thatching is an antiquated, obsolete roofing system, it has evolved into a modern craft. Thatched roofs share many of the advantages of other modern roofing materials and still have much to recommend them for use in many undeveloped areas, as well as in the modern resource-affluent world. Although they are labor intensive, materials are not expensive.

Some of the best thatching materials are straw and grasses, making them appropriate for buildings that have walls of the same renewable materials. Certain varieties, particularly those with tall, rigid stems, can last fifty years or more in a roof if the work is done carefully. Rye, wheat, rice, and other cereal

Thatched roof on Elizabeth Nuzom's palapa, Alamos, Sonora, Mexico.

straws are very well suited to this work, as are other uncultivated wild grasses. Specially managed thatch made with Phragmites australis (water reed) can last up to a hundred years when correctly used. Palm thatch usually has a much shorter life.

Modern combine harvesters effectively destroy cereal straws for use as a thatching material by crushing and splitting the stalks into piles of intermingled butts and tips. The butt end is the more weather resistant part of the stalk, and thatching bundles should be assembled with the butt ends all at one end. One alternative is to use straw that is harvested by a binder, an antiquated and hard-to-find machine still sold in Europe, that does not destroy the straw stalks. Another is to use combed wheat, which is produced when the grain is removed from the straw by combing or stripping rather than threshing. In combing, the straw remains uncrushed and oriented with the butt ends all pointed in the same direction.

Were it possible to overcome the difficulty of acquiring good thatching material and develop simpler methods of construction, thatch could provide beautiful, well-insulated, nontoxic roofs capable of breathing like a bale wall. English thatchers say that organic thatch from Eastern Europe lasts longer than modern straw, probably due to lower nitrogen levels.

As presently practiced, thatching requires only the simplest of tools, and, while it may never become popular with developers of mass-produced housing, it remains a creative and satisfying craft capable of converting easily produced resources into beautiful and functional roofs. Thatched roofs also require a relatively simple roof structure compared to other heavier systems like tile.

One straw bale house in Sonora, Mexico has been built with a palm thatch roof. Perhaps others will follow, using thatch in both traditional and innovative ways.

BAMBOO TRUSSES

It is difficult to think of a material better suited to alternative roof construction than bamboo. It is easy to grow under a wide variety of conditions, wider than most people would imagine. Given a little water, it grows quickly, and many timber bamboos are hardy to zero degrees F. Like straw, it is a renewable resource and can be sustainably grown. It has excellent tensile strength and is used to reinforce concrete in many areas.

In some areas, however, the harvesting of bamboo is creating ecological disasters similar to the cutting down of old-growth or tropical rain forests.

Bamboo forests are complex ecological systems, and, as with all materials, it is wise to know the impact of the decision to use it.

Bamboo does have some disadvantages. Its natural durability is lower than wood, and it must be treated with preservatives to last in exposed locations. Due to variation in its diameter, it is not well suited to standardization or large-scale commercial applications. Also, bamboo connections often require extra time and special skills.

As part of a project of the Methodist Church of Mexico near Puebla, Mexico, bamboo trusses were used in conjunction with a straw bale building, the first known to use bamboo in the roof structure. The trusses were topped with cross sections, or purlins, of carrizo reed (a bamboo-like grass), roofing felt, several inches of dirt, and then finished with clay tile.

There are a number of good books and manuals available on the use of bamboo as a building material, all listed in the appendix. One basic guide is called *Building with Bamboo* by Jules Janssen and is published by Intermediate Technology Publications. Other more in-depth works include *Bamboo — Its Use*, by the Chinese Academy of Forestry and *The Bamboo Construction Handbook* (in Spanish) by Oscar Hidalgo; both are available from Tradewinds in Gold Beach, Oregon.

Above and left: Bamboo trusses, Puebla, Mexico.

Another booklet, *Bamboo on the Farm,* by Daphne Lewis, explains how to commercially grow and harvest bamboo for shoot, pole, and plant production. Suppliers of bamboo for cultivation are also listed in the appendix. Timber bamboo poles are available from Bamboo Gardens in Seattle, Washington (see appendix). Some care must be exercised to prevent the escape of bamboo as an invasive weed. In some areas there are laws governing the growing of bamboo, since it can supplant native trees and vegetation if allowed to grow unconfined.

METAL TRUSSES

Roofs made from galvanized light-gauge steel framing are well suited for bale buildings. Metal trusses can be either prebuilt or manufactured on site. They are lightweight and capable of spanning large distances without center supports, which make them good structural candidates for large buildings and barns. They can be connected with hurricane ties (small metal plates to strengthen connections) to either wood or metal roof plates. The EOS Institute of Laguna Beach, California, constructed a temporary straw bale build-

Metal trusses, EOS Institute Demonstration straw bale Eco house.

ing using lightweight steel trusses for the Southern California Home Show in 1993. Again, in load-bearing bale buildings, care must be taken to assess how loads are transferred to bale walls on large-span roofs.

PORCHES AND DORMERS

Hip, pyramid, and gable roofs are well suited for the addition of porches and dormers. Roof lines can be easily extended to create partial or complete wrap-around porches, which are an inexpensive way to obtain useful living space. For example, a wrap-around porch could be screened on one side of the house for outdoor living, dining, or sleeping during the hot and insect-laden periods, left open on other sides for use during bug-free seasons, and glazed on the south side to create a greenhouse for plants or a sunroom for solar gain. Smaller porches can be developed for specific seasons and uses. Porches further protect the bale wall surfaces from moisture and general weathering.

Dormers can increase useful space when used as sleeping and sitting nooks. When adding dormers to create usable attic space, all the issues regarding second-story design, such as the additional loads imposed on the walls

Dormer windows on house in northern New Mexico.

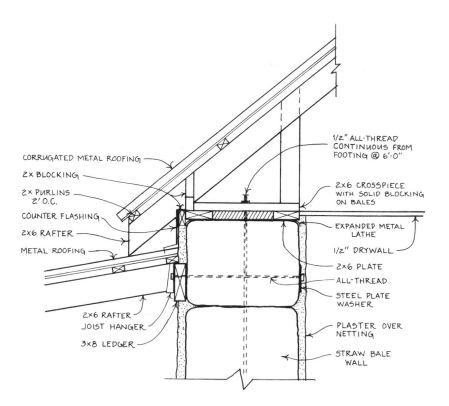

Labels on diagram:

CORRUGATED METAL ROOFING

2× BLOCKING

2× PURLINS 2' O.C.

COUNTER FLASHING

2×6 RAFTER

METAL ROOFING

2×6 RAFTER

JOIST HANGER

3×8 LEDGER

1/2" ALL-THREAD CONTINUOUS FROM FOOTING @ 6'-0"

2×6 CROSSPIECE WITH SOLID BLOCKING ON BALES

EXPANDED METAL LATHE

1/2" DRYWALL

2×6 PLATE

ALL-THREAD

STEEL PLATE WASHER

PLASTER OVER NETTING

STRAW BALE WALL

Attaching a porch to a load-bearing wall.

from the floor structure, furnishings, and occupants, must be considered. Many of the historic Nebraska houses have dormers and second-story space.

In structures using load-bearing bale walls, a method of attaching porches is needed unless the porch is attached to the overhanging rafters. At the Tree of Life Rejuvenation Center, long bolts were inserted through the bale wall to attach a wooden ledger on the exterior of the wall just below roof level. Large metal plates, serving like washers, were used on the inside of the wall to keep the bolts from pulling through the bale wall. The wooden ledger was also attached to the roof rafter with hangers.

ROOF INSULATION

Most modern bale buildings have used fiberglass roof insulation, but recent studies suggest that this type of insulation poses health risks. Concerns about its safety, along with reports that fiberglass insulation may actually diminish in R-value as the temperature drops, have led many bale builders to look for other roof-insulation products.

One of the easiest and most cost-effective ways of insulating the roof is to use straw. Whole bales have been used when the ceiling and roof structure possess sufficient strength. Otherwise, loose straw or flakes can be used. An interesting straw-insulating technique was used by Matts Myhrman and Judy Knox in their Tucson straw bale building. With the installation of each ceiling section of sheet rock, loose straw was stuffed into plastic garbage bags, which were pushed into the space above the sheetrock and between the rafters. Then the bags were quickly withdrawn, leaving the straw, which was tamped into place with a hoe. When it came time for the last section of sheetrock, wires were stretched between rafters to hold the flakes of straw in place before the sheetrock was installed.

There have been many suggestions about ways to flame proof loose straw for attic or roof insulation. One is to spray the straw with a borax solution. Instead of directly treating the straw, burlap bags can also be dipped in borax, allowed to dry, and then stuffed with straw. There are other commercially available flame retardant materials, but it would be best to carefully evaluate the toxicity of these materials before using them in your home.

Clay-coated rye straw was used in eighteenth-century Swiss-German houses between floor joists and in ceilings for insulation. Straw-clay construction, which uses walls made of clay-coated straw, uses the same mix for roof insulation.

In addition to straw, other environmentally friendly insulation products have been developed. One of these is Woolex, which is made from pure cellulose without the addition of colored inks or plastics. It is available in loose fill or spray from the Central Fiber Corporation in Wellsville, Kansas (see appendix). Another option is cotton insulation made from 100 percent recycled cotton by Greenwood Cotton Insulation Products in Roswell, Georgia, which is available in batts and rolls, or can be blown in.

The Noland straw bale house in Lone Pine, California, used a product called Air Krete, a cementitous foam material derived mainly from minerals in sea water. It has good R-value, no known toxicity, good acoustical qualities, is resistant to fire, and as a foam it seals all cavities well. It can be used throughout the building as well as in the roof.

Insulation made from recycled paper is now widely available, as well.

CHAPTER 9

FLOORS

BALE BUILDINGS CAN USE almost any floor system. Often the most convenient floor, at least in the United States, is a concrete slab-on-grade, which can be colored, textured, carpeted, or tiled. It can be cold in the winter, however, if no perimeter insulation is used, and uncomfortable due to its hardness. Soil or adobe floors are inexpensive, and can be made sufficiently durable for residential use, at least in areas with light traffic. Tile or brick on sand is another cost-effective option. All of these have good thermal mass properties; that is, they store heat or cool and help stabilize the indoor temperature. An interesting possibility might be the use of some type of lightweight concrete that would be sufficiently hard to withstand traffic and yet soft enough to be more comfortable to stand on. Wood makes a beautiful floor, but in an age when lumber reduction in buildings is critical, it may be an unreasonable choice.

Athena's adobe floor in Santa Fe, New Mexico.

A good strategy might be to use different floors throughout the house, to meet specific needs. Harder materials capable of withstanding heavy traffic could be used in the more public areas, while softer and less expensive materials could be used in the more private, intimate spaces.

The thermal efficiency of most houses in cold climates can be improved with insulation under the floor to augment the perimeter foundation. Rigid foam insulation is most commonly used for that purpose; bales have also been used in France and by ArchiBio (see pages 142 and 179).

CONCRETE FLOORS

If the concrete truck is coming to pour a foundation or grade beam, it may make sense to pour a concrete floor as well. They are quick, durable, and moderately priced. They can be finished in many ways and when used with area rugs can provide a very serviceable floor. Colored pigments can be mixed into the concrete in the truck, providing integral color that extends all the

Above left: Forms for concrete pavers, Steve and Nena MacDonald's house, Gila, New Mexico. Above right: Soil-cement pavers, poured by Cadmon Whitty, Corrales, New Mexico.

way through the concrete. During a pour, pigments can be dusted onto the surface and floated, often giving a slightly mottled color. Or, the concrete can be stained after completion with a variety of treatments. Some of the more interesting options are acid-based stains which give a somewhat irregular finish, as do ferric nitrate and ferrous sulfate, which lend beautiful shades of brown and orange. Stained floors should be sealed and waxed. Oil-based pigments can also be mixed with turpentine or penetrating oil sealers to color concrete floors.

Concrete floors can be stamped or scored to look like tile, brick, or flagstone, using one of several stamping systems that are available. An interesting and inexpensive way of creating a concrete floor is to make forms for homemade pavers out of 2-by-4s, or 1-by-4s and 1-by-2s, and pour them a few at a time. They definitely go slower than pouring a slab, but they can be done by one person with a wheelbarrow and a few forms. The joints can then be grouted, filled with exposed aggregate or small mortared stone, or simply loose gravel. This makes an excellent floor in a greenhouse because of its ability to simultaneously drain and provide a hard surface.

A stonelike appearance can be achieved with concrete pavers by pulling the forms soon after pouring and tamping. A plastic bag is then draped over the paver, and the edges are rounded and shaped by hand. Troweling after they have dried a little gives a smooth finish. Finishing with an acidbased stain or ferric nitrate increases the stonelike effect. Concrete also makes an excellent base for tile, other types of pavers, carpet, and even mud adobe.

Soil cement can also suffice for this application. When done correctly, soil cement can make a very hard surface. According to retired engineer Franklin "Doc" Vaughan, a longtime proponent of soil cement, the trick is using the right soil with the right percentage of cement. Very high clay soils and dark-colored top soils will not work. Moderate clay soils require 12 to 13 percent cement, while sandy, more gravely soils need less; 10 percent will usually work.

Polished stones, shells, and other objects can be embedded in the concrete for an interesting effect. Care should be taken that such objects do not stick up and create a hazard for someone to trip on. Another beautiful effect is to use leaves to make an imprint in the concrete when it is ready to finish-trowel, creating very low-relief images in the surface of the concrete. This was done nicely in some exterior concrete at the Tree of Life Nursery in southern California.

STRAW BALE AND CONCRETE SLAB

The ArchiBio group has this to say about constructing concrete floors without steel reinforcement:

> One of the great qualities of straw is its insulating capacity. Also, straw is like a miniature bamboo and has reinforcing capacities that cannot be easily disregarded. Loose or chopped straw is commonly used as reinforcement with a number of building materials that range from mud to concrete.
>
> ArchiBio operates in a cold climate, in eastern Canada, where winters are long and demanding. A concrete slab floor has developed a very bad reputation because of its capacity to act as a heat and humidity sink. A slab can be cold and uncomfortable for a long, long time.
>
> Since bales can be used in walls to create a high level of insulation, we thought, why not do the same with a floor? We also decided to try to develop a straw floor that required no steel reinforcing, thus eliminating the Faraday effect created by the gridwork of the steel reinforcement, making the house a little more environmentally friendly for its

inhabitants. In the mid–1980s when the team at ArchiBio began doing research and testing, Michel Bergeron, one of our members, first began using chopped straw as a replacement for iron rods in slab on grade work, and then as reinforcement in straw bale concrete slabs.

When pouring a slab, the forms have to be a good 20 inches high, since the bales are roughly 14 inches when laid sideways. You need to allow for 2 to 3 inches of poured concrete over and under the bales.

Be prepared for funny looks when you tell the drivers of the concrete trucks that you want to add chopped straw for reinforcing to the concrete mix in the truck. Since the truck is already on site, you will want to take advantage of its capability to easily mix the straw thoroughly with the concrete. We add one bale for every three cubic yards of concrete. You will need the help of additional friends or workers for this part of the operation, because the trucks are high and bales are heavy. A good way to chop the straw quickly is to make two chain saw runs along the strings of the bales and then cut the strings. The added straw will eat up a lot of water, so you will have to have the driver add water as the mix thickens. Add just enough water to be able to pour; remember that too much water weakens the concrete.

When the mix is ready, pour the straw-reinforced concrete. This first pour should be 2 to 3 inches deep. Immediately after pouring and rake leveling the concrete, proceed to cover the entire surface with straw bales, leaving about 2 to 3 inches free around each bale, maybe 4 inches for the course near the forms.

The next part of the floor is the touchiest part of the entire operation. Straw is mixed once again with the concrete in the truck, but this time 25 percent more concrete will be needed than for the first pour. Both pours can be done on the same day.

The straw concrete is poured around the bales, creating a honeycomblike web. The concrete should be poured carefully on top of the bales, *with overflow to the sides. Otherwise, the bales will want to move and slip sideways. You can also use small sheets of plywood on top of the bales on which to pour the concrete. Take your time and pour the concrete slowly. This part is critical and needs to be done well, since this is where the slab gets its strength and ability to provide even insulation. The pour is stopped when the concrete is just about level with the top of the bales. An inch or two below is ideal.*

The next day, or when the first pour has firmly set, the cover coat is poured. No straw is added to the mix this time, because the straw will

A: Form for concrete and straw bale slab—first pour.
B: Placement of bales.
C: Second concrete pour around bales.
D: Finished slab.

A

B

C

D

make it very difficult to float the slab, as strands stick out, especially if the surface is finished mechanically. A high-density, 4,000 psi mix works best for a well-floated and finished slab. Regular concrete without bales should be used wherever a chimney is to be raised or anywhere a strong structural base is required.

This slab will take a good 20 to 30 percent more concrete than a regular 6-inch pour, but the result is a strong, super-insulated slab that will work for you twelve months a year. It is a cheap investment for what it gives in return.

Our experience has shown that these straw bale slabs are fantastic. They work well, are efficient and strong, and since the straw is fully coated by the concrete, they will not rot. When all parts of the house are equally well insulated, the slab will never be a humidity sink or source of discomfort.

Author's note: For more information on the concrete and straw bale slab, contact ArchiBio (see appendix).

EARTHEN FLOORS

Earthen floors are one of the oldest floors in history, and have been used all over the world. In the southwestern United States, poured earthen, or "adobe," floors were the standard, used prior to the introduction of wood flooring, brick, and concrete. They can be beautiful, soft, and warm, and when carefully done and finished with a good surface treatment, provide a comfortable, practical, and all-natural floor. Because the soil on-site can usually be used and the skill level required is minimal, earthen floors can be very inexpensive—almost free.

In the Southwest, there has been a recent renaissance of earthen floors. They have been used in very expensive homes as well as in simpler structures where materials, skills, and funds were limited. Plants of the Southwest, a nursery in Santa Fe, used an earthen floor in their main retail building.

Specific formulas for earthen floors vary according to available materials, cultural traditions, and individual preferences. Most adobe floors are more fragile than other masonry-type floors; they may crack and need occasional care and repair. Depending on the mixture and the construction process, however, the floor can be strong and durable, requiring no maintenance or special attention.

There are numerous ways to construct earth floors. If attempting to install one with no previous experience, there may be some experimentation involved. A number of individuals who are quite skilled at this craft are available for consulting, including Anita Rodriguez of Taos, New Mexico, and Robert LaPorte of Fairfield, Iowa. Anita's approach was born out of the Enjarradora tradition in Hispanic New Mexico, where women were entrusted with the work of making and caring for adobe floors. Robert LaPorte's approach has its roots in the earth construction traditions of Europe (see appendix).

Outlined here are the basic steps of earthen floor construction, summarized from a diversity of traditions and builders.

Earthen floors of good quality can be constructed in just about any climate. The main prerequisite is a site that drains well and is free from moisture problems. The characteristics of soil, slope, exposure, and precipitation need to be analyzed. In dry climates, it has been the tradition to pour an earthen slab on top of an unprepared sub-grade 3 to 4 inches below the finished floor level. In wetter and/or colder climates, more extensive sub-grade preparation is needed, as was the custom in European countries. A 12- to 18-inch sub-grade is established. Chalk lines can be snapped around the walls to establish the height of the finished floor. All organic material needs to be removed, and it is a good idea to shape the center part of the floor 2 to 3 inches higher than the perimeter to ensure good drainage. A porous base is then used, usually 6 to 12 inches deep of 1- to 3-inch stone compacted by hand or with a mechanical tamper. In some applications where moisture is less of a problem, several inches of sand in place of the stone may be sufficient. Moisture barriers can make an inexpensive sub-floor preparation, although the breathability of the floor is sacrificed.

In the case of a stone base, some type of barrier is needed to prevent the subsequent levels of floor material from sifting down and filling the spaces between the stones, thus depriving the base of its moisture-resisting and insulating properties. One method, used by Robert Laporte, is the application of 2 to 3 inches of wheat straw covered by a clay slip (a thin mixture of clay and water), and then compacted to $^1/_2$ to $^3/_4$ inch. The ideal barrier has sufficient bulk and texture, is decay resistant, and accepts a clay slip.

A sub-floor is often used between the base and the actual floor. Three inches of a sandy-silty mix of dirt, compacted to 1 to 2 inches, is common. About 50 percent sand makes a good ratio. If radiant heating is to be installed, the plastic tubing is placed on top of the sub-floor or sub-grade. This sub-floor can also serve as a temporary floor during the construction process.

There are several ways to prepare the mud mix for the finished floor. Soils containing a maximum of 35 percent clay were traditionally used in the southwestern United States and Mexico. A ratio of 80 percent aggregate to 20 percent clay and silts is often considered ideal. European tradition calls for a mix of 5 parts sand to 1 part of a milky-consistency clay slip made from soil that is 50 percent clay. The old mason-jar test is a simple way to evaluate soil properties: One needs a glass jar filled

"I guarantee my adobe floors for life. They never crack; they hold up to excessive wear—from high heels, children, or even puddles of beer. You can do just about anything on them but chop wood."

—Anita Rodriguez

with $\frac{2}{3}$ soil and $\frac{1}{3}$ water. Add 2 teaspoons of salt, which will aid in the settling of clays. Shake the contents well and allow it to settle for four to eight hours. Sand will be at the bottom, silt next, and clay on top, allowing you to see the proportions of each.

The strength of the floor is in the aggregate, while the clay and silts are the binders. To give additional hardness to the floor, various substances are typically added. Traditionally, the southwestern and Mexican floors were often mixed with various combinations of manure and blood. In the Bob Munk house of Santa Fe (see the color section), builder Max Aragon used a mix of 1 part dried blood and manure and 2 parts soil for the adobe floors. Dried blood meal can be bought anywhere soil amendments or fertilizers can be found. Straw was sometimes added in traditional floors to help reduce shrinkage and minimize cracking. Soil cement can also be used for the floor by adding 10 percent cement to sandy and gravelly soil, and 12 to 13 percent to high-clay soils. Wheat paste was sometimes used at a rate of approximately one pound for every 10 square feet. Casein-based products like white glue have also been used successfully in earthen floors at a rate of about 1 quart for every 10 square feet. (For the sake of measurement, a large contractor's wheelbarrow converts to about 10 square feet at 4 inches of depth.) The gel produced from boiling prickly pear cactus or cholla may also work.

Adobe floor mixing at Canelo Project workshop.

Facing page: Adobe floor being poured at Bob Munk's house, Santa Fe, New Mexico.

The amount of water added to the earthen mixture varies from no water, installing the mixture dry and compacting it, to very wet, in which case it is poured, screeded off, and left to dry. At the Plants of the Southwest nursery, dry "crusher" or rock fines were used, then mechanically compacted and sealed with boiled linseed oil.

Other mixes have used a slightly damp mixture that is screeded and tamped down. The mix should be damp enough that when squeezed it binds and holds together, yet does not drip water, and it should be wet enough to be poured. Dirt used for the floor need not be sifted. The actual mixing of the mud is done in a wheelbarrow or in a mortar mixer and then poured and screeded to the appropriate level.

One of the more entertaining and enjoyable methods is mixing the mud in place. The room is filled with the dry mud floor mixture, water is added with a hose, and everybody—friends and children—helps mix the floor, using their bare feet and hands.

If the floor is to be screeded off, 2-by-4s on edge, or some other appropriate material should be set in place before beginning the pour. Opinions differ on how thick the floor should be. The most common depth is 3 to 4 inches.

Satisfactory floors can also be built with the aid of a level, working off chalk lines snapped on the walls. The floor can be poured a little at a time, leveled, and tamped.

If using screeds, they need to be removed when the pour is completed and the resulting voids filled with mud, and both the filled areas and any remaining footprints troweled on retreat.

The final step is tamping or compacting the floor, which can be done with the aid of a homemade tamping device made from a piece of plywood and an upright 2-by-4, or any device used for compacting concrete. Commercially made tampers are nice in that they have wire mesh on top and allow the excess water to rise up through it.

Note: Earthen floors are best poured during the driest times of the year. They cure by evaporation and can take anywhere from ten days to six weeks to dry depending on climatic conditions.

A gridwork of 2-by-4s can be laid throughout the floor before pouring, as is sometimes done with concrete floors. These can be filled one by one and leveled at the same time. Large earthen pavers can be poured with the use of removable forms and later grouted with a different colored mud mix for a patterned floor.

If using a drier mix, the slab may be thicker than a poured slab. Tamping can be done by hand or with the aid of a standard concrete tamper. When the floor is dry enough to support weight, the surface can be troweled with the aid of knee boards. A pair of 18-inch oiled plywood squares will suffice, moving them in tandem. Another possibility at this stage is to cut grout joints in the floor, which helps control the cracking and gives the appearance of a floor made with earth pavers. The Noland house of Lone Pine, California, (see the color section) used that strategy.

As most earthen floors cure, there will most likely be cracking. A wet mud slab can sometimes shrink up to $1/2$ inch, depending on the thickness, amount of clay, and amount of water used. These resulting cracks can be filled as they are or can be made slightly larger and filled with a different colored mud (pigments can be used), creating the appearance of a flagstone floor. The grouting dirt mix should be sifted through an $1/8$-inch hardware screen and mixed with water. The mix is then easily poured from coffee cans or passed through masonry grouting bags.

A different approach, in contrast to filling the cracks, is giving the entire floor a thin finish coat of sifted soil. A beautiful colored soil can be used for this final coat, adding to the beauty of the floor. European tradition used a mix of 3 parts sand to 1 part milky clay slip of 50 percent clay soil with 0.1 percent oil. This coat is usually applied about $1/2$ inch thick. If there is any cracking in this coat, an additional, even thinner coat can be applied. Many earthen floors are commonly poured in two to three layers.

The final step is applying a hardener to the finished dry floor. Without some type of hardener, the earth floor will wear excessively and will not resist moisture. Boiled linseed oil in combination with either paint thinner or turpentine has been the most commonly used. It has proven to be both cheap and reliable. Two coats are usually ap-

plied using a mix of 1 part paint thinner or turpentine to 1 part boiled linseed oil, and allowing the first coat to dry thoroughly before applying the second. A final third coat of 3 parts linseed oil to 1 part thinner or turpentine completes the process. A paint roller is the easiest way to apply the mix, using a brush for corners. Some people have used full-strength linseed oil for the first coat, followed with a one to one mix for the second and third coats. Chevron floor hardener has also been used as well as adobe and masonry sealants.

There are now a number of citrus-based thinners available that, although more expensive, should work well and are less toxic than paint thinner. A company called Bioshield makes an excellent product called Penetrating Oil Sealer (see appendix), that is a mix of boiled linseed oil, herbal oils, and lead-free drier. In bulk, it costs about twice as much as a conventional thinner-linseed mix, but its nontoxic qualities may make it well worth the extra price.

Earth floors, several thousand years old, plastered with what was probably a lime-based mix, have been found in very good condition in excavated sites in the Mideast. A lime plaster or a hard gypsum plaster such as Red Top Hardwall or Imperial may, when sealed, provide a sufficiently strong coating for a mud floor. Since those plasters are neutral-to-white in color, they could be tinted with any number of different colors before sealing. A thin coat of cement plaster might also work if used in combination with a masonry bonder. Max Aragon gave some of the Munk adobe floors a final coating of structolite plaster mixed with cornmeal for strength, color, and texture.

Finally, the floor can be waxed with a standard floor wax or beeswax for an extra measure of protection.

Wherever there is a crack, the floor is weakened, and with wear, small chunks of the floor may eventually work loose. If not repaired, the hole will grow in size, much like a "pothole." Repair, if needed, is simple. A little of the extra mud mixture used, (it is wise to put some aside during construction for later repair work), mixed with water, can then be worked into the hole with a trowel or finger. After the mud has dried, it can be resealed.

BRICK OR TILE ON SAND

Brick and tile have been a preferred floor material by many different cultures throughout history, and there are many good reasons for using them now. For the most part, they are easy to install, and they make durable, inexpensive, and attractive floors. They also provide good thermal mass for passive solar buildings. If earthen floors are used in low-traffic areas of a building, brick or tile can be used wherever more durable surfaces are required. The most eco-

Facing page
Top: Adobe floor with grouted joints at the Noland house, Lone Pine, California.
Bottom: Cracks in adobe floor grouted with different color adobe at Bob Munk's house.

Above left: Brick floor at Joan Chandler's house in Gila, New Mexico. Above right: Radiant floor tubing before concrete pour, Tree of Life Rejuvenation Center, Patagonia, Arizona.

nomical application is to lay them on a base of approximately 1 1/2 inches of sand rather than a concrete slab. Plastic grids are sold to make layout faster and easier. When set tightly, or carefully grouted in the case of tile, they will not shift or settle. Masonry wall cap blocks, wood blocks, and stone are also inexpensive choices for this type of floor.

An additional benefit of brick or tile on sand, when used in conjunction with radiant floor heating, is that the floor can be easily removed and re-installed if a problem develops with the piping. This is a considerable advantage over radiant heating under concrete floors, which usually require costly demolition and repair work to the slab to repair the heating system.

There are numerous references and source books about how to construct a brick or sand floor. *The Earthbuilders Encyclopedia* contains an easy to follow how-to section on the subject (see appendix).

STONE FLOORS

Flat stone, if available, can make an inexpensive and beautiful floor. It is usually easiest to work with when set in sand. The spaces between the stones can be grouted with a clay soil and sand mortar or with Portland cement mortar. Loose gravel or small, smooth river stones can also be used to fill the spaces between the stones if good drainage is required in spaces like a greenhouse.

FLOOR HEATING

Radiant floor heat systems operate by moving warm water or air through plastic tubing or metal pipe embedded in a concrete slab, the sand be-

neath a brick floor, or the poured mud of an earthen floor. They can be heated by solar energy, natural gas, propane, or electricity. A common concern of many people is whether the water system will develop leaks. Older systems, which used copper and steel pipes, have occasionally developed leaks, but the systems with flexible plastic tubing have a better record so far. As mentioned earlier, if installed with brick on sand or earth floors rather than a concrete slab, future repairs would be greatly simplified. Radiant floor heat provides a very comfortable, safe, and economical heating system for use with bale buildings.

The traditional and simple Korean ondol system can provide backup heat, while making secondary use of heat that comes from cooking and heating stoves. In this system, flues are run under the floor of the house from the cooking and heating units to chimneys on the opposite side of the house, thus providing radiant floor heat. The ondol can be further backed up with solar hot air from collectors or a greenhouse and with cool air in the summer from other passive sources.

A modern version of this old technique can be accomplished by using masonry blocks with hollow cores. Blocks can be laid on their sides in rows with their cores aligned so that hot air from some type of collector can be fed in one end and allowed to travel the length of the floor before returning to the collector through a cool-air duct at the other end. The warm air heats the blocks and the mass in the floor above. The floor can be concrete slab, brick, or earth. For more information on this type of floor, refer to *Fine Homebuilding's Guide to Foundations and Masonry.*

CHAPTER 10

INTERIOR ELEMENTS

INTERIOR WALLS

Interior walls can be constructed of almost any material, including straw bales. All the wonderful qualities of bales as exterior walls can be carried to the inside of the house as well. It is with interior walls that people have the most daily contact. The soft thick walls of plastered bales can create an instant sense of stillness and quiet within. Their superior sound-insulation qualities make them ideal for music or meditation rooms, teenagers' rooms, recording studios, and partitions between apartments.

Interior straw bale wall at Bob Munk's house (arch is wood-framed).

Katherine Wells incorporated an interior bale wall between the living room and the bedroom of her New Mexico house for sound insulation. Bob Munk's house in Santa Fe also uses straw bale interior walls. Bill and Athena Steen used bales to create an interior, 4-foot-high partition wall in their home in Canelo. The three-string bales were laid on edge and added a wonderful adobe-like feel to the room. Laying the bales on edge can help save on interior floor space.

Most people, even those in straw bale homes, resort to conventional frame walls with sheetrock for interior walls, often because of interior space limitations. Interior frame walls are constructed in bale buildings as they are in conventional buildings, the main difference being the method of attachment where the frame meets the bale wall. The approach used at the Tree of Life Healing Center used large metal bolts inserted through the bale wall from the outside to connect the frame. Four-inch steel plates were used on the outside surface of the wall to prevent the bolts from pulling through the bales.

In load-bearing buildings, the use of non-compressible interior walls requires some careful attention to detailing, or the interior walls may unintentionally become load-bearing and cause differential settling problems. The

192

Above: Connection of interior frame wall to straw bale wall with bolts and metal plate washers. Above right: Interior straw bale wall at Katherine Wells's house in northern New Mexico.

simplest way to deal with this, for framed interior walls, is to let the interior walls extend through the ceiling and be attached to the ceiling framing by means of nails or screws in slotted holes, which allow vertical movement. It is critical to recognize the possibility of vertical movement, and design to accommodate it.

Another option for interior walls is a product made in England called the Stramit Easiwall system, which is a nonstructural compressed straw building board ranging from 1 inch to 3.25 inches in thickness. The compressed straw panels are paper coated on each side, ready for finishing with thin plaster and paint. The Perryton Economic Development Corporation of Perryton, Texas, is entering into a joint venture with Stramit International to manufacture its product here in the United States.

Other straw-board products are being manufactured in the United States. Meadowwood Industries in Albany, Oregon, makes straw panels that are $1/16$ to 1 inch thick and use a natural resin to bind the straw. They come sealed with a varnish and can be used as they are without any further finishing.

With solar designs, it can be advantageous to build interior walls out of masonry materials as a way of including additional thermal mass in the structure. Adobe walls provide good mass. Obviously, in developed areas they are more expensive and take more time than frame and sheetrock, but in areas

Above top: Interior adobe brick wall used for shower enclosure and solar thermal mass, Canelo, Arizona.

Above: Soil-filled sandbag wall.

where clay soil is available and speed is not as important, they are a good choice for use with bale structures.

A simpler, mortar-free adobe wall can be built using sandbags, which are filled in place with moist dirt and plastered directly over the bag material. Reinforcing can be provided by running parallel strands of barbed wire between the courses. Basically, this method is just a fast way of making adobes in their place in the wall, using the bags as forms. When the moist fill-dirt dries, it leaves a very hard, bag-encased, adobe brick which can then be plastered as with regular adobes.

Straw that has been coated with a thin clay slip, as with cob construction (see page 118), can also be used to make interior walls, especially where straw and clay soil are available. One drawback, mentioned earlier, is that walls built using the cob method can take a long time to dry. Although the technique has not been tested, we are intrigued by the possibility of using sandbags filled with a similar straw-clay mix instead of soil.

Ken Haggard of the San Luis Solar Group of San Luis Obispo developed a unique method of building simple, high-mass interior walls. The wall uses a 2x4 wood frame filled with poured concrete and stained with ferrous sulfate. Prior to pouring the concrete, several pieces of rebar are positioned within the frame, and a simple form is set up to hold the wet concrete. The surface of the wall ends up very irregular with exposed aggregate showing, but it makes an unusual and attractive wall surface, nonetheless.

In a greenhouse attached to a bale retrofit building in Amarillo, Texas, Pliny Fisk developed an interior partition wall that also served as a heat sink opposite a south wall. A wire basket, or gabion, was filled with rock to create the wall. Both wire and rock were left exposed. Rock has excel-

Rock Gabion wall, "The Great Texas Retrofit," Amarillo, Texas

lent heat retention qualities, yet the process of building a stone wall takes a great deal of time. Using wire fencing shaped to the dimensions desired is an efficient use of this age-old technique. Cage ring clips, often available at feed stores, are a convenient way of connecting sections of wire fence.

A simple frame wall can be built out of small-diameter bamboo or split bamboo, and then plastered. Variations of this technique are used throughout the world. For that matter, almost any fiber, whether straw or century-plant leaves, can be used for this type of wall.

ELECTRICAL AND PLUMBING

Electrical and plumbing layouts will not be any different in a straw bale house than in a conventional building. When conduit or electrical wire such as Romex or UF must be run in the wall, it can be laid in the joints between the bales as the walls are stacked, or it can easily be tucked between the bales with a stick later.

If the wire needs to be routed to a location that does not coincide with a joint, a channel or groove can be cut across the surface of the bale for the wire. Any sharp and pointed tool will suffice, but chainsaws are most commonly used by inserting the tip of the blade partially into the bales. If a channel of even depth is desired, a hole could be drilled through a chainsaw bar at a distance from the end of the bar that is equal to the depth of the cut desired. A bolt can then be inserted and secured in the hole. Consequently, when a channel is cut in the wall, the bar of the chain will penetrate only to the depth of the bolt. Skil saws with double blades have also been used to cut uniform channels. Holes can be drilled through the bales with a wood auger.

Electrical boxes and recessed light fixtures can be solidly mounted by attaching them to wooden stakes driven into cavities cut in the bales. The edge of the box or fixture should sit about 1 to 1 1/2 inches out to finish level with the finish coat of plaster. Care should be taken to leave adequate clearance for anything combustible. A fire-retardant spray such as clay and borate can be sprayed on or applied behind junction boxes, lights, and other heat sources to reassure building inspectors.

In general, it is a wise idea to keep plumbing out of the bale walls, since water is the main danger to these walls; pipes occasionally break and water can condense on cold pipes. Plumbing can be run in interior partition walls, under the floor, or in furred-out walls in front of the bales. If a pipe must run through the walls, it is best to run it in a plastic sleeve in case of any future mishap. It is highly undesirable to have a water pipe break in a bale wall.

Any electric utility channels that have been cut into the bale walls must be filled with some type of stuffing to cover the electrical wire if cement stucco is to be used. Most codes specify that electrical cable cannot come into contact with cement. Fiberglass insulation has been satisfactorily used, and adobe plaster or a straw-clay mix could also work.

ELECTROMAGNETIC INFLUENCES

When installing the electrical system of a house there are several ways to minimize the electromagnetic fields (EMFs), which can adversely affect the human body by creating generalized stress and weakening the bodily functions. In addition to EMFs emitted by specific electronic appliances, potentially harmful fields are created by the basic wiring in a building. Twisted electric wires gener-

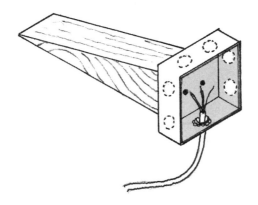

Top: Electrical box attached to wooden stake.
Middle: Electrical box in bale cavity.
Bottom: Fiberglass insulation stuffed in channels to protect wire from stucco.

ate half the field of that generated by more commonly used parallel wires. Wire in conduit produces half as much field as that produced by exposed wire. Electric wires also decrease in power in a logarithmic relationship with distance from the source. Depending on the location in the house and the amount of time that various spaces will be occupied, one or more of these techniques can be used to reduce the EMF influence.

The walls surrounding the bed is an area where wiring should be kept to a minimum or even avoided. Areas such as the kitchen, offices, and entertainment areas can be fed with twisted wire in conduit for maximum reduction. A master switch that prevents any current in the wires of a room as long as there is no user in need of electricity there can be incorporated in the overall electrical plan.

Books and videos on the subject of EMFs, as well as Gauss Meters (which detect and measure EMFs), are available through IBE, The International Institute for Bau-Biologie & Ecology, Inc., P.O. Box 387, Clearwater, Florida 34615.

ATTACHMENT POINTS

Because bales do not provide a good nailing surface, provisions must be made for hanging cabinets, shelves, and other assorted items, especially with load-bearing bale walls. Lightweight items that require small nails can often rely on the plaster on the interior walls.

An easy way to provide a nailing surface is to attach a number of sharpened wooden stakes to the back of a 2-by-4 and drive them into the bale until the 2-by-4 comes to rest flat against the bales. An alternative is to drive the wooden stakes first and screw the 2-by-4 or a 1-by-4 to the stakes. The protruding 2-by-4 can serve as a screed or level for the plaster on the wall, which means that the wood would remain exposed after the plaster has been applied. That makes attaching whatever is to be fastened to the wood surface a lot easier because the wood is visible.

If it is not predetermined where everything is to be hung, 1-by-4s can be used instead of 2-by-4s and randomly placed throughout the interior walls wherever it seems likely that something might be hung in the future. The 1-by-4s are narrow enough to be embedded beneath the plaster. They can be covered with building paper and wired along with the rest of the wall. Care should be taken to note the location of these boards for future reference, although they might reveal themselves; because the plaster is thinner over these

Two-by-four blocking for cabinet attachment, "Mom's Place."

boards, it may crack. When fastening something to them, care is also required to keep screws from breaking off chunks of plaster when they hit the wood.

David Eisenberg has suggested cutting off one side of a wooden I-beam, inserting the plywood part between a course of bales and pinning it in place with dowels.

Inevitably, the problem arises when the building is completed and there is a need to hang something where no nailer has been provided. A hole can be drilled through the plaster and a large diameter dowel driven into the bale as a nailer. If really heavy items are to be hung, bolts could be run all the way through the wall and out the other side as an attachment point.

CHAPTER II

FINISHING BALE WALLS

FOR ANYONE WHO ENJOYS BEAUTIFUL, colored wall surfaces, the finishing steps of plastering and coloring bale interior and exterior walls can be one of the most satisfying experiences of building a bale structure. Bales are a very flexible wall material that can be easily molded into a variety of shapes and forms. Of course they can be finished to appear virtually straight and can even be covered with sheetrock or wood siding, but they naturally lend themselves to a somewhat irregular flowing wall surface characteristic of old-world, thick-walled buildings.

Plastering party for straw bale walls.

In addition to aesthetics, one of the major factors that influences the choice of plaster and color is the question of whether the breathability of the wall is to be maintained. Walls can be finished so that they are sealed to varying degrees or so that they are allowed to breathe. A breathing wall allows outside air to be heated or cooled as it passes through the mass of the wall before mixing with the interior air. If the wall is finished with a vapor barrier, cement plaster, elastomeric coating, and a latex vinyl emulsion paint, it will be well sealed and will allow a lower level of air exchange. One danger with a completely sealed wall is that if for any reason moisture enters, it will have a very difficult time getting out, leaving the bales in the wall highly susceptible to molds, fungus, and decomposition.

In contrast, a wall plastered with lime, gypsum, or earth and colored with a lime wash or calcimine distemper paint will be very breathable, allowing natural evaporation of moisture and a high rate of air exchange. Walls with vapor barriers allow between 0.2 and 0.5 air exchanges per hour, whereas a breathable bale wall may provide between 1.5 and 3 exchanges per hour. The high level of air exchange provided by breathing wall systems creates a vital and healthy interior environment. The whole house becomes an air-to-air heat exchanger.

PLASTERING

A wide range of plasters exist that are suitable for use in conjunction with bale walls. Selecting a plaster will depend on the desired hardness, level of maintenance, texture, and feel. Most modern cement plasters seek to minimize maintenance but sacrifice many desirable qualities in the process. Soft plasters, like earth and gypsum, are pleasing to touch, easy to repair, easy to nail, and have good acoustics but are not as easy to clean as some harder plasters, which are cold and hard to the touch, hard to nail and repair, and have poor acoustic properties.

Plaster can be finished smooth, rough, or textured. The finish coat can be floated to bring out the sand so that the surface is slightly pebbled or troweled very smooth. Soft and natural plasters can be easily textured by hand to create a variety of beautiful patterns as is often done in India and Africa. Relief work is also commonly practiced with the same materials.

Plastering is one object of bale construction that may cost more and use more material than would be necessary for other types of buildings. The irregular surface and the small cavities between bales make them plaster consumptive. The extra care taken to keep walls straight and aligned during a bale wall-raising is greatly appreciated at the time of plastering, as trying to work out irregularities at that stage is more difficult than doing so as the walls go up. Depending on how plaster is applied and finished, there can be an increase of 20 to 70 percent in the amount of material used for straw bale structures than that used in conventional homes. Filling any cavities in the wall ahead of time with a mix of mud and straw also helps reduce the amount of plaster needed. On the positive side, the plaster adds significant structural strength to a load-bearing bale-wall building, especially when the plaster is sprayed on, forcing it into all the cavities. The additional plaster adds to the thermal mass on the interior, improving the thermal performance of the building.

Applying sheetrock on the interior or black board (celotex) on the exterior of bale in-fill walls can greatly reduce the amount of plaster needed, though it gives the building a more conventional appearance, lessening some of the natural unevenness of bale walls. Exterior and interior wood siding and paneling have also been used with bale buildings.

Bale houses have been plastered with and without stucco netting, or reinforcing wire. Stucco netting provides a mechanical connection for the plaster, which some plasters need in order to adhere well to the wall. Netting also helps reinforce cement-based plasters and, when firmly attached to both the roof plate and the foundation, greatly adds to the strength of the structure as

Asphalt-impregnated Celotex with cement plaster over a straw bale wall.

a whole. However, the brittle and rigid shell of stucco presents an element of incompatibility with straw. Straw is a flexible and soft material and is better suited to plaster and forms of reinforcement that have similar characteristics.

Working with stucco netting can be time consuming, and adds to the cost of the house. It is also debatable whether the increased strength of the netting is necessary for bale walls in many situations. In undeveloped parts of the world, stucco netting is often unavailable, and some people believe it causes disturbances in the electromagnetic field.

Some bale homes have been plastered without stucco netting. Cement plasters and mud or adobe plasters have been applied directly to the bales. Since the bale walls have a rough texture (rougher when the bales are laid flat), the plaster usually has no problem adhering. Time will tell how well these walls hold up, but in most cases they appear to be doing fine as are some of the historic houses built without netting.

Stucco netting comes in various strengths. Because of the increased amount of plaster required by bale walls, a number of plasterers prefer using a heavier, 17-gauge wire, which is designed for three-coat application. Twenty-gauge wire is designed for use with one-coat, fiber-reinforced stucco applications. The netting can be nailed to the roof plate and to a wooden nailer in the foundation if one has been installed. When bales are stacked on edge, the stucco netting can be tied directly to the baling wires or polypropylene strings on the surface of the wall. When bales are laid flat, as they most often are in load-bearing buildings, other techniques are necessary to attach the stucco netting to the surface of the bale wall.

In the early Nebraska houses, wooden stakes were often driven into the bale wall as attachment points for the stucco netting. Recent efforts have focused on finding a simpler method. Weaving wire back and forth through the bale walls to secure the stucco netting to the wall surface is frequently done, but is laborious and time consuming. One could also use baling twine, which is easier to work with than wire. If the bale needle has a small groove filed in its tip, the twine could be pushed through the bales without being threaded through the needle. A length of twine on the other side of the wall can be fed through the loops by a second person, and the loops pulled tight, much in the way a sewing machine would do.

John Parsons of Rimrock, Arizona developed a very efficient system for attaching stucco netting to his straw bale house. Using inexpensive, 17-gauge, galvanized electric fence wire, which come in $\frac{1}{4}$-mile-long rolls, John cut lengths of wire and folded them in half. The wires were long enough to allow the doubled end to be pushed through the bales with the tip of a needle

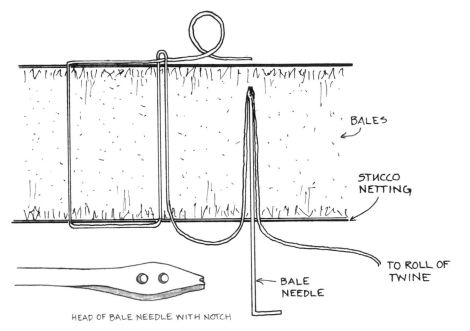

BALES

STUCCO NETTING

TO ROLL OF TWINE

BALE NEEDLE

HEAD OF BALE NEEDLE WITH NOTCH

Sewing stucco netting to bale wall.

and fastened to the stucco netting on one side of the wall, then, on the other side, to be separated, so that each wire could be pulled over to an adjacent wire, pulled taut, and twisted together.

One of the more successful methods was developed by Max Aragon while working on the Munk house. He made pins, slightly longer than the width of the bale, out of approximately 9-gauge wire with a hook on one end. He then drove the pin through the wall until the hook pinned the stucco netting to the bale on one side. A co-worker on the other side of the bale would bend the wire over the stucco netting on that side with a pair of pliers.

Some heavier-gauge wires bend more readily than others; use the most flexible available. U-hank wires, which are commonly packaged in bundles and used for hanging ceiling panels, are used by a plastering company in Tucson. It comes prefolded and can be unbent, one end attached to a bale needle, and pushed through the wall. The ends are then attached to the stucco netting on opposite sides of the wall and tightened.

Smaller, site-made, U-shaped wire pins can be useful for pinning the stucco netting at odd spots throughout the walls. The heavier the wire, the better, but also the more expensive. Find what works with the least amount of material. The wire can be bent against its natural curve so that the ends flare out, helping them stay more firmly anchored in the bales. Commercially avail-

Window opening prepared for plastering with metal lath, stucco netting, and roofing felt.

able U-shaped pins made from 11-gauge wire, called sod-staples, would also work. They are used to anchor erosion-control geo-textiles, and are available in 12-inch lengths. The trick in applying the stucco netting is to get it tight and yet leave it loose enough so that the plaster can get between the wire and the bale.

Stucco contractors have also used metal lath on the entire surface of the bale wall in place of stucco netting. Because of the irregular surface of the bale wall and all the cavities that need to be filled, relying on the metal lath as the primary surface for the stucco to attach to, rather than the surface of the bales, is considered to be more efficient and cost-effective. Consequently, the first coat is applied principally to the lath, which will leave many air pockets and cavities behind the plaster. Using this approach, even with the increase in cost for the lath, is probably cheaper. However, some people think that this approach is questionable since most of the strength of the plaster coat will be in the metal lath and not incorporated into the structure of the wall.

If stucco netting is undesirable yet some type of reinforcing is wanted, a natural fabric netting like jute or coco, used for erosion control, would be an alternative. Coco netting has a tighter weave than jute. Both are usually available from outlets that deal in erosion-control materials. One supplier for jute netting is Arizona Bag Company in Phoenix. Other non-metallic nettings recommended for use with synthetic stuccos should work well as substitutes.

Black felt paper beneath the stucco netting has occasionally been used to cover bale walls before plastering. It can save on the amount of plaster, but the rigid paper does not conform well with the surface of a bale wall, and as a result many air pockets and cavities can remain throughout the wall. Most plasterers do not recommend this approach. If paper is used, many more wire ties will be needed to attach the stucco netting to help keep the paper flat against the bales.

The draft code for straw bale buildings in New Mexico doesn't allow the use of a moisture barrier under the stucco, in order to allow for the natural transpiration of water from the bale walls. In the draft code for Tucson and Pima County, Arizona, a moisture barrier may only be used on the lower third of the exterior wall, to protect it from splash, driven rain, or snow. It is thought by many that the use of any type of building paper, vapor barrier, or other non-breathing material is not a good practice for bale walls.

Applying plaster by hand is one of the more time-consuming parts of bale construction. For that reason, sprayed-on stucco has become a popular option. It turns the most laborious part of the bale-building process into one of the fastest, next to stacking the bale walls.

Traditionally, three coats of plaster are applied: the scratch, the brown, and the finish coat. One option that can save a great deal of time and labor is to spray the first, or scratch coat, then apply the last two coats by hand. The scratch coat is by far the most difficult because it is the one that has to work out irregularities and give shape to the wall, and spraying the first coat provides the additional advantage of forcing the stucco into all the cavities in the wall. Steve Kramer of Tucson, a plasterer by trade, has sprayed at least a dozen bale buildings in the southern Arizona area. In his experience, bale buildings sprayed with a cement-based stucco exhibit less cracking than conventional buildings. As of early 1994, he was charging $1 per square foot to spray three coats of cement stucco on a bale building, $2 per square foot including application of stucco netting.

Tony Perry, president of the Straw Bale Construction Association and Straw Bale Construction Management in Santa Fe, has become a distributor for a very efficient machine, called Quick Spray, for spraying stucco. Quick Spray is simpler to operate, less prone to complications, and less expensive than most conventional machines, and it is easily transported in the back of a pickup or station wagon.

A contractor in California has suggested spraying the bale walls with gunite, a dry cement mix that is wetted at the spray nozzle as it is applied. Because it is drier than regular sprayed-on stucco, it is very strong and can be applied in one coat. Gunite machines are being used by builder David Easton, with a mix of soil, sand, and cement to build rammed-earth walls. The same mix could be used on straw bale walls.

Stucco being sprayed on straw bale walls.

Stucco get-togethers and plaster parties have been held for a number of different buildings and wall raisings; it takes much less time for ten people to plaster a wall than for two to do it. Such parties are a great way to get the building plastered quickly, and many people enjoy plastering for a while. The finished product may not be as perfect as it would be if professional plasterers were used, but it will usually be adequate. Some plasters are more difficult to work with than others, cement being one of them. It can be helpful to use a plaster that is a little forgiving, mud probably being the easiest. In many parts of the world, including among the Hispanic communities and Indian Pueblos of the southwestern United States, women, and often children, traditionally did the plastering of adobe houses. Their tools usually consisted of their bare hands and a stone or sheepskin to polish the finish coat. For the modern plasterer, swimming-pool trowels with rounded corners are easier to use than the more common square-cornered ones. Smaller trowels are easier to handle, and the rounded edges slide around irregular surfaces and curves without leaving scratch marks or catching on the stucco nettings. Putty knives and scrapers are useful for detailing.

A very important point to remember is that a load-bearing bale-wall must be allowed to complete its settling process, unless it was precompressed, before the plastering is done. In-fill bale buildings and mortared bale-wall buildings can be plastered immediately after the walls have gone up.

TYPES OF PLASTER

CEMENT STUCCO

Cement is one of the hardest plasters. It bonds well with straw, has a long life, and is very weather resistant. Cement can be irritating to the skin, however, so wear gloves unless you possess the plastering skills to keep the mix off your hands.

Every plasterer seems to favor a slightly different formula for cement stucco. Rather than indulge in a debate over which one might be better, the mix used by Tucson plasterer Steve Kramer, which has worked satisfactorily on over a dozen bale buildings, is included here. Mixes will tend to vary according to climate and location. Consultation with local plasterers can be helpful in determining the best mix and curing times for each area. The mix should not be too rich in cement; otherwise, the wall will be susceptible to shrinkage cracks.

SCRATCH COAT:

    2 bags of cement

    1 bag of lime

    37 rounded shovels of screened clean sand

BROWN COAT:

    1 bag cement

    1 bag lime

    45 rounded shovels of screened, clean sand

FINISH COAT:

    1 bag cement

    1 bag lime

    40 rounded shovels of screened, clean sand

    Fine or silica sand for a smooth finish

The brown coat is applied after the scratch coat has set, which could be immediately or within a few days. Otherwise an acrylic bonder might be needed for adhesion. With the deep cavities in a straw bale wall, additional drying time may be required. The finish coat is generally applied about four days to a week after the brown coat.

The plastered wall should be misted or covered with damp cloth for the first few days to obtain greater strength and reduce shrinkage, especially in hot, dry weather. It is less critical to mist interior walls if doors and windows are kept shut because humidity and temperature are much more stable inside, but all freshly plastered surfaces should be misted at least the first day or two if it becomes apparent that they are drying out. Be careful not to oversoak the walls. Cement stucco generally cures in thirty days.

Another option with cement stucco is to use a fiber-reinforced cement-based stucco mix. It is designed for one-coat applications $1/2$-inch thick, but has been used by several straw bale builders in thicker applications with a finish coat. Fibers can be purchased separately and added to the mix, thereby avoiding the cost of a prepackaged product. Chopped, short lengths of straw could work just as well—they now are being used by ArchiBio in Canada to reinforce concrete slabs.

Cement stucco mixes once utilized a lower percentage of cement than those currently being used. These earlier mixes sometimes used ratios in the vicinity of 1 cement and 1 lime to 7 or 8 sand. This resulted in a softer stucco, which was known as a soft mix.

The cement for stucco or plaster can also be made from locally available waste materials in many cases. Pozzolanas, materials containing reactive silica and alumina, which will react with lime to form cementlike products, can replace up to 25 percent of the Portland cement without adversely affecting strength. Rice hull ash makes one of the better pozzolanas; some coal fly ash and other ashes can also make good pozzolanic cement. The Intermediate Technology Development Group offers a forty-eight-page booklet called *Rice Husk Ash Cement: Progress in Development and Application*. Pozzolanas purportedly can also be added to lime and water to make a product that is strong like cement, yet remains flexible. Refer to the *Earth Construction Manual*, from the United Nations Center for Human Settlement, 1984.

LIME PLASTERS

Until the relatively recent introduction of cement plaster, a plaster of lime and sand was the traditional plaster mix used throughout the world. Although it is rarely used today in the United States, lime-based plaster remains popular in other parts of the world, especially Mexico. It makes a somewhat durable plaster that is porous and evaporates moisture. Lime also inhibits the growth of mold and mildew and repels many insects. It is very workable, making troweling much easier than with cement stucco. It can be beautifully finished with soft matte washed-on colors. These qualities make it very worthy of consideration as a plaster for bale walls.

Lime is notoriously slow to set (requiring extra floating), and takes longer to cure. One reason that cement and gypsum plasters have become more popular is because they set much more quickly.

Commercially manufactured lime requires more energy to manufacture than cement, but it can also be locally produced within small communities using the most basic technology. Any environmental problems connected to the manufacture of lime are usually associated with large-scale exploitation. Impact is minimal when it is produced on a small scale close to where it is to be used. Caliche soils have frequently been used as a source of lime in New Mexico. Limestone is roasted, which produces calcium oxide, or quicklime. In the Southwest and Mexico, limestone was often roasted in the adobe bread ovens, or *hornos*. It is screened and then slaked or hydrated by mixing it with water to produce calcium hydroxide. The slaked or hydrated lime is then mixed with sand and water for plastering.

The base coat often includes some type of natural fiber, animal hair, or plant material as a binder before a finer finish coat is applied. Other additives used to improve its overall quality have included linseed oil for durability and adhesion; tallow for plasticity and adhesion; skim milk or whey to increase impermeability; and casein glue to increase strength and adhesion. Small amounts of cement are now commonly added to provide extra strength.

A program entitled Churches, Symbols of Community, conducted by the New Mexico Community Foundation in an effort to restore historic adobe churches and provide employment based on traditional earthen construction techniques, has worked extensively with lime plasters. They researched different plasters, analyzed samples, and collected oral traditions before finally developing their own specs. Ed Crocker, technical director of the program, graciously and generously provided the following information on lime-plaster formulas, which makes a significant contribution to this book, as this information is very difficult to obtain.

As is the case with most traditional formulas and methods, there is a great deal of variation, which often depends on local climates, soils, availability of materials, and composition of the wall surface being plastered. For example, lime adheres differently to varying soils, some responding more poorly than others.

Type-N lime is used in all applications and formulas that require the use of lime. It is often used for soil stabilization projects and has better adhesion qualities, especially with earth or adobe walls. It is higher in calcium than the commonly available type-S lime, which has more magnesium.

FORMULAS FOR LIME PLASTER

LIME WATER (2 TO 3 PERCENT LIME)

This is used to dampen the wall surface prior to plastering, to improve adhesion. It is also used as a liquid to mix with earth mortars and plasters.

⅓ shovel of type-N lime
Mix with a 55 gallon drum of water

LIME PUTTY

This is combined with sand and water to make a lime plaster. It is made by mixing 5 bags of type-N lime in a 55-gallon drum of water. It is then allowed to soak as long as possible. The longer it sits, the more plastic it becomes. It has no limit to its shelf life and can sit indefinitely. It is not uncommon for one- to two-year old batches of this putty to be used. Even though this type of lime is already hydrated, better results are attained by rehydrating it.

BASIC LIME PLASTER

FIRST COAT

5 parts sand

1 part lime putty

The walls are wetted with lime water before the lime plaster is applied. When the lime on the wall mixes with the lime in the plaster, it recarbonates, thereby improving the bond. Lime water can be applied by dashing with a brush or with a small recirculating pump that has an attached garden hose.

SECOND COAT

3 parts sand

1 part lime putty

The second coat can be applied almost immediately, even before the first coat has dried.

THIRD COAT

1 ½ parts sand

1 part lime putty

It is preferable to apply lime plaster on adobe walls without the aid of any reinforcing wire. The same could hold true for straw bale walls. If the bale walls are very uneven, they can be given a leveling coat of earth plaster to reduce the amount of lime plaster needed. Any cavities which have been filled prior to applying the plaster can also have small rocks inserted in them that project ½ to ¾ inch to act as a lath.

LIME PLASTER WITH NOPAL (PRICKLY PEAR CACTUS) MUCILAGE.

The mucilage of the prickly pear cactus is often added to lime plaster in Mexico and provides several benefits. It helps the lime set, increases adhesion, improves workability, and makes the plaster more water repellent. Ficus Indica, commonly called the Burbank variety, is preferred because it is relatively spineless, easy to propagate, and produces prolific new growth. It is hardy through USDA zone 8. It is extensively grown in towns throughout California, the southwestern United States, and Mexico. The cooked leaf pads also make a wonderful food. If prickly pear is not available, the stems of the cholla cactus can be used as an equivalent substitute. Other mucilaginous products might work equally as well. Agricultural grade psyllium seed or kelp derivatives are other possibilities. (See appendix).

—Mix 1 part lime putty and 3 parts sand. Dump it on the ground and let it dry for at least a month; the longer the better.

—Two weeks prior to plastering, fill a large container with chopped up prickly pear leaves or cholla stems. Fill with water and let stand for one to two weeks. A thick mucilage will be formed. It can also be boiled for immediate use but must then be used right away, as it spoils once it has been cooked.

—Dilute the mucilage with approximately 4 parts water to 1 part mucilage.

—Add the diluted mucilage to the dried putty and sand; mix until a workable plaster is attained.

—The plaster is traditionally slapped or thrown on the wall thickly with a pointed mason's trowel.

—A board or darby is then dragged across the wall for leveling, leaving a somewhat rough surface.

—An additional two to three coats of plaster can be applied with a trowel for a smooth finish.

—After the initial set, the finish coat can be polished with a 6-inch diameter smooth river stone to give a compacted and polished finish.

On a restoration project at San Xavier Mission in Tucson, a final sealant of blended neutral soap and alum was applied to the lime/prickly pear plaster. This combination produces aluminum stearate, a water repellent that allows the evaporation of moisture.

LIME PLASTER WITH NOPAL GEL—FORMULA NO. 2

This formula is another one from southern Mexico, but begins with quicklime rather than a hydrated lime.

—Fill a barrel or container with chopped nopal or prickly pear, and cover with water. Let set for one week.

—Mix 1 part of the nopal liquid with 2 parts quicklime or calcium oxide.

—Wait 24 hours and screen any lumps. Dilute with water and mix with 3 to 4 shovels of sand to make plaster.

Additional undiluted mucilage can be added to the plaster to make it smoother and more workable.

LIME PLASTER WITH PORTLAND CEMENT FROM NORTHERN MEXICO

This mix is frequently used throughout Sonora, Mexico, and may be common in other parts of Mexico as well. The Portland cement adds an element of additional strength to the lime.

4 parts lime

1 part cement

17 shovels of sand

Adobe on Katherine Wells's studio.

EARTH PLASTER

Earth and straw, as well as grass fibers, have been combined as building materials for as long as anyone can remember. They are combined in the making of adobe or earth bricks and plasters. The natural affinity between the two materials makes this an excellent material for plastering bale walls. Besides being highly breathable, earth plaster can be both durable and beautiful. It can be highly finished as well as easily textured or used in relief.

The use of mud plaster is enjoying a renaissance throughout the world as its favorable qualities are once again being appreciated. Its main disadvantage is that it is not very moisture resistant, although it allows for the rapid evaporation of moisture. With earth or adobe structures, it has been a common practice in many parts of the world to annually repair the exterior mud plaster or to replaster the entire building. This event often coincided with feast days or other significant events, and was looked on as a yearly ritual.

In most situations mud is very suitable for an interior plaster. For exterior use, it is best suited to drier climates, although with a certain amount of protection it can be workable in a variety of conditions. The use of wider eaves and overhangs will help an exterior earth plaster wear better, as would the inclusion of porches all the way around the exterior of the building, and a greenhouse or sun room on the south. The Dey straw bale residence in Fairfield, Iowa, uses deep eaves to protect the exterior earth plaster. A single porch could also be used on the side of the house that receives the worst weather throughout the year. Simpler, less expensive thatched or vine covered trellises, or *ramadas* as they are called in the Southwest, could also be employed.

Despite the restrictions for exterior use, earth plaster has numerous advantages. It is probably the easiest plaster for anyone of any age group to apply. It requires only the most basic tools and can even be applied by hand. In India, beautiful textured earth walls are created by the women, who finish the walls by patterning with their hands. It is inexpensive, requires no energy to manufacture, is environmentally friendly (it *is* the environment), and is very easy to repair. Unfortunately, these are not the common standards of measurement for the construction industry.

Earth plaster begins with soil which has less than 30 percent clay. As with earth floors, a combination of 80 percent aggregate to 20 percent clay and silt is preferred. The glass jar method can help determine percentages (see page 183). This simple method, combined with some test wall samples, will help determine whether to add more sand or clay. If the mix cracks excessively, more sand is needed.

There is no basic mix which can be universally used. Earth plasters probably vary more than any other mix. Each locality usually develops a formula which draws upon its available resources and meets its climatic requirements. Consequently, only basic guidelines can be given. The best approach is to experiment with different mixes on test walls. Soils almost always need to be manipulated by adding more sand or clay. If it is too sticky, the mix has too much clay; if it won't bind, it has too much sand. The dirt can be sifted with $^1/_4$-inch screen.

Fibers such as straw, grass, animal hair, and plant fibers are usually added as reinforcement to the interior base coat as well as the exterior. Of all these fibers, straw is the most frequently used. Short lengths of 1 to 1 $^1/_2$ inches are used at a rate of 1 large handful for every 10 shovels of dirt. Straw is regarded as a critical ingredient in earth or adobe plasters in the Southwest and Mexico, where it is said that adobe without straw is like a person without a soul.

Ed Crocker of the New Mexico Community Foundation has commented that an essential element of applying earth plaster is to apply it by dragging it across the wall surface in a horizontal movement, which forces the straw into horizontal alignment. This is important because when rain hits the horizontally positioned straw, the water will split and sheet down the wall rather than running in rivulets and eroding the wall, as would happen if the straw was aligned vertically.

Ed has also said that adding lime to earth plaster is a successful practice that improves the quality and workability of earth plaster. In the foundation's historic-preservation work, lime is incorporated by using lime water (2 to 3 percent) in place of regular water to mix the plaster. (Refer to the Lime Plaster Section for the lime-water formula.) The New Mexico Community Foundation has bulletins on earth construction (see appendix).

Natural stabilizers are often added. Nopal, cholla, and agave mucilage is sometimes used with earth plasters, as with lime plaster. Saps of different plants are used throughout the world. Six to seven percent rye flour can be boiled in water and added to increase surface hardness. Animal manures are also used as stabilizing and binding agents. Ash can be added to improve the workability. It has also been reported that a solution of Borax, added at 5 to 10 percent of the total mix, along with casein, greatly improves the ability of an earth plaster to resist moisture. Skim milk could conceivably be added to the mix in the place of water to provide the caesin.

A thin finish coat called an *alis* is often applied to earth-plastered walls. An alis is essentially a slip coat in which finely sifted clay is mixed to a paintlike consistency and applied with a brush or roller. A variety of colored clay soils can be used. All have different characteristics which require either familiarity or experimentation. Whitish soils often contain lime, are very workable, and adhere well. Red soils are typically heavy in clay and will require the addition of sand. Alis that uses tierra amarilla, or yellow dirt, was normally applied with a woolen mitt and worked to bring mica to the surface. Blue Raven Construction of Santa Fe mixes powdered colored clay with fine silica sand and a little sheetrock compound for body. Different colored clays could be combined in the same wall to create variegated color surfaces. Mica can also be added to the mix.

The alis is polished with a river or cobble stone while it is still damp. Polishing helps reduce cracking and gives the wall a distinct surface. Wooden trowels are also used.

Though not the most pleasant material to work with, asphalt (emulsified asphalt, driveway sealer) is sometimes used to stabilize mud plaster. One gallon of asphalt is premixed with water and then added to 30 shovelfuls of clay soil. Asphalt helps make a very durable exterior plaster. Cement can also be used as a stabilizer, 10 percent for sandy soil, 12 to 13 percent for moderate clay soil.

European traditional earthen plasters are often made from a clay slip mixed with fiber and sand. The base coat can be 1 part slip to 2 parts sand to $1/2$ part fiber. The fiber can be eliminated in the final coat, finer sand used, and 1 percent oil added.

The Dey residence mentioned earlier used a mix of 1 part clay soil, 2 parts silica sand, 1 percent linseed oil, 8 percent borax (for fire and fungus prevention), and 5 percent $1/2$-inch straw. The finish coat was the same, minus the straw fiber.

Steve MacDonald used two coats of earth plaster over his straw bale walls and then applied a finish coat of sheetrock compound.

A thin earthen finish coat can be used over two coats of gypsum and sand plaster on interior walls. The interior of Carol Anthony's straw bale cloister (see the color section) was done that way, as was Bob Munk's house, which also had mica flakes (a natural glitter) added to the finish coat.

INTERIOR GYPSUM PLASTER

Gypsum is a major ingredient in many interior plaster finishes. It is not suitable for exterior use because it is highly moisture-absorbent, but it has a number of advantages for interior use. It is easy to work with and soft to the touch, sets quickly, and is porous and breathes. It is an excellent choice for those who do not want to use cement or lime plaster but who want something harder than earth.

Gypsum is hydrated sulfate of calcium, occurring naturally in sedimentary rocks. It is commercially available in a number of products manufactured by US&G, the United States Gypsum Company. Gypsum plasters are available for numerous applications in both finish and base coats.

One of the most versatile all-around gypsum plaster products is called Red Top, which comes in regular and fibered mixes. Sand can be added for

Adobe plaster with straw.

either hand or machine application. Perlite can be added for a lightweight insulating mix that must be hand applied. It is very easy to work with, especially for beginning plasterers. Gypsum is recommended as a basecoat, but it can be used for all three coats: scratch, brown, and finish. Blue Raven Construction of Santa Fe used it for all three coats on some walls in the Hughes-Rhodes straw bale house (see the color section) and then sealed it without the addition of color with a product called Okon. Linseed oil could have been used, but it slightly yellows the wall. When choosing a sealant, it would be better to choose one that breathes. Red Top also bonds well with mud,

Finish coat of adobe plaster (alis with mica), niche in Hughes-Rhodes house.

making it possible to use mud fill in wall crevices and low spots under the application of the basecoat, or earth-based plaster for a finish coat.

Structolite is a lightweight basecoat to which perlite has already been added. It weighs half as much as other sanded gypsum basecoats; some users have commented that it is like plastering with whipped cream.

Fibered gypsum is also popular as a basecoat and is said to counteract cracking. US&G reports that it does not add strength as is sometimes believed. It was originally designed as a plaster that would adhere to the old-style wood lath.

Tom Luecke of Boulder, Colorado has been experimenting with agricultural grade gypsum mixed with sand as an interior plaster for bale walls. He has also been adding it at a rate of 35 percent with interior earth plasters.

Joint compound, an extremely soft interior plaster, is easy for beginners to use. It is available premixed and is very forgiving. Silica sand can be added to it for texture, or it can be sanded when dried for a smooth finish. Other, harder plasters such as Red Top, adobe, or cement, can be used as a base coat and thinly coated with joint compound for the final coat.

A variety of gypsum finish plasters are available, and any of the basecoat plasters can also be used as a finish coat. Gypsum plasters can be mixed with lime putty for a harder finish. Structo Gauge, when mixed with lime, produces a high-strength, crack-resistant durable white finish that sets quicker than lime when used by itself. It is good for use in high traffic areas and has good abrasion resistance.

US&G has an excellent technical bulletin available that lists all of their plaster products and their applications (see appendix).

BASIC PLASTERING TECHNIQUES

Plastering of exterior walls is best done under moderate conditions. Temperature extremes should be avoided, as well as rain and wind. Wind can burn the plaster and make it set too quickly. Plastering interior walls, on the other hand, can be undertaken almost any time of the year, as the interior climate of a building is relatively easy to control.

The preparation work for a bale structure is much the same as for any other type of building. However, as mentioned previously, it is essential that with load-bearing bale-wall structures all settling be complete before plastering commences.

PREPARATION

Any wood that will be plastered should be covered with black felt paper to keep the moisture from swelling the wood and cracking the plaster and, wherever black paper is used, some kind of reinforcing netting is needed over it so the plaster has something to adhere to.

Strips of expanded metal lath around doors, windows, and joints increases the strength and ease of plastering. With in-fill buildings, it is usually a good idea to connect the top course of bales in the wall to the beam that supports the roof.

The floor should be covered with drop cloths or some other material; cheap, plastic drop cloths are commonly available. The covering chosen should be taped to the floor to prevent plaster from working its way underneath. Tape and cover doors, windows, frames, and lintels to save cleanup.

Finally, fill any obvious low spots in the wall with plaster and let it set before plastering over it.

TOOLS FOR PLASTERING

— Good clean trowels. Old trowels with dried plaster are virtually impossible to work with. Swimming-pool trowels can be a good choice for beginning plasterers due to the absence of square corners. A square trowel is necessary, however, for corners and wherever else 90-degree angles occur. A corner trowel, bent in the middle, makes wall corners much easier to finish.

— A 3- to 4-inch putty knife or sheetrock knife can be a useful tool for detailing hard-to-reach areas, or anywhere the larger trowels do not fit comfortably.

— A plaster hawk holds the plaster while you apply it. These can be purchased or easily made by attaching a 10-inch-square piece of plywood to a handle.

— Hands can be more effective in applying earth plaster than trowels, which are only needed for creating a smooth finish coat.

— A darby, essentially a long skinny trowel, is used to level larger sections of wall area. These can be purchased, or made from a 36-inch length of 1-by-4 redwood with handles on one side.

— A clean brush and a bucket for water.

— A plaster rake (scratch tool).

— A powered mortar mixer or homemade mortar box for mixing the plaster can be made out of plywood. A convenient size is around 6 feet in length, 3 feet in width, and 1 foot in depth. A wheelbarrow will suffice, but holds limited amounts of plaster.

— A wheelbarrow to move plaster from the mixing location to where it is being applied.

— A mudboard where the plaster can be transferred from the wheelbarrow and placed on the hawks of the plasterers. A 2.5-foot-square piece of plywood on a moveable stand is a convenient size.

— A scaffold if the height of the walls requires it.

Ideally, one person is needed to screen sand and to mix the plaster, one person to move the plaster and transfer it to the mudboard, and one or more people to apply the plaster. Mix a small test batch to begin with to see how the plaster behaves. Dry mix the materials first, gradually adding water. Stiffer mixes tend to hold to the wall surface better. If the mix is too stiff, however, it will be too hard to work with.

APPLYING THE SCRATCH AND BROWN COATS

A good place to begin plastering is the middle of the wall, working in segments across the surface of the wall. Some plasterers prefer starting at the top and moving down. Apply the plaster with an upward sweep, left to right for right-handed people and the reverse for left-handed people. When using earth plaster, it is often easiest to apply it by hand and then trowel it smooth. That approach avoids trapping air between the bales and the plaster as happens when plaster is cut directly from the hawk. The scratch coat can be applied as thickly as

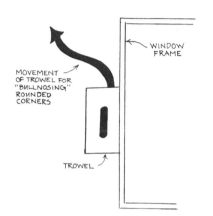

Above: Motion of trowel when rounding or bullnosing a curved wall surface at windows and doors.
Right: Cutting plaster from a hawk.

necessary to even-out the wall surface, if desired. The brown coat should give the wall its final shape and form in preparation for the finish coat.

Moving the plaster off the hawk onto the wall with the trowel takes a little practice. This is sometimes referred to as "cutting from the hawk." It is done by cutting the trowel into the plaster on the hawk and scooping it onto the wall in a sweeping arc. The movement requires a twist of the wrist while tilting the hawk up toward the wall. For some people the hawk is too bulky and heavy; they prefer using their free hand to hold the plaster.

Creating rounded corners at door and window frames is called "bullnosing." Plaster is first applied in a regular manner onto the wall around the frames. Once the plaster is applied, it is rounded, or bullnosed, by pulling an empty trowel up and horizontally across the curved surface. The same motion applies when a darby is used instead of a trowel. Clean water can be sprinkled on the wall with a brush to improve workability. A 3- to 4-inch putty knife can be useful in tight areas.

The darby is used to even out larger sections of plaster on the wall. It is not used to apply plaster, only to smooth it out. As when using the trowel, water can be sprinkled on the wall if needed. After the walls have been darbied, touch-up work should be done around all windows, doors, outlet boxes, etc.

The surface of the scratch coat can be raked with a small plaster rake, also known as a scratch tool, made especially for that purpose, to improve adhesion of the brown coat. The brown coat can be applied anytime after the scratch coat has set, or hardened. After the initial set, the plaster should be kept moist for several days to help it cure. Keeping the doors and windows closed helps the curing process for interior plaster.

A thorough cleanup should be done immediately after each coat—dried plaster can be extremely difficult to clean up.

APPLYING THE FINISH COAT

The final coat of plaster is a thin application that gives the wall its appearance. Finely screened sand and silica sand are often used because they offer more control and make a smoother finish possible. The final coat can be given any texture finish that might be desired.

A textured sand finish is accomplished by using a wet sponge float. The sponge float is moved in a circular pattern across the wall while sprinkling water at the same time. This technique exposes the sand in the plaster.

A smooth finish is a little more difficult to accomplish and takes some practice. It is achieved with repeated passes of the trowel and sprinkling of water. Some plasterers drag their wet brush across the wall and follow it with the trowel to achieve this effect.

COLORING THE WALLS

While the plastering is being done, it is a good idea to plaster several additional bales, which can be used for experimenting with color before applying it to the newly finished walls. Make samples of both interior and exterior plasters if they are different.

The most common way to decorate and protect a plastered wall is with latex or vinyl emulsion paint, modern, water-based paints that are commercially produced from polyvinyl acetate or acrylic polymers. Most are polymer based, and seal the surface of the wall with a plastic film, which as it ages may blister and peel. These paints come in a great variety of colors but are very flat in texture and lacking in character.

There are many alternatives to these water-based plastic paints, many more than most people realize, all with different textures, degrees of luminosity, breathability, and application techniques. There are a number of traditional classic formulas that can be used on plastered bale walls and offer a refreshing variation. The thickness and uneven surface of a plastered bale wall affords the opportunity to create a beautiful hand-crafted surface by drawing upon these traditional methods.

In contrast to latex paints, many traditional formulas penetrate and are absorbed into the surface of the wall. Many allow the wall to breathe rather than sealing it. In general, they are made from environmentally friendly ingredients and do not rely on the petroleum industry for their manufacture. Most originated from people living in the country, who developed formulas based on available local materials such as lime, chalk, clay, milk, eggs, and oil.

This section contains a sampling of some of those formulas, which can be reproduced today without a great deal of difficulty and with the satisfaction of producing a homemade, functional, and unique colored wall. As with many environmentally friendly ingredients, though, these traditional formulas are not created with the same ease as when one goes to the local paint or hardware store and purchases a gallon of paint.

SEALANTS AND INTEGRAL COLOR

The finish coats of some plasters are so beautiful that they may require no additional color. A penetrating oil sealer will not only protect the wall, but will also give it a slightly aged appearance. The textured surface of earth plaster, which often contains fibers of straw or grass, is usually sufficiently beautiful by itself. However, a single or any combination of different colored clays can be applied to give more intensity to the finish coat. Such an application can be done with a thin coat of plaster or a clay wash the consistency of a paint.

Oxides or pigments can be added to almost any type of plaster to give color to the finish coat. These can be evenly mixed to create a uniform color or mixed irregularly to give more variation in color tone and texture. The final exterior coat of cement-based plaster is commonly referred to as the color coat. Sheetrock compound is sometimes tinted prior to application with pigments or latex paint to produce a particular effect.

The use of integral color saves labor and time with some very interesting results, but it is very difficult to match when repairing cracks and damaged wall sections, especially with cement plaster.

LIMEWASH

Historically, most buildings in Europe, the Americas, and other parts of the world were limewashed on a regular basis. Limewash does not have the hard elastic quality of latex paint and must be applied more frequently, but it has numerous advantages. It has a soft, matte quality that has a pleasant feel and, when prepared properly, is adequately hard and durable. It is porous and will allow any moisture trapped inside the wall to evaporate. It will not blister and peel, but rather will mature and mellow with age. It also acts as a disinfectant.

Limewash is very stable when used as an interior plaster, but will probably need annual or bi-annual application when used as an exterior plaster, depending upon local climate conditions. It can be applied to any lime-, earth-, or gypsum-plastered wall. It cannot be applied over modern emulsion or oil paints, but it must be applied directly to the plastered surface. Normally it is white, but it can be colored with the addition of pigment. Not all pigments combine well with lime; lime-proof pigments are needed. As lime is alkaline, it destroys any acid-based pigment. Lime-resistant pigments include yellow ocher, sienna, umber, cerulean blue, cobalt blue, ultramarine, red oxide, and oxide of chromium. When acquiring different pigments, inquire as to whether they are lime-resistant. Natural earth pigments are fine, as they are inert. Limewash can also be mixed with milk to make casein or milk paint. It is caustic when wet and must be handled carefully.

BASIC LIMEWASH FORMULA

A short bristled brush will work well with limewash, as it tends to have a runnier consistency than normal paint.

— Mix four handfuls of slaked or hydrated lime with one half gallon of water. This combination will bubble and steam; be careful not to inhale the vapors.
— Stir to dissolve any lumps once the reaction has stopped. Add enough water until the desired consistency is reached.
— Strain to remove any further lumps.
— Mix any pigments separately in a small amount of water and add to the wash. Remember to use only lime-compatible pigments (see above list). The color will always dry lighter than the wet mix.

LIMEWASH FORMULA No. 2

This formula is reported to be a durable exterior limewash finish. Lime-resistant pigments can be added for color.

— Add 12 gallons of hot water to a bag of slaked lime.
— Add 1 pound of zinc sulfate.
— Add 2 tablespoons of salt that have been dissolved in 2 gallons of hot or boiling water.
— Mix the above with 2 gallons of skim milk.

LIMEWASH ADDITIVES

Around the world, various substances are added to limewash to improve its durability, especially as an exterior finish. Some of these include linseed oil, acrylic bonder, and salt. The gel from the prickly pear cactus is used in Mexico, and it seems feasible that the mucilaginous gel from other plants would work. Agricultural-grade psyllium seed, xanthan gum, and other plant materials are worth considering.

Chuck Bruner added one cup of concrete bonder to each gallon of the lime wash he applied to the straw bale house he built in 1949 in Douglas, Wyoming. The lime wash may last as much as five years longer with the bonder added, according to Chuck.

LIME CASEIN PAINT

Sour skim milk is used to make casein-based paint, with many regional variations and formulas. Basically, the curd is separated from the soured milk and then washed, dried, and powdered. It develops binding power when an alkali material (most often slaked lime) is added to hydrolyze it, creating casein glue. Lime casein powder can also be commercially bought or dried, and powdered curds can be mixed with slaked lime putty. Skim milk might suffice just as well.

Lime casein makes a flat and stable paint with a rough texture that is more durable than basic limewash.

LIME CASEIN FORMULA

— Mix equal parts of water and lime casein powder until the powder has been completely integrated.
— Add water until the desired consistency is reached.
— Add lime-resistant pigments for any desired color.

AMMONIUM CASEIN PAINT

A milk-based paint that gives a very transparent finish, ammonium casein uses ammonium carbonate instead of lime. White pigment is usually added to make it more opaque.

AMMONIUM CASEIN FORMULA

— Mix 1 part casein powder with 4 parts water until all lumps are dissolved.
— Add 1 part ammonium carbonate and allow to stand for 30 minutes.
— Add additional water if necessary to reach the desired consistency.
— Add pigment.

CALCIMINE DISTEMPER PAINTS

Calcimine distemper is made from a mix of whiting, water, and glue size. It produces a very smooth and highly finished surface. Like limewash, it is permeable and allows for the evaporation of moisture from the wall. When pigments are added, the resulting color is flat and soft but very much alive.

It should be applied over a freshly plastered surface or one that has been treated with a similar finish. Regular calcimine distemper can be used for interior walls, while it is necessary to use oil-bound distemper—available only as a manufactured paint—on exterior walls. Oil-bound can also be used on interior walls.

Calcimine distemper is traditionally applied in one coat, so the paint edge should be kept wet and not allowed to dry. It is most often applied in straight lines.

WALL PREPARATION

The surface of a newly plastered wall should be prepared with glue size to reduce the porosity before calcimine distemper paint is applied. Most glue sizes are animal products such as rabbit skin, which is the most commonly available, and calfskin. Isinglass, which is made from fish, does not require heating like the others do, but it is not as durable.

GLUE-SIZE MIX

— Mix 1 part size to 20 parts water.
— Heat until the granules melt and a sticky liquid forms. Do not boil, as it will become brittle.
— Apply while warm.

CALCIMINE DISTEMPER FORMULA
— Mix 7.75 pounds of whiting with 3 gallons of water. Stir well, remove any lumps, and allow to sit so that the whiting settles to the bottom.
— Combine 4 ounces of concentrated calfskin granules with 2.5 cups of hot water, and let sit for three hours or longer.
— Thoroughly mix ingredients and heat in a double boiler until it becomes a liquid.
— Remove any surplus water from the whiting.
— Add 1 teaspoon of ultramarine pigment to the whiting to counteract the color of the glue size and to whiten the mix.
— Strain and add the heated size to the whiting. Mix well.
— Before the mix cools, add pigment to achieve desired colors. If an even finish is desired, pigments should be first diluted with water before adding.
— Allow to cool; a thick gel will result. Use soon after mixing, as the calcimine distemper mix will not last long.

SIMPLE OIL PAINT

Oil paint can be made from almost any vegetable oil that dries; linseed oil is the most common. Olive oil does not dry.
— Mix pigment with boiled linseed oil or other oil. Mix it thick enough so that it becomes like a heavy dough.
—Add enough oil to make the mix more liquid, until it flows.
— Add turpentine until the mix becomes like a chocolate sauce.
— Strain through cheesecloth, muslin, or nylon.

COLORED WASHES

Colored washes applied directly to the plaster or onto a neutral-colored basecoat or primer can add a soft, varied texture and sense of depth to any wall. By building up layers of different colored washes of both light and dark shades, a glowing, translucent finish can be created. Applied directly onto freshly plastered white walls, a color washed wall can appear much like the old frescos of Europe.

Washes can be made by diluting any water-based paint, like an acrylic, gouache, or emulsion (latex) paint, with water. Oil paints can be diluted with mineral spirits. A simple latex color wash uses 1 part latex paint to 5–9 parts water. These washes should be applied loosely, leaving plenty of the basecoat or wash beneath uncovered. Each coat needs to be dried thoroughly before adding more to avoid displacing the previous color.

There are various techniques used to apply the wash, each creating its own unique texture. Dragging a clean brush down through freshly applied wash will create a striped effect; a crumpled rag rolled across the surface will produce a soft, variegated finish; while a wall dabbed loosely with a sponge takes on a marbled texture. The easiest and fastest method is to use a large brush to paint the wash on with crisscrossing motions, producing a warm, weathered look. The approach used in applying color will depend upon the effect desired for the room.

Two excellent books on color washes, paint mixtures, and other painting techniques are *The New Paint Magic* by Jocasta Innes, and *Classic Paints and Faux Finishes* by Annie Sloan and Kate Gwynn.

NATURAL WALL PAINTS

The Eco Design Company of Santa Fe (see appendix) carries its own line of Bio Shield natural wall paints, casein paints, earth pigments, and other natural sealers and coatings. The wall paint is a water-based dispersion of natural resin, oils, beeswax, pigments, and fillers that is produced with a minimum of environmental damage. It is intended as an interior wall finish and is suitable for use over a variety of finishes.

The Euro-American Trading Corporation carries a line called Nature's Paints by van Wyse, as well as a variety of other products that are natural and environmentally safe. The company's interior wall paint is both durable and breathable.

FERRIC NITRATE AND FERROUS SULFATE

Ferric nitrate and ferrous sulfate, two iron-based products available through chemical or garden supply houses, can be diluted with water and used to color finished interior or exterior plaster. They can be mixed at a rate of around 50 to 80 pounds of water. It is an inexpensive way to color the surface of a wall and gives a very beautiful golden brown finish that is irregular and textured in appearance. The Noland House of Lone Pine, California (see the color section) was finished on the exterior with ferrous sulfate, and Lane McClelland's and Laurie Roberts's round straw bale house (see the color section) was finished with ferric nitrate. A mix of 1 part ferrous sulfate to 1 part water has been reported to work well.

Left: Brophy Chapel.
Facing page:
Top left: Carol Anthony;
right, Mary Diamond.
Bottom left: Laurie
Roberts and Lane
McClelland;
right, Kate Brown.

TRUTH WINDOWS

After bale buildings are completely plastered and finished, they often look no different than other buildings. Therefore, many bale buildings have continued a recent tradition of leaving a section of the bale wall exposed to verify that the building has been built from bales. Initially, these openings were made of some type of glazing or plexiglass with a frame around it. As time passed, they became more sophisticated and artistic in their expression. Some documentations of truth-window styles follow.

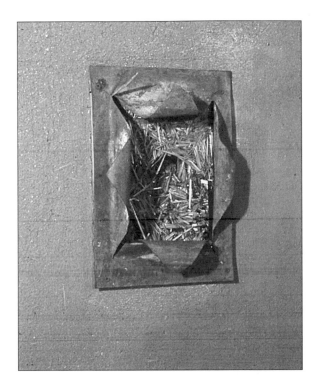

CHAPTER 12

OTHER USES FOR STRAW BALES

IN ADDITION TO HOUSES, straw bales have been used for a variety of other structures, including patio or privacy walls, agricultural buildings, emergency housing, and children's housing. Their flexibility, low cost, high insulation, and ease of construction make them ideal for such structures. The options for straw bales are endless, limited only by the imagination.

PATIO WALLS

Children playing on a straw bale patio wall in Elgin, Arizona.

Walls made from straw bales can protect homes, gardens, and patios. Bales can help define spaces that encourage social activities for much less labor and expense than many other materials. The width of the bales allows the easy creation of thick walls for children to play on, cozy seating areas, and excellent sound protection.

Landscape architect Bill Hayes and builder Cadmon Whitty, both of Albuquerque, New Mexico, have built a number of beautiful straw bale patio walls. They have worked together, as well as independently, on wall projects that range from small entryways to large patio enclosures. Their walls have achieved overnight popularity because they create much the same effect desired from an adobe wall, at a reduced price. In fact, straw bale walls, in combination with landscaping, made up the majority of Bill's business within one year of completing the first wall he designed. His early 1994 prices were running approximately $32 a linear foot for an average 4-foot high wall, and about $40 a linear foot for a wall up to 7 feet in height.

Cadmon played a principal role in developing the construction techniques presently being used in Albuquerque for straw bale patio walls. In the beginning, he was concerned about potential stability problems, the ability of an unprotected stucco wall to withstand moisture and weather, the expense of an extra-wide footing, and the disputable aesthetics of a thick wall.

With those concerns in mind, he began building his first bale wall in a very conservative fashion—almost laughably, he later realized. He used a massive footing, 18 inches wide and 18 inches deep, with 12 inches extending up above grade. The bales were stacked cautiously, only 3 feet high and in only two courses. All were pinned with 24-inch wooden stakes, two per bale. When the wall was done and plastered, it looked far better than he had envisioned, and he was impressed by its sturdiness.

Having discovered that it was possible to build a sturdy and attractive straw bale wall, he set out to build more straw bale walls accommodating the budgets and tastes of different clients. Deciding that the straw bale wall possessed sufficient strength, he proceeded to design a wall minimizing the width of the footing by turning the bales on edge, which also saved on the thicker stucco application on the top of the wall. To further save on concrete, he used a footing constructed of two railroad ties set above ground, capped with cement, and connected to cement block piers which were set into the ground. The piers anchored the ties to the ground and connected them to the next set of ties in sequence. Eventually, he decided that although this footing method was inexpensive, it proved to be labor-intensive.

Bales used as foundation forms with nailer for stucco wire.

Later Cadmon discovered the concept of grade beams, and had them engineered to match the weight of the straw and the soil drainage of northern New Mexico. This proved to be the most efficient, cost-effective way to provide a footing and protect the bales from moisture. To further facilitate the process, he used bales as forms to pour the concrete grade beam.

Growing progressively more confident, Cadmon was soon stacking bales up to 7 feet in height, modifying bale lengths to $1/2$, $1/4$, and $1/8$ sizes, cutting niches and arches, and stepping the elevations in the walls, or, as they say in New Mexico, "Santa Feing it." He also created thinner, 6- to 9-inch walls from bales modified to $1/2$ and $1/3$ widths. The wooden stakes gave way to 40-inch lengths of rebar, which provide much more stability than the 24-inch wooden stakes.

A good stucco finish is crucial for protecting bale walls. Cadmon uses 20-gauge stucco netting, which seems to be the best solution for the best price. He uses a rich mix of chopped straw mixed with stucco to shape the tops of the wall for better drainage. He also adds straw to the scratch coat of stucco.

Although Cadmon and Bill have experienced no major problems with their walls, some straw bale walls (as with frame and masonry walls), especially those with long runs, have shown a tendency to crack. The cracking appears to take place along the vertical joints where the bales come together. Ted

Above: Castillo patio wall, Albuquerque, New Mexico; designed by Bill Hayes, built by Cadmon Whitty.

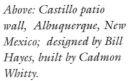

Top: Cap of stucco mixed with straw on top of bale wall.
Middle: Steps in bale wall.
Bottom: Bale wall built by Cadmon Whitty.

Above: Bale wall with bale over entrance, Albuquerque, New Mexico.
Right: Castillo wall, Albuquerque.

Varney has considered using expansion joints every 6 to 8 feet. Free-standing straw-bale walls would probably benefit from having stucco or gunite blown on, allowing it to penetrate deeply into any spaces in the joints and thereby giving it greater structural stability. Another strategy would be to incorporate more corners by breaking any long expanse of wall surface with enclosed seating, planting, or accent areas.

Straw bale patio walls appear capable of resisting moisture when it comes to rain and snow, but unlike historic bale houses which have stood the test of time, there are no similar examples of historic straw bale walls. The fundamental difference between a bale patio wall and a bale wall in a building is that there is no roof covering the top of the patio wall to protect it from moisture. The stucco which covers the bales in the wall is being asked to perform the same protective function as a roof. Initial observations would suggest that it is capable of doing so.

It is advisable to seal or waterproof the top of the wall, and critical that the bottom course of bales be well protected from moisture by sufficiently elevating them above grade and moisture-proofing the foundation. To protect the top of the wall from moisture, materials such as tile or stone, in addition to various sealants, could be used as a top course. The cap of mixed straw and stucco developed by Cadmon provides protection for the bales in the wall, especially when sealed. Good drainage should keep water away from the wall; drains can be set into the portion of the foundation that is above grade for water to pass through whenever necessary. Irrigated flower and growing beds should be kept away from the base of the walls.

OTHER STRUCTURES

STORAGE

Some of the oldest straw-insulated structures known are apple storage sheds in England. These lightweight, wood-frame structures that have lattice walls hung with bundles of straw make a well-ventilated, well-insulated shed that is excellent for storing produce. These were once common on estates throughout England, but only a few remain in use.

Straw bales have been used for many years to build super-insulated storage sheds for potatoes and other crops and may last for years without plaster. They could be used for many other applications on the farm if they were reinforced with pins and plastered. The Tree of Life Nursery in California is ex-

Tree of Life Nursery seed storage room.

tremely pleased with its plastered-bale seed storage room; owner Mike Evans reports a fluctuation of only 5 degrees in temperature throughout the year.

INSULATED TANKS AND QUICK WATER STORAGE

Plastered bales can be used to encase above-ground concrete or gunite water-storage tanks, or a plastic pool liner could be used to line stacked, plastered bales for water storage. Careful attention to waterproofing will be necessary to ensure longevity in the plastered tank.

WORKSPACES

Plastered bale construction is ideal for workshops or garages that will be used for manufacturing, woodworking, equipment storage, and maintenance. The high thermal mass and insulating properties make them pleasant to work in and reduce noise transmission to neighboring properties.

COMMERCIAL BUILDINGS

The high insulation value, noise suppression, economy, and durability of bales make them a good choice of material to be used in combination with tilt-up and light-frame construction for commercial space. The incorporation of bales into

Friederike Almstedt at work in her straw bale studio.

one- and two-story light commercial building is quite straightforward. Concrete can be used between bales for the two-story buildings with engineered wall-to-wall ties.

Larger commercial buildings can also incorporate bale construction. The most obvious candidates are metal and concrete frame construction with the bales used as in-fill, where the super-insulation, thermal mass, and fire-resistant properties of plastered bales will prove especially appropriate.

Retrofitting older brick and tilt-up commercial buildings with straw bales should also be considered. Bales could be added either inside or outside existing walls, to turn uncomfortable and energy-demanding buildings into pleasant and economical sanctuaries. For unreinforced masonry buildings which pose a severe safety risk in areas affected by earthquakes, a bale and bond-beam wall system could be used to insulate and reinforce the building.

EMERGENCY HOUSING

In areas where straw or hay is common and available, comfortable emergency housing could be thrown together in a matter of hours. Communities could recover more quickly from a natural disaster with warm, dry shelters constructed quickly of low-cost bales. Emergency response teams could conceivably be equipped to construct temporary bale structures.

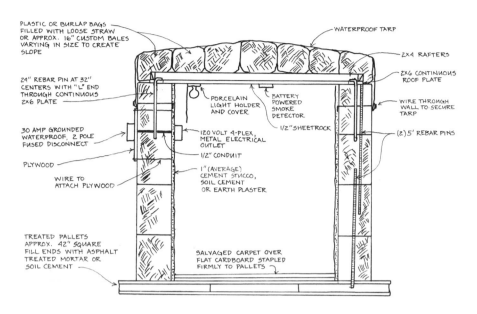

PLASTIC OR BURLAP BAGS FILLED WITH LOOSE STRAW OR APPROX. 16" CUSTOM BALES VARYING IN SIZE TO CREATE SLOPE

WATERPROOF TARP

2X4 RAFTERS

24" REBAR PIN AT 32" CENTERS WITH "L" END THROUGH CONTINUOUS 2X6 PLATE

2X6 CONTINUOUS ROOF PLATE

PORCELAIN LIGHT HOLDER AND COVER

BATTERY POWERED SMOKE DETECTOR

WIRE THROUGH WALL TO SECURE TARP

30 AMP GROUNDED WATERPROOF, 2 POLE FUSED DISCONNECT

120 VOLT 4-PLEX, METAL ELECTRICAL OUTLET

1/2" SHEETROCK

(2) 5' REBAR PINS

PLYWOOD

1/2" CONDUIT

WIRE TO ATTACH PLYWOOD

1" (AVERAGE) CEMENT STUCCO, SOIL CEMENT OR EARTH PLASTER

TREATED PALLETS APPROX. 42" SQUARE FILL ENDS WITH ASPHALT TREATED MORTAR OR SOIL CEMENT

SALVAGED CARPET OVER FLAT CARDBOARD STAPLED FIRMLY TO PALLETS

EMERGENCY SHELTER

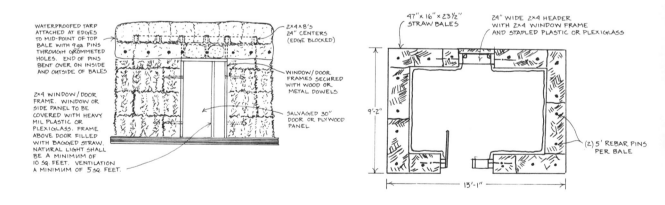

WATERPROOFED TARP ATTACHED AT EDGES TO MID-POINT OF TOP BALE WITH 9ga PINS THROUGH GROMMETED HOLES. END OF PINS BENT OVER ON INSIDE AND OUTSIDE OF BALES

2X4 WINDOW/DOOR FRAME. WINDOW OR SIDE PANEL TO BE COVERED WITH HEAVY MIL PLASTIC OR PLEXIGLASS. FRAME ABOVE DOOR FILLED WITH BAGGED STRAW. NATURAL LIGHT SHALL BE A MINIMUM OF 10 SQ. FEET. VENTILATION A MINIMUM OF 5 SQ. FEET.

2X4X8'S 24" CENTERS (EDGE BLOCKED)

WINDOW/DOOR FRAMES SECURED WITH WOOD OR METAL DOWELS

SALVAGED 30" DOOR OR PLYWOOD PANEL

47" X 16" X 23½" STRAW BALES

24" WIDE 2X4 HEADER WITH 2X4 WINDOW FRAME AND STAPLED PLASTIC OR PLEXIGLASS

9'-2"

(2) 5' REBAR PINS PER BALE

13'-1"

A cooperative project of the Development Center for Appropriate Technology and Out On Bale, with help from Tucson architect Bill Ford, has created a design for a temporary emergency shelter for victims of homelessness or disasters. The city of Tucson will issue permits to construct this straw-bale shelter, which can be inexpensively built, especially when using salvaged and donated materials. For further information, contact David Eisenberg of the Development Center for Appropriate Technology (see appendix).

Straw bales used for exterior seating in Bill and Athena's patio.

SEATING SPACES

A simple, unplastered bale can serve as instant, informal seating and can last for many years. It can be covered with a blanket or pad to make it more comfortable.

For more permanent seating, the bale or bales should be lifted off the ground and protected from moisture. Most exterior bale seats have simply been plastered with cement stucco; however, capping the top with flagstone or tile could give variation. Using the bale in conjunction with patio walls or exterior house walls gives the seat a backing, adding to its comfort. A slope can even be built into the backing, much like a couch, and cushions can be added. However, the height of the three-string bales is just about perfect as is, and the extra height of a thick cushion is often too much. Thicker padding can be added to two-string bales, which are usually lower. Built-in seats also serve as a thickening effect to the base of the wall, which adds to both its aesthetic appeal and its structural strength.

SOUND-CONTROL WALLS

Freeway noise is a severe problem in many transportation corridors. Conventional sound-control walls are expensive and cannot be built by unskilled labor. There is a backlog of over 220 sound-control projects in California alone.

Straw bales would make less-costly and potentially safer sound walls possible, and much of the labor could be provided by the community that will benefit from the wall.

AGRICULTURAL AND GARDEN USES

ANIMAL SHELTERS AND BARNS

There is little doubt that the first shelter built with bales was a barn, and plastered and unplastered bale buildings are still ideal for barns and other animal shelters. The ease and economy of building with bales made on the site can't be beat, with costs of baling running about 50–90¢ a bale. If bales are left unplastered, they must be protected with fencing, or they may be eaten by animals. Snow fence or chain link can be used to protect the walls.

Dexter Johnson, a retired agricultural engineer from North Dakota State University, has been researching and promoting temporary bale buildings for prairie farms. Test projects and on-farm experience have yielded excellent results, even with structures built with ungainly large, round bales.

Temporary bale-barn building systems from Blacke Lyon Associates in Norfolk, England, use large Hesston bales (4-by-4-by-6 feet), with a modular metal frame and plastic roof. These buildings can be made in almost any size and erected very quickly.

Bale buildings are particularly effective for pigs, which have comfort requirements similar to humans. A pig farmer in Alberta, Canada, who has used very large buildings up to 16,000 square feet, found he could build a temporary bale building for less than the annual interest on a conventional building. At the end of each season the bales are burned to sanitize the site. The size of the structure is adjusted year to year based on projected meat prices. The improved structure helped to increase pig weight gain and eliminate tail biting and fighting. The farmer's profits increased, and he was providing more humane quarters for his animals. A much more elegant and costly system for piggeries has been proposed in Denmark using a tension roof.

Another story about the effects on pigs living in bale shelters as opposed to those living in standard small, metal shelters, was related to Tony Perry by Arthur Staniforth, the Strawmaster of England—arguably the world's foremost authority on straw. The pigs in the straw bale piggeries seemed much happier and no longer ran away from people who entered their pens. They also ate less and yielded more meat.

Steve and Nena MacDonald's chicken coop.

Permanent farm buildings can be built using any of the methods described earlier in the book. Nebraska-style buildings are appropriate for some uses. Pliny Fisk developed a model farm for the Texas Department of Agriculture using truss-bale walls. The folded metal lightweight trusses and metal roofs are worth considering for other sites as well. The project included five plastered bale buildings, three with a sprayed concrete finish, and two hand troweled. These structures were featured in *Architecture* magazine in May of 1991.

For farm buildings that require many openings for access of equipment or storage, a frame structure with bale in-fill will be more appropriate. Pole barns, timber frames, and metal frames can all be used.

GREENHOUSES AND GROWING FRAMES

The walls of greenhouses and growing frames can be constructed easily from bales of straw, providing excellent insulation and a growing environment. For temporary structures the bales can be left unplastered and renewed each year. Permanent structures should be plastered and detailed to keep water out of the straw.

TEMPORARY GARDEN WALLS

Bales can be used to construct temporary walls to protect gardens from wind and predators prior to establishing a more permanent fencing system. When a wall has served its purpose, it can be turned into mulch or compost.

In areas where newly planted seedlings or other plants are subjected to strong spring winds, bales can be placed on their upwind side for instant protection. As with walls, the bales can be converted to mulch for the plants when they have outgrown the bale.

RAINWATER CATCHMENTS

Bales can be placed in a line on the contour of the ground to create an embankment for catching rainwater without excavating and mounding the dirt. As they decompose, they will help establish a permanent berm on the contour. They can also be used on downward slopes to make smaller catchments for individual trees or plants.

COMPOST PILES

Excellent compost piles can be constructed from bales. They can be constructed to any desired height, shape, and size. Eliot Coleman gives a good description in his book *Four Season Harvest*.

Right: Steve Kemble's straw bale workspace in Bisbee, Arizona.

Right: Tree of Life Nursery work building.

Left: Interior of Catherine Wanek's straw bale greenhouse, Kingston, New Mexico.

Below: Utility farm building, Ciudad Obregon, Sonora, Mexico.

Left : Cold frame at the Tree of Life Rejuvenation Center.

Above: Sue Mullen's straw bale cold frame.

CHAPTER 13

DESIGNING THE STRAW BALE HOUSE

Olivier Brill and Stephanie Duisberg's straw bale cottage in the Dragoon mountains, southeastern Arizona.

ARCHITECT BOB THEIS HAS DESCRIBED the critical issues of straw bale design at this historical moment:

The early history of straw bale construction was characterized by fairly conventional buildings, with bales incorporated in wall systems and traditional components used over, under, and around these walls. In such cases, the straw bales were used simply as large dimensional blocks. However, as soon as you have built with bales it is apparent that this is not just a "substitute" wall system. Bales are unlike any other material: they are massive, but not heavy like stone or earth; simple to work with, but the result has a very rich feeling; quick to erect, but very adaptable. Most unique to this kind of construction is its flexibility. Literally, the walls have a lot of give. They permit site adaptation and a relaxation of dimensional tolerances.

It is this flexibility that is the key to straw bale's potential. Bales offer informality and the opportunity to personalize our environments, which we lost when we traded our vernacular building traditions for industrial building. Elements which are difficult to build with our present wall systems become straightforward: buttresses; buildings that are only roughly rectangular; curved walls where we want them; benches growing out of walls; niches carved into walls; walls that are relaxed about being straight, relaxed about being flat. We have never had walls that could be simultaneously so substantial and yet so adaptable.

We have a lot of technical data to assemble and to generate, but the real work in helping straw bale building to evolve is to perceive the material anew without being dominated by the weight of images and concepts that belong to other materials. The deeper issue remains of

243

defining a straw bale language based on the material itself without viewing it as an imitation of something else, such as adobe or stone.

Deciding to build with straw bales is only one step in a larger sequence of choices. After you've made the decision to build with straw, you will need to ask other questions:

Will you build the structure yourself, like Chuck Bruner (see page 245), or hire professional contractors?

Will you plug conventional heating and cooling equipment into your straw bale building, or commit yourself to a higher level of energy consciousness, including the incorporation of passive solar features into your design?

Will you use the bales as a load-bearing wall or use straw as in-fill within a modified post-and-beam frame?

Will you build a square or rectangular structure, or experiment with other shapes?

The decision to build is an opportunity to be aware of the whole context you are living within, including the seasonal conditions of your climate, the materials that are local and traditional to your region, and the larger environment, including the other people who live around you.

Ultimately the question to ask is this: How can we build most appropriately, given our personal resources as well as the ecological resources of the planet? The sections of this chapter, some of which have been written by others who have been exploring the potential of straw as a building material, will show that when working with straw bales you have a greater range of design and structural options than you might realize initially.

Mary and Chuck Bruner outside their straw bale home.

THE PIONEER BALE-BUILDER'S APPROACH

—CHUCK BRUNER, September, 1992

In January of 1948, I moved with my wife and two sons into a rented shack. It was a mess but the only thing available. Rent was $30 a month. I was a World War Two veteran, so we started looking for a house to buy under the GI Bill. Everyone with money we talked to said, "Forget it," as they could loan the money to other folks for a higher interest rate than the GI Bill would allow. We started looking at lots so we could build, but the lots cost more than the money we had, and one had to own the ground to use GI loans to build with.

Time moved on, and in the spring of 1949 we found a string of lots that included a well in what was then east Douglas, Wyoming. The price was $500, half down and a note for one year on the balance. In the meantime, I was acquainted with a friend who had built a grocery store with straw bale walls the year before, in Glendo, thirty miles away. I was so impressed with his total cost, and the results, that we began thinking of using straw bales for our house.

We drew up the plans for a post and-beam-type construction, the best we could. It would have three bedrooms, one bath (a big mistake), kitchen, living room, and utility room. It would have a 3:12 pitch roof so we could have storage space in the attic. We would have to settle for cement floors throughout, as cement was much lower-priced than wood joists and flooring. No money for basement walls, either. The foundation would be 16 inches wide (to allow for two-string bales laid on edge rather than flat), 12 inches thick, with two rebars imbedded. The top surface of the foundation would have to be even with the top of the ground on the upper end of the grade (even though I know this was a mistake, it has not caused us any problems—perhaps because we only have about 14 inches annual rainfall).

I hand-loaded all the sand and gravel and hauled it to the location, unloading it the same way. Dad and I went together and bought a cement mixer, and I fixed up a washing machine engine to run it with. Portland cement was 97¢ a sack, as I recall. We mixed all the concrete and mortar on location. All the sand and gravel had to be hand-screened, of course. A friend who had a 14-inch stationary baler moved it out to a straw stack and we baled the straw. He fed the thing, and I set the blocks and hand-tied each bale. I think this cost us $30. What lumber we needed was green, sawed from the local sawmill thirty miles away. I hauled it in as we needed it. (This lumber caused me all kinds of trouble, as it twisted and warped very badly.)

The 6-by-6 posts were set on the foundation, if it can be called that, and braced. The straw bales were laid with fresh mortar on the bottom and on each end, just like bricks and cement blocks are. Window frames were made out of 2-by-12 native pine, placed as desired then plumbed and braced; door frames, the same. When the walls were up, I made a form all around the top and poured a concrete plate, with two rebars imbedded (this has never cracked). Then the roof beams were cut and put in place on top of the posts. As I was not a good carpenter (I'm still not), I had quite a time with the roof construction, but it has stood the test of time, so far.

Then the plastering began. By this time, we had electricity at the pole and a pump on the well. I would spray the straw, wait long enough so the plaster would stick, then start troweling the plaster right onto the damp straw. When it set up a bit, a broom was used to scratch it so it would be rough enough for the next coat of plaster to stick. Each additional coat brought the surface of the walls straighter, and I kept at it until they were nice and straight. (In 1955, we could afford to have a professional stucco man apply an oriental white spatter coat.) The inside walls were handled in the same manner, except I used more lime in the plaster.

We started digging the foundation in April and moved in about the end of September. I worked a nine-hour day, six days a week as an auto mechanic during this time. The house was worked on in the early morning hours and late into the night, and on Sundays. We had quite a bit of help from my father, and my brother at times, when the work required two or more people. I also had several friends who would give me a hand as the occasion demanded.

Our house was built on a pay-as-we-go basis. If we could pay for it, we bought it and built with it. We have never had a mortgage or interest to pay. There are a few spots that never have been finished, however.

The stucco and plaster have not caused us any trouble, nor the straw. The wood has been the problem, as we must have built right over a termite nest. After many years, I have finally finished off the termites. I have also replaced window sills with concrete. No major cracks have shown in the house. Frost line here is close to five feet deep, so apparently the whole house, foundation and all, must rise and fall when the frost comes and goes.

I know there were lots of mistakes made in design and construction of our house, but it has been a very forgiving structure. Our heating bills have been roughly half of our friends' bills for the same-size house. We have no air conditioning and have no need for it. The size is about 1,300 square feet. The house has been lived in for forty-three years, and we are still here. There is much more that could be said, or written, but I think this covers the subject pretty well.

EDITOR'S NOTE:
Mary Bruner, when asked what it's been like to live in their home, said, "Fabulous! Just fabulous!" When pressed to share the disadvantages, she thought long and hard before responding, "The kitchen window is too high, and there aren't enough electrical outlets."

In 1984 Chuck's and Mary's house sailed virtually unscathed through an earthquake centered thirty-three miles from Douglas that measured 5.5 on the Richter scale. Damage to the Douglas town hall, built in the early 1900s of brick and stone, was so severe that the building had to be razed.

Chuck and Mary attended the first national straw bale building conference in Arthur, Nebraska, in 1993.

BUILDING GUIDELINES

1. KEEP IT SMALL AND SIMPLE.

Small and simple structures require fewer materials, are easier to build, cost less, use less energy, and are in everyone's best interest. A house need not be large to be both beautiful and functional; space is often a wasted commodity. Smaller spaces can be more intimate, connecting people both to the building and to each other.

2. LIMIT THE DESIGN AND PLANS.

Modern building relies heavily on plans that include detailed drawings of every facet of the house, and provide guidelines for each phase of construction. We find that people produce the most creative results, however, when they are allowed to learn from what they are doing and make adjustments and improvements during the process.

3. USE BALES AS BALES.

Design and build to take advantage of the natural characteristics of bales rather than attempting to make them conform to designs and methods for which they are not well suited. Let an understanding of both the limitations and the advantages of bale-wall systems be the starting point for the design and building process.

4. USE LOCAL MATERIALS.

Before the advent of modern transportation, most structures relied on local building materials and designs that effectively met the demands of the climate. Regional styles could be developed again that are truly a product of local materials, climate, and culture, whether native or grown, and that meet the conditions of each particular context. Buildings that are created from the natural environment around them are often more beautiful, sustainable, and ecologically thoughtful than conventional buildings.

5. USE ENVIRONMENTALLY SAFE AND NATURAL MATERIALS.

Choose the most responsible product possible. Use both salvaged and recycled materials without sacrificing energy and water efficiency. Look for products that are safely manufactured and don't cause an increase in carbon or a depletion of ozone. Natural materials with a low embodied energy, such as wood, earth, and stone, are preferable to materials that require significant amounts of energy to be produced, such as cement and metal. Avoid the use of wood products that require the logging of old-growth forests or tropical hardwoods.

6. SELECT A GOOD SITE.

Avoid the tops of hills. Besides being highly susceptible to wind, erosion, and fire, buildings placed on the top of a hill are often disruptive to the natural landscape. Big deciduous trees to the east and west of the building are important to block early-morning and late-afternoon summer heat. Evergreens employed as windbreaks can be used on the north or northwest sides of the house to block severe winter winds. South-facing slopes offer good solar access as well as providing good air drainage and frost protection, and generally provide one of the most versatile building sites.

7. DESIGN AND BUILD WITH FAMILY, FRIENDS, AND COMMUNITY.

Not only will it reduce costs to build with family and friends, but the resulting building will have a much more personal feel. All members of the family can

Laying the first rice-straw bale at the Shenoa Retreat Center wall raising in northern California.

play a part, as in many cultures where the women and children are responsible for the majority of the building and maintenance. People who have actually been a part of building something are more likely to want to take care of it.

8. RELATE SPACE AND FORM TO CONTEXT.

The more a structure takes on the characteristics of its natural context, the more it will belong to the place. Let the space be defined slowly and carefully so that all the subtleties of that context and place can be heard. Reflect the native forms and allow what you are building to be molded through time.

PASSIVE SOLAR FUNDAMENTALS

While construction of a straw bale building can be accomplished without deliberate incorporation of active or passive solar features, the performance of straw bale buildings is greatly enhanced if builders acknowledge solar considerations in choosing their site, in positioning their building on the site, and in designing their windows and doors, roof, and other elements.

The basic ingredients of a well-built solar structure include a well-insulated shell, thermal mass, east-west orientation, a suitable building shape for a given environment, good window placement, and direct solar gain, which takes place through south-facing glazing. All of these factors can work together to create a building that provides most or all of its own heat, and requires little or no artificial or auxiliary cooling: in essence, a house that heats and cools itself.

1. INSULATED EXTERIOR SHELL

The better the insulation in the walls, roof, foundation, floor, doors, and windows (the shell of the house), the slower the leakage rate of heat or cold from the inside of the house to the outside, and vice versa. Often it is initial cost considerations that determine the amount of insulation that gets added to a structure. Even when the rest of the house is well insulated, it is often difficult to insulate doors and windows to the same degree, therefore these can be one of the biggest heat-loss or heat-gain areas in a house. A super-insulated, well-sealed structure, with few or no openings, would be extremely energy efficient in the sense that it would effectively conserve whatever heat or cold is inside the building. Window openings for light and ventilation will decrease the amount of heat conserved, but can allow for solar gain, a free source of heating. A building capable of collecting and storing heat in the colder months through passive solar absorption can balance out any loss through areas of lower insulation. Furthermore, heat gain can be limited during the summer months, when extra heat is undesirable, if the house is properly oriented in order to work with the natural cyclic movement of the sun, receiving heat from sunlight in winter and excluding hot sunlight by shading in summer.

2. GOOD SOLAR ORIENTATION

Solar design requires a basic understanding of how the sun moves in the sky over the year, and how this movement affects the sunlight that reaches a specific location at different times. In the summer in the northern hemisphere, the sun rises as well as sets to the north of the east-west line, and is high overhead at noon. In the winter, the sun is much lower at noon and rises and sets at points that are further to the south. It is possible by taking advantage of those changes to build a house that is naturally cool in the summer and warm in the winter.

The key to solar design is proper solar orientation. Ideally, a house should face true south, not magnetic south, but a house that is within 15 degrees east or west of true south will still collect 90 percent of the available sun. Any good compass manual or map will help determine true south for a given location; using the north star to represent the pole opposite true south also works. If the house is rectangular, align the longer side of the rectangle with the east-west axis.

3. WINDOW PLACEMENT

The challenge in placing windows is to arrange a variety of sizes and orientations of window so that there will be maximum heat and light gain in the winter months and minimum heat gain in the summer months, while allowing good ventilation and views.

In a house properly oriented, south-facing windows will allow the sun to enter the house during the winter, yet because of the difference in solar trajectory in the summer, there will be less direct sunlight entering during the hot season. North-facing windows will have no direct gain in either the winter or summer. East-facing windows will always have morning sun, which can be very effective for early-morning heating during the winter. West-facing windows will always have afternoon sun, which is highly undesirable during the summer. Overhead skylights will let heat and light in all day long, year-round.

Generally, there should be more windows on the south, fewer on the north, and even fewer on the east and west. Overhead glazing or skylights should probably be avoided. Compromises are usually inevitable, but the effects of undesirable heat gain or loss can be reduced with shading systems and insulating curtains.

4. SOUTH GLAZING

In solar designs, the south-facing glazing is the main heat-generating element. The greater the surface area of south-facing glass, the more heat gain there will be. The more glass, however, the less insulation, so the ability of the house to conserve heat will also be reduced, thus increasing the amount of heat lost at night and during times of no solar gain, and increasing the amount of heat that enters in the summer. The ratio of heat-loss to heat-gain will vary constantly, on a daily basis and according to climate, available sun, and the amount of thermal mass, insulation, and shading incorporated into the design of the structure.

In cold climates with low levels of winter sun, it is better to have a minimal area of south glass, perhaps 4 to 10 percent of the square footage of the house, with as much insulation as possible in the walls in order to rely more on the heat retention of insulated walls than on solar gain. On the other hand, in cold climates with a great deal of available sun, including northern New Mexico and Arizona, Nevada, and Utah, it is more effective to increase the amount of south-facing glazing, relying more on high amounts of heat gain than on high insulation. In Santa Fe, for example, it is common practice to incorporate as much as 20 to 30 percent (or more) of south-glazing. Solar buildings in warmer climates, with high levels of winter sun, will most likely perform better with the lower (4 to 10 percent) levels of south-glazing, minimizing unwanted heat gain. Edward Mazria's *The Passive Solar Home Book* provides formulas for computing this optimal ratio of glazing to insulation. Another excellent publication on passive solar design is *Passive Solar Design Strategies: Guidelines for Home Builders,* published by the Passive Solar Industries Council (see appendix for other solar-design resources).

5. INTERIOR THERMAL MASS

Thermal mass on the interior of a building is able to store heat or cold and then slowly release it back out to the surrounding air. Heat from a sunny winter day as well as the coolness of a summer night can be retained inside the insulated shell of the exterior walls if the building incorporates adequate thermal mass. Thermal mass is needed to prevent daytime overheating of the structure and to stabilize its ambient temperature through nights and periods of cloudy weather; the more mass available, the more stable the interior temperature. Also, the more directly the winter sun hits the mass, the higher the heat gain.

Floors can provide a good source of mass. Concrete, brick, flagstone, or other masonry materials work especially well. Earth floors can be used, but do not perform as well. Insulating beneath the floor helps return the heat gained to the interior of the building more quickly. Interior walls in houses are often framed with wood, but if built out of masonry materials such as rock or adobe these can provide excellent mass, especially those interior walls hit directly by the sun. Concrete poured between studs is a quick way to add mass.

Water is one of the best thermal mass materials. Water has a very high heat capacity, which means it can hold a lot of heat (or cold) before releasing it to the surrounding air. It was common in early solar buildings to see 55-gallon drums filled with water and painted black to store solar gain. Water walls or seats can be fabricated out of metal and incorporated into the south wall of a building or placed near a wood-burning stove. Water storage has the disadvantage of possible leaks.

Although its heat capacity is less than that of water, stone can also be used for thermal mass. An easy way to create an instant rock wall is to use gabions or heavy-gauged wire baskets filled with rock. They could make nice partitions, and could also be used for cooling in the summer if water were set up to drip down through the rocks.

6. INSULATED GLASS

Double-pane or insulated windows minimize the heat loss through these openings and will be advantageous in all but the mildest climates. There are many factors and variables to consider in selecting appropriate glazing materials. Consulting with local sources is often the best way to determine which type of insulated glazing will be best for a given area.

Double-pane windows are available with an air space that varies from $1/8$ to 1 inch. The larger the gap between the panes, the higher the insulation value. However, too large an air space between the glass (more than one inch) will allow air to flow and conduct heat rather than insulate. It will also create a shading effect, where one pane of glass shades the other, cutting down the solar gain.

Buying pre-sized, tempered, double-pane or insulated glass units and framing the openings accordingly is usually much more cost effective than having windows made to order in odd sizes. Pre-manufactured window units that can be opened and closed are of course good for ventilation. Inexpensive double-pane windows can be made at home by doubling up salvaged single pane windows with a ½- to 1-inch gap between the glass. These assemblies should be framed in with their stops screwed into place so that the pieces can be easily taken apart if the windows fog up on the inside, which happens occasionally even with pre-manufactured units.

For straw bale applications, custom windows with wide sills can be ordered from manufacturers such as Marvin Windows. A very effective alternative to wood stops for mounting glazing to structural framing is a product called SureSeal™, sold by Brother Sun of Santa Fe (see appendix), which uses leak-proof, no-maintenance exterior metal extrusions.

There are new high-performance window glazings available, such as low-E2. These windows redirect the heat back into the house but block out a large amount of sunlight, and should not be used on south-facing glass, but may be useful for other orientations (especially the west and north). An insulated glass called Energy Advantage, manufactured by LOF, is a much better choice for south-facing windows. Low-e window film, available through Real Goods (see appendix), can be applied over most single-pane and double-pane glass windows with great results. It installs easily, like wallpaper, using a squeegee and other common household tools. It can be purchased at a fraction of the cost of factory applied low-e films and has a lifetime of about fifteen years.

Storm windows will improve window performance. Insulated shutters or curtains on the inside of even single-pane windows can help retain heat at night. These can either be hand-made or bought.

7. SOLAR OVERHANGS AND SHADING

Allowing sunlight to enter the windows only when heat is needed is virtually impossible. Since without provisions for shading, there will most likely be heat gain during times when extra heat is undesirable, shading is an extremely important element of solar design.

A well-placed overhang can be used to shade south-facing windows in the summer, yet allow sunlight to enter when the sun is lower during the winter. Generally, in colder climates such an overhang should be narrower, allowing the sun to enter earlier in the fall and later in the spring, whereas in warmer climates, the overhang can extend further out, thereby eliminating solar gain early in the spring and delaying its entrance until later in the fall. Overhangs can run anywhere from 1 foot wide in colder areas to 3 to 4 feet wide in hot desert areas. They are easiest to design when all south-facing glazing is the same height and depth in the wall.

To correctly size an overhang, calculate what are called the "winter noon sun angle" and the "summer noon sun angle." (Winter noon = 90 degrees minus the latitude, minus the declination. Summer noon = 90 degrees minus the latitude, plus the declination.) Draw a cross-section of the south wall showing the location of glass in the wall. Project the summer noon angle from the bottom of the glazing and then the winter noon angle from the top of the glazing. The intersecting point of the two is the end point of the overhang.

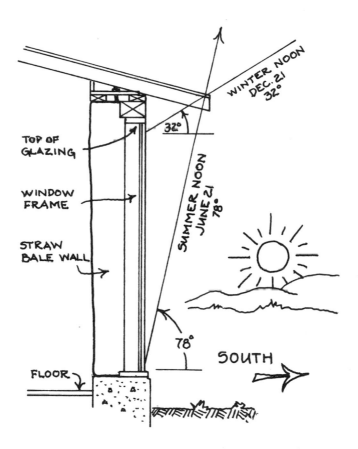

Even with a well-designed, permanent overhang, there are always compromises. For instance, if the overhang is designed to be wide enough to block out a good portion of the sun entering in the warmer fall months, it then begins blocking out needed sun early in the cool spring months, and vice versa. Portable or moveable overhangs and shades will allow for greater control and flexibility than permanent overhangs. With certain types of roofs, these can be made to slide into place for the summer months and withdrawn to the top of the roof for the winter. A louver-type window shade with moveable slats is even simpler, and is completely adjustable as conditions vary. A ramada-type structure may work as nicely as an extended overhang. Removable coverings such as shade cloth, burlap, palm leaves, or branches can be placed on the ramada for the summer and removed for the winter. A well-placed deciduous tree will serve the same function.

East-facing and west-facing windows need to be shaded in the summer from the rising and setting sun, which enters at lower angles. A tremendous amount of air conditioning is required to offset the blistering heat from just one picture window facing west. Vertically placed shading is much more appropriate for this purpose than overhangs. Trellises with fabric, shade cloth, or vines can be used, as can deciduous shrubs and trees. Shade curtains can be hung on the outside of the windows and can be easily made out of local materials, including branches or bamboo woven with wire or cord.

Shading is important not only where direct solar gain comes through the windows, since unshaded areas around the perimeter of the house including bare ground and paved surfaces may also reflect a lot of heat into the building. Either hanging shades directly over the windows or shading the perimeter surface itself will help to block a significant amount of that heat.

8. INDIRECT GAIN

Solar gain can also be harvested through indirect means, for instance through a greenhouse or sunroom on the south side of the building from which heat can be distributed to the rest of the house. During the day, a sunroom heats up, and in a well-designed system this heat will enter the main house through vents, windows, or doors. The sunroom can then be shut off from the rest of the building at night because it will not hold its heat as effectively as the better-insulated parts of the house, which have more thermal mass and less window area.

Trombe walls can be used for similar results if privacy is needed or if it is desirable to delay the passage of solar gain to the interior of the building. Trombe walls are basically glazing framed over a mass wall, with a small air space between the glazing and the wall. The mass is usually a dark color in order to absorb as much energy as possible. Heat then passes to interior living areas by direct conduction or through vents in the wall. To function optimally, trombe walls must be the proper thickness, which is a function of local climate and materials used. Trombe walls can also have openings or windows to provide visual access to the outdoors.

9. BALANCE OF SOLAR COMPONENTS

Determining the best combination of components in a passive solar structure in its specific location and climate is an art in itself. Computer programs designed to simulate the thermal properties of a structure may help reduce the amount of guesswork involved. The Canelo Project has developed a computer program that can track the thermal behavior of a building given its structural materials, insulation, window openings, solar orientation, thermal storage capacity, and weather conditions. This is an excellent tool for understanding how to combine materials in a building as well as for determining the percentage of window to wall area. The program also analyzes heat storage (mass) and insulation requirements.

Using this program allows a designer to organize interior spaces with knowledge of actual heating and cooling capabilities. Windows and doors can be situated in the most thermally efficient locations, incorporating local weather data, solar characteristics of the site, and latitude of the region.

The simulation becomes more accurate with each factor that is added to the description of the building. Since the process is a simulation, its results cannot be perfectly accurate, but the values provided need not be completely accurate in order to be useful in making intelligent design decisions. Even without absolute calibration, one can compare the relative results of alternative designs and thermal-gain strategies. For example, it is easy to observe the overall thermal effects of changing the size of a window or adding more insulation. The program is not yet available for general distribution, but technical consultations are available from the Canelo Project, to help builders analyze their designs (see the Resources section).

10. BACK-UP HEATING AND NATURAL COOLING

In a moderate climate, a super-insulated building with adequate solar gain, proper shading, and good thermal mass will move through the seasons of the year with little need for additional heating or cooling. However, for extended cloudy days when there is no solar gain, a back-up heating system may be needed.

In addition to incorporating the basics of a good solar design, care should be taken to eliminate leakage of heat or cool air to further minimize the need for back-up systems. Weather-stripping doors and windows, caulking, and sealing can dramatically reduce unwanted losses. In most houses, walls are capable of breathing well and can provide a continuous source of fresh pre-heated air. If for some reason the walls have been completely sealed, an air-to-air heat exchanger can be used.

Back-up heating can be provided by a simple, clean-burning wood stove. If a back-up system receives limited use, burning sustainably harvested wood makes a lot of sense. Newer EPA-approved stoves with catalyzers are very efficient, as are European-style tile ovens, which are sources of radiant heat and burn very small amounts of wood compared to other wood stoves (see *The Book of Masonry Stoves* by David Lyle).

Radiant heat is by far the most comfortable and efficient form of heat. Where larger back-up systems are required, heat can be distributed using a small pump that moves hot water from a boiler through plastic tubing embedded in the concrete, earth, or brick floor of the building. This water can be pre-heated with solar panels, and in climates with good solar gain, a super-insulated house may require only the solar-heated water.

Other methods of providing backup heat vary according to climate and circumstance. In places where there is an inexhaustible supply of compost, a compost pile can generate significant amounts of heat. Some designs use a heat-collecting coil run through the compost pile, while others place the pile against the wall of the greenhouse.

Cooling can often be provided through a number of simple strategies without employing sophisticated air-conditioning systems. To begin with, all buildings should be designed to capture cooling breezes in the summer. Every area has predominant directions for its seasonal winds, and windows can be placed to take advantage of these. Trees and shrubs can be planted to provide corridors for those breezes if exact window alignment is not possible.

Screened vents in the wall that can be covered in cold times of the year with insulated panels are more economical than operable windows. To encourage circulation, some vents should be placed just above floor level for the intake of cooler air and others high in the wall to allow warmer air to exit.

Where nocturnal temperatures are cool, the house can be opened at night to let the cool air enter and be stored in the mass of the interior space. Early in the morning before temperatures rise, the house can be closed off and circulating fans used to provide air movement during the day. If nights are not sufficiently cool, an evaporative cooler can be run into the early hours of the morning. Evaporative coolers work much more efficiently with the cool evening air than with the blistering heat of mid-day. Some models have been developed to run off photovoltaic panels and 12-volt DC.

Extensive vegetation around the outside of the house will help significantly in reducing its temperature. The plants' shade, transpiration of mois-

Courtyard in the Nuzum residence, Alamos, Sonora, Mexico.

ture, and oxygen will create an oasislike microclimate, especially in drier areas. Interior courtyards can also be delightful during summer months, with arbors, vines, shade cloth, and large shade trees used to help moderate temperatures. Two-story courtyards are easier to ventilate, because of their height, as they create more of an updraft (like a chimney), but a one-story shaded courtyard with good door placement around the perimeter will work fine.

In some parts of the world, shade houses or rooms can provide a comfortable environment or a source of cool air for the rest of the house, utilizing the opposite principle of a greenhouse or sunroom. A structure can be built on the cooler side of the house, usually the north or east, covered with some type of netting or burlap, and filled with vegetation and even a pond or fountain. Overhead misters can be used to keep the space and the burlap walls damp. Mulch can be placed on the floor to absorb moisture and keep the floor cool. The shade house is then vented into the rest of the house.

Exterior porches also provide a cool, comfortable outdoor living area during hot periods of the year.

The Environmental Research Lab, at the University of Arizona in Tucson, has developed passive down-draft cooling towers that provide good indirect cooling in situations where evaporative coolers may not work. Mary Diamond's straw bale house (see page 26) in southeastern Arizona has a built-in cooling tower.

EVALUATING BALE WALL OPTIONS:
THE LOAD-BEARING VERSUS
THE MODIFIED POST-AND-BEAM

—BY PAUL WEINER

For the past four years my company, Design and Building Consultants, has been involved in building structures with plastered bales of straw. During that time, many questions have arisen about the pros and cons of building this way; questions ranging from concept to detail. Probably the most interesting and frequently discussed question is whether to use load-bearing bale walls or a modified post-and-beam system. The big issues in question include cost-effectiveness, building settlement, architectural flexibility, quantity of materials, and the perspective of building authorities.

Dedication ceremony for the Tree of Life Rejuvenation Center in Patagonia, Arizona.

Although it was not planned as an experiment, two of my associates, Bob Lanning and Karin Rosenquist, and I recently had the opportunity to build the same building (only slightly modified) on two different sites using these two different systems. The exterior of the building is L-shaped, totaling 900 square feet, and uses a pitched metal roof with a combination of hip and gable ends. Our original plan had been to build both structures with load-bearing bale walls. However, developments during the construction process of the first building convinced us to redesign the second.

It so happened that both buildings utilized the same design because we needed to quickly design and build a construction office and worker mess hall for the Tree of Life Rejuvenation Center in Patagonia, Arizona. Rather than begin from scratch, we decided to slightly modify the load-bearing bale-wall design we had drawn up but not yet built for another client, Pam Tillman, and use it for the Tree of Life building.

Having made that decision, we went about the process of securing a permit for a load-bearing structure in Santa Cruz County, Arizona, where the Tree of Life building was to be built. This was somewhat facilitated because the city of Tucson had already issued a load-bearing permit for the Tillman residence. After some discussion and a letter absolving the county of any liability related to the structural safety of the building, the building officials allowed this one permit, but quickly stated that they would not allow another load-bearing permit until a prescriptive building standard for load-bearing straw bale construction had been written and approved by regional building officials.

The Tree of Life building was the fourth significant straw bale structure for which I was to direct the building effort, and I was very interested in carefully observing the process and making determinations regarding labor and materials related to load-bearing bale-wall structures. We were also looking carefully to evaluate the window and door systems that we had developed for this structure in terms of flexibility and cost-effectiveness. And, we were looking for more general architectural control. Because a load-bearing building settles differentially at points along the wall and top plate, a simple, pleasing design can be turned into an irregular mess. To avoid that, we started to look at greater controls in the building methodology to keep the structure true to the design intent.

The walls of the Tree of Life building were built with what has become a fairly standard load-bearing bale-wall assembly. To begin with, it is assumed that a load-bearing straw bale wall of seven courses will settle 1.5 to 3 inches over a couple of months under a normal roof load. One might assume that by dividing the amount of settlement into the number of courses, you would arrive at the amount of settlement per course. If it weren't for door and window

Wall raising at Tree of Life Rejuvenation Center.

bucks varying the number of bales in any given wall section, that assumption would hold true. However, door bucks bear on the foundation and don't compress, while the section of wall around a window frame will settle differentially, depending on whether lintels are used above the window frame or a structural window frame transfers the loads above to the one or two courses of bales below.

If lintels (most often steel) are used over door and window frames, the loads from above the length of the lintel are concentrated at the two points where the lintel rests on the bale wall on either side of the frame. Since bales compress, the concentrated loads at those two points will cause the bales to compress more than the bales at other points in the wall. This can be further complicated if poorly compressed custom-sized bales have been included in the wall section directly under the bearing points of the lintels. If lintels are used with door frames, space needs to be allotted above the door frame to allow for settlement.

If window frames are structural, they transfer the loads from above the frame to the one or two bales below the frame. The problem is that those bales

Window shim at Tree of Life building.

are being required to compact as much as the seven courses of bales on either side of the frame.

With either method, potential settling problems occur. In the process of attempting to maintain enough control over the roof plate to attain a clean roof line, it is crucial to understand how much settlement will occur at all of these different points in a load-bearing bale-wall section. This can be a difficult analysis.

With the Tree of Life building, we began by designing the door and window frames as structural units, and decided against using any type of lintels. We felt that we could handle any differential settling by using an adjustable shimming process in the field. At some point in the process I reconsidered our earlier decision and came to believe that undersizing the outside dimensions of window and door bucks, and using steel lintels in combination with a shimming system, would ultimately give us more control.

Despite our most careful and calculated efforts to keep the roof plate level by adjusting the shims over the door and window frames as well as precompressing the walls with the aid of a transit, we still ended up with an uneven line of rafter tails, which were eventually corrected only by extensive shimming of the roof plate—sometimes as much as 2 to 3 inches. Despite the shimming, the rafter tails were finally aligned by creating a level line along the bottom of the drip cap. The load-bearing bale-wall system comes with several inherent problems that require some form of resolution. My experience with this building, coupled with the building authorities' unwillingness to permit any additional load-bearing bale-wall structures, led me to explore other possible bale building systems for future straw bale structures at the Tree of Life Center.

While engaged in that process, I had the opportunity to visit another straw bale house, which, oddly enough, was under construction at the same time on a site almost adjacent to the Tree of Life Center. The house had been designed by Sonoita, Arizona, architect Bill Cook, and reflected some sound thinking in terms of structural straw-bale design. It was a highly efficient, modified post-and-beam structure with bale in-fill that was very appropriate to straw bale construction. What Bill had done was to assume that bearing posts would be placed only at the corners of the building and in conjunction with window and door jambs. The 2-by-4 sheathed frames used for the jambs became structural bearing supports. This was the brilliance of the system.

Within minutes of being inside this building, I realized that it potentially solved all the problems we had encountered with the load-bearing bale-wall building for the Tree of Life project. The one concern was cost. Could this system resolve all the messy little problems of load-bearing work and be built for the same cost or less?

Since we had not yet begun construction on Pam Tillman's residence, which had almost the same floor plan as the load-bearing bale-wall building we were completing, it occurred to me that it was a perfect opportunity to experiment with this new system if the client was willing and time permitted. With Pam's approval, we set to work making the necessary changes to retrofit the design of her load-bearing structure into a modified post-and-beam.

As we worked on the design, the cleverness and cost-effectiveness of this particular method became quantitatively clear. To begin with, the same window bucks that had been designed as sheathed and framed units for the load-bearing structure needed to be changed only by adding an

Window frames in Tillman wall.

extension beneath the sill to allow the frames to bear directly on the foundation. An additional extension to the top of the frame would also be needed for the frame to reach and support the roof beam. With these minimal modifications each window and door frame could become a bearing structural support. A positive feature of these plywood-sheathed window and door frames is their flexibility. They can be sized to accommodate any-width wall. In this case they were 24 inches wide, the same width as the bales, and consequently no notching of the bales had to be done to incorporate the frames into the walls. They would simply

Glu lam beam.

extend from the inside edge of the wall to the outside edge.

In addition to these modifications of the frames, corner posts (4-by-4s) needed to be added. Since there were a few gaps remaining in the structural framework where posts would be required, we began to ask ourselves simple questions like: If we placed another column in the wall, could we reduce the size of the main beam and keep the cost down? Such questions led to other discoveries such as realizing that we could build a shelving unit into the wall and use it for bearing in place of another column. Had the building been

designed from scratch, bearing door and window frames could have been better distributed throughout the perimeter of the structure, possibly eliminating or at least reducing the need for any additional bearing posts.

The final component to the design was a $3\,^1/_8$ by $7\,^1/_2$-inch glue lam beam, which we sized by trying to efficiently accommodate the roof loads over the longest span between windows, doors, and corners.

By the time we had completed retrofitting the design, it became clear that this method of building with straw bales would be much more efficient than the load-bearing wall approach we had used, and that it would eliminate the problems we had faced during the construction of the Tree of Life Center building. The new structural framework would immediately remove the most frustrating part of the load-bearing wall system, the many hours spent pre-tensioning the walls and leveling the roof plate. Besides reducing the amount of labor needed, the new framework eliminated the need for the doubled 2-by-6 roof plate that we had to use to meet the requirements of the county building officials. The glue lam we had chosen for the main beam would result in a 5 percent increase in cost, but when compared with the savings in labor that was realized, a net gain for the post-and-beam system resulted. Furthermore, the glue lam was fabricated from second-growth lumber that has a quick maturation rate.

Using this modified post-and-beam system also enabled us to eliminate the use of all-thread sections running from the foundation to the roof plate. Not only did this result in a savings in materials, but the time spent carefully and precisely impaling bales over all-thread sections during the wall raising would be eliminated. Door and window frame lintels could also be eliminated.

The most fascinating discovery we made came from analyzing the amount of lumber used in the two buildings. It is commonly assumed that load-bearing structures will always use less lumber than post-and-beam construction, but in this case our analysis clearly showed that the load-bearing structure had consumed more lumber. The two designs used the same door and window frames with slightly more material in the frames for the post-and-beam structure because they extend from the foundation to the roof beam. The post-and-beam structure also used an additional nine 4-by-4 posts, six of them in the corners. However, when the $3\frac{1}{8}$ by $7\frac{1}{2}$ glue lam beam is compared with the load-bearing roof plate, which was constructed from a pair of doubled 2-by-6s with 2-by-6 cross rungs, the glue lam clearly represented a 40 percent reduction in lumber.

We calculated the total volume of board feet of lumber used in each structure by multiplying the length of each lumber component with its cross-sectional width. The results of those calculations follow:

BUILDING MATERIAL COMPARISON

	TREE OF LIFE	TILLMAN
Doors and Windows		
2-by-4s	164	281
2-by-6s	73	73
2-by-4s (treated plate)	6	13
plywood ($\frac{1}{2}$-inch CDX)	equal	equal
Other Structural Components		
4-by-4 wood posts		81
glu-lam beam ($3\frac{1}{8}$-by-$7\frac{1}{2}$)		284
2-by-6 roof plate	530	
Totals	773	732

As can be seen by this analysis, the Tillman residence used less lumber. Further efficiency is revealed when one considers that 38 feet of 24-inch-wide steel ladder-type lintels and 240 linear feet of $\frac{1}{2}$-inch all-thread that were used in the load-bearing structure were not needed in the post-and-beam structure. The lintels represent a cost of approximately $400, and the all-thread another $160.

Frame with bale in-fill at Tillman residence.

Through our design modification process we addressed many what-if scenarios. After a thorough analysis, we comfortably concluded that although there may be many ways of approaching a post-and-beam straw-bale structure, if it is done with efficiency in mind, it can be done more quickly, efficiently, and inexpensively than a load-bearing bale-wall structure. My personal feeling is that you end up with a better product, one that is not subject to the inevitable settlement of load-bearing bale walls and one whose behavior and maintenance is therefore more predictable. The exception to this thinking might be smaller structures (16 feet by 16 feet maximum) with small window openings, or structures with simple one-way roof systems over a moderate span (shed roofs of 20 feet or less).

One of the most satisfying elements of this discovery was realizing that numerous potential straw bale homebuilders, who had given up the idea of building with straw because they were discouraged at the prospects of securing a load-bearing permit, and who had decided that the financial benefits would be lost if they resorted to a structural framework, could once again entertain the possibility of building with straw.

The criteria on which I am basing this analysis was developed in response to a particular style of building and its architectural guidelines, and may differ from that of an owner-builder. If a different roof system were used, one that did not require such precise alignment, our analysis could change. An improved roof plate that used less material could also have an impact on the load-bearing design. If it were possible to efficiently and cost-effectively design and build a more rigid roof plate, the differential settling issues could be minimized.

Both systems have validity, depending on the skill of the builder, the size of the structure, the sizes of wall openings, and the need for architectural control. As professionals in the building field, we continually look for efficiencies of labor and material use, some standardization of building methodology (for the sake of efficiency), and flexibility in design opportunities. We want things to go together in a predictable manner and to be able to estimate how they will look and feel once they have stopped being just materials and have started to create the final product. Optimally, we seek to achieve a high level of predictability without sacrificing creativity. The modified post-and-beam system affords us that opportunity.

BUILDING SHAPES

THE OCTAGON

Steve Kemble of Sustainable Systems Design designed and built a 450-square-foot, eight-sided structure styled after a traditional Navajo hogan in southeastern Arizona. Salvaged utility poles were used in a post-and-beam structural stystem with bale in-fill walls, using bales laid on edge. The basic structure of the building and the bale walls provided no noticeable increase in complications from a regular post-and-beam-type structure.

The walls meet at 135-degree interior angles, forming a gap at each corner where the bales butted up to the poles, which was filled with loose straw. Stacking the bales on edge saved usable interior space and cut costs by reducing the number of bales needed by one third. There was no significant decrease in insulation value because the R-value of the straw increases when the stems are perpendicular to the ground, as they are when the bales are on edge.

The octagonal shape creates a wonderful interior space and has lots of straight wall surface to accommodate furniture, appliances, shelves, etc.

Straw bale octagon designed and built by Steve Kemble in southeastern Arizona.

Even though the structural framework and the bale walls of the building presented little problem, roof construction on the eight-sided structure was much more complicated. The eight sides translated into eight hips, a vented ridge cap, and a lot of calculating to cut the roof decking without wasting large amounts of material. Shingles were chosen as a roof surface because of the difficulty involved in cutting metal roofing to this shape. Cutting the ceiling material (not completed at the time of this publication) would be an equally challenging endeavor.

In essence, this building creates a unique interior space and an attractive exterior at the cost of constructing a labor-intensive and time-consuming roof system. The octagon shape might be a good candidate for a traditional type of roof like the turf roofs used on old Scandinavian buildings, which were essentially soil with grass or herbs growing in it.

T-SHAPED GUEST CABIN

This small building was built as a T for different reasons. Steve Kemble and Carol Escott of Sustainable Systems Design wanted to demonstrate that a straw bale building did not necessarily have to be a rectangle or a square. The

Steve Kemble and Carol Escott's T-shaped guest cabin featured in the video, "How to Build Your Elegant Home with Straw Bales."

dimensions of the T-shape fit the site well without disturbing native vegetation and water run-off patterns. The house is the minimum size that would comfortably serve its intended function.

The cabin has an interior space of 250 square feet, and cost approximately $24 per square foot to build. This amount reflects only the cost of materials, however; all the labor was provided by Steve, Carol, and friends.

Upon completion of the project, Steve and Carol reviewed the construction process and discovered a number of interesting facts. They realized that by using the T-shape, they added considerably to the complexity of the project—the amount of materials and work required—while adding only 40 square feet of usable interior space. The addition of a single bale length to the east and west walls would have increased usable floor area by 40 percent or 100 square feet. With a small building like this one, small increases in dimension can make a large difference in usable space.

Had the building been a square shape with the same overall dimensions, the usable interior area would have increased from 250 square feet to 400 square feet (an increase of 60 percent). The square shape would mean a 25 percent increase for the additional slab and roof area, while the amount of

Floor plan of Steve and Carol's T-shaped guest cabin.

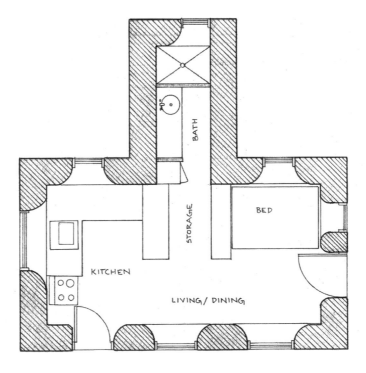

structural bale wall would remain the same. The roof would be easier to build, since the valleys for the T-shape would be eliminated. With this change, the overall cost would increase only 5 percent but would result in a 60 percent gain in usable space. The overall cost per square foot, $16, would be lower than the $25 per square foot required for the more complex T-structure.

The how-to video documents the entire construction of building, and a detailed analysis of the building process is available as well.

ROUND STRUCTURES

A number of round straw bale structures have been built, including one by Lane McClelland and Laurie Roberts and another at the Tree of Life Nursery, both in southern California. Both buildings have load-bearing walls.

Constructing curved bale walls, as is the case with octagons, presents little problem. The bales need to curve only slightly, and this can be easily accomplished as described earlier in the chapter Working with Bales.

The most complicated part of a round structure if the walls are load-bearing is the roof and the roof plate. Round straw bale structures require a different and more flexible roof system. Cutting the decking for the roof can be a wasteful and time-consuming process, and circular roof plates are difficult to design because there are no straight wall spans to allow for the long lengths of lumber usually necessary to provide adequate stiffness in the plate. Consequently, building a roof plate for a round structure involves ingenuity. A roof design that allows for irregularity in the rafter line will help compensate for any differential settling. The load-bearing McClelland-Roberts building uses a decorative and attractive palm thatch around the circumference of the roof, which covers all the rafter tails.

Nonetheless, these difficulties with the roofs of round structures are usually offset by the charm and beauty of round buildings.

Rafters, blocking, and decking on top of roof plate for round, load-bearing straw bale building, Tree of Life Nursery, Southern California.

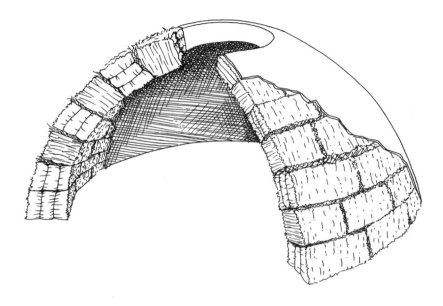

Roxanne Swentzell's dome.

ROXANNE SWENTZELL'S DREAM

Roxanne Swentzell lives in Santa Clara Pueblo, where she sculpts figures from clay and teaches permaculture.

I've had this dream. In this dream I live like the people used to live, because I choose to—in a way that gives me power, power on my level, a human creative level.

I made a small dome out of straw bales with the help of my husband Joel and my children, Porter and Rosie. It is about 15 feet in diameter and easily holds us all. We laid the bales on stones that we gathered into a circle. As we went upwards, one row of bales at a time, we slowly tilted and wedged the bales inward. They held each other up, compressing inward to tighten and strengthen the dome.

We slept in it. I chose to leave a small hole at the top to look out at the sky. It was quiet and very beautiful to lie there looking up at the walls around me curved in, holding me safe. "We will plaster it with mud," I thought, "and someday it will all fall down back into the earth, welcomed, and many things will grow here in the mulch our little house has made."

The simplicity made me feel cleaned and clear. My mind could rest, and it seemed easier to just be. "This is a good step," I thought, "for getting to my dream."

FLOOR PLANS

To design a house that will be comfortable and be used, the patterns of the inhabitants' lives need to be closely matched with the layout of the house. The flow of movement within the house will influence the way people relate to the house itself and each other. Combining spaces and giving them multifunctional uses can reduce the number of interior walls needed and help keep the square footage and costs to a minimum. Incorporating alcoves and large sitting or sleeping nooks throughout the house can help create a feeling of privacy without actually building separate rooms. An excellent reference for those wishing to design their own homes is *A Pattern Language* by Christopher Alexander.

These floor plans are intended to give the reader an idea of how straw bale houses can be laid out. There are five different examples, ranging from small guest-sized units to a two-bedroom, 2,700-square-foot house. Several different bale-wall construction methods are represented, from simple post-and-beam to load-bearing walls. Complete sets of plans are available from the different designers.

BILL AND NANCY COOK'S GUEST HOUSE—SONOITA, ARIZONA

The Cook's guest house, designed by Bill Cook, has a 640-square-foot exterior, and a 432-square-foot interior, with one bedroom, bath, living room and kitchen. The house is post-and-beam construction, with TJI joists with flat roof. The north wall is frame construction to accommodate the kitchen, glass patio doors, and floating glass window in the northeast corner. This guesthouse is attractive and simple.

South elevation of Bill and Nancy Cook's guest house.

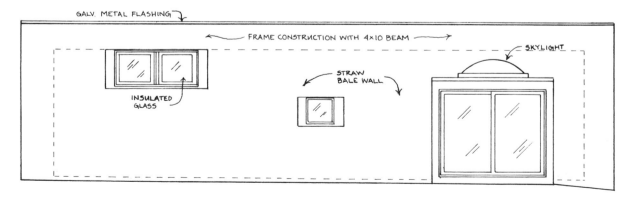

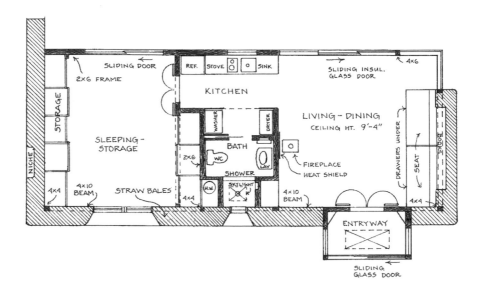

Bill and Nancy Cook's guest house floor plan.

THE LAVINA RESIDENCE—DRIPPING SPRINGS, TEXAS

This building was designed by Steve Kemble of Sustainable Systems Support of Bisbee, Arizona. It has an exterior dimension of 900 square feet, and an interior dimension of 730 square feet. It is a post-and-beam construction using box columns in the wall in place of single posts. They are the width of the wall, 18 inches, and constructed from a pair of 4-by-4s sheathed in plywood. The beam is a rough-cut 3-by-10. The building has one bedroom, one bath, living room, kitchen, and loft.

North elevation of the Lavina residence.

NORTH ELEVATION

The Lavina residence floor plan.

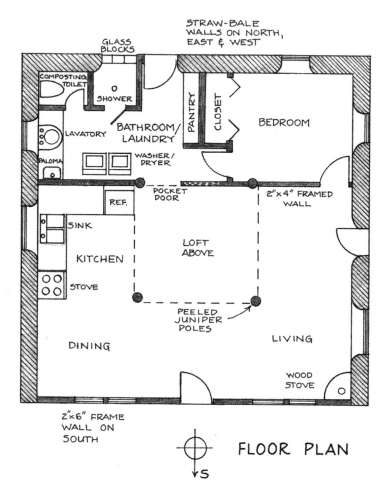

STRAW-BALE WALLS ON NORTH, EAST & WEST

GLASS BLOCKS

COMPOSTING TOILET

SHOWER

LAVATORY

PALOMA

BATHROOM/ LAUNDRY

WASHER/ DRYER

PANTRY

CLOSET

BEDROOM

POCKET DOOR

2"×4" FRAMED WALL

REF.

SINK

KITCHEN

LOFT ABOVE

STOVE

PEELED JUNIPER POLES

DINING

LIVING

WOOD STOVE

2"×6" FRAME WALL ON SOUTH

FLOOR PLAN

S

THE PAM TILLMAN RESIDENCE—TUCSON, ARIZONA

The Tillman residence has a 900-square-foot exterior with a 742-square-foot interior. It was designed by Paul Weiner of Design and Building Consultants. It has one bedroom, one bath, kitchen and living area. The roof incorporates both a hip and gable design. Although designed as a load-bearing structure, this building was actually built as a post-and-beam. It reveals a clean and simple design that lends itself to being constructed a number of different ways.

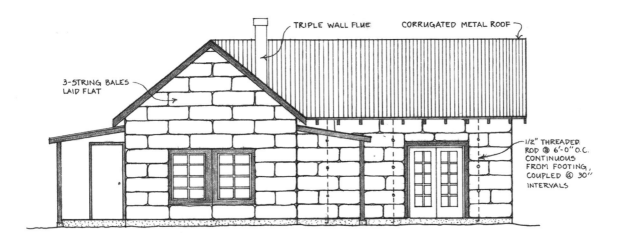

TRIPLE WALL FLUE

CORRUGATED METAL ROOF

3-STRING BALES
LAID FLAT

1/2" THREADED
ROD @ 6'-0" O.C.
CONTINUOUS
FROM FOOTING,
COUPLED @ 30"
INTERVALS

SOUTH ELEVATION

*South elevation of the
Pam Tillman residence.*

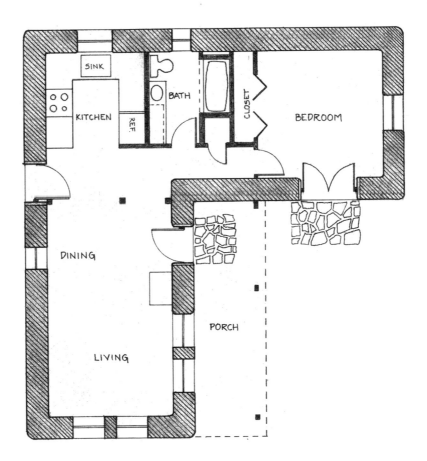

SINK

KITCHEN

REF.

BATH

CLOSET

BEDROOM

DINING

PORCH

LIVING

*The Pam Tillman
residence floorplan.*

SOLAR STRAW BALE FAMILY RESIDENCE—CONCEPTUAL

This floorplan, although designed for a high desert environment, could work in a variety of climates. It incorporates south glazing for direct solar gain and has a small courtyard which can function as an outdoor living area during the warmer months. The top of the courtyard could be screened. Adobe interior walls provide thermal mass, along with water walls/drums positioned along the south wall. The outdoor south patio has been designed for removable shading to regulate the amount of solar gain. The west wing of the house functions as a children's realm with sleeping nooks and a common living and play area. The east wing serves as an adult's realm with a bedroom and office or workspace. A rooftop sleeping and living area is located over the adult bedroom. The interior floor space is 2,700 square feet.

Floor plan of a passive solar family residence.

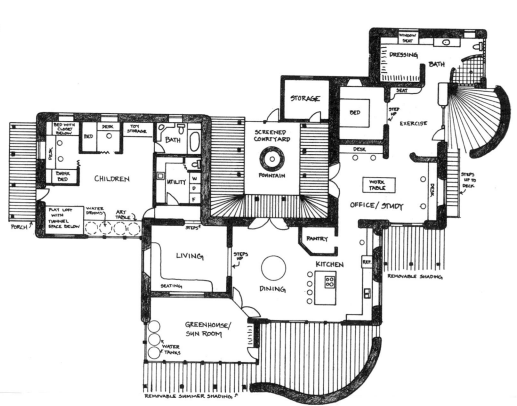

THE GENIUS LOCUS MULTI-STORY PROTOTYPE

This is a prototype design from Genius Loci, a group from northern New Mexico working on natural housing. The house is a small, highly adaptable design, that with minimal changes can be modified to meet regional variations in climate and site.

The exterior dimensions of the house are 26 by 26 feet, with a square footage of 676 feet. The interior living area is 576 square feet; however, an additional 500 square feet is gained through the addition of the second floor, which involves only a minimal amount of extra work. Since the interior living space almost doubled (1,076 square feet) while using the same foundation and roof structure, the cost per square foot of effective living area is greatly reduced. Three extra courses of bales and the addition of a floor are required for the upper story. The total wall height is 12 feet, with 9-foot-high ceilings for the first floor, and a 3-foot knee-wall upstairs. The ridge beam for the roof runs north-south, the south gable end is framed with glazing for solar gain, and an open cathedral ceiling is used.

The roof pitch is steep to allow maximum second-story headroom. The roof can be easily raised one or two bale courses if additional height is desired for minimal expense.

South-facing perspective drawing of the Genius Locus multi-story prototype.

The Genius Locus multi-story prototype floor plans.

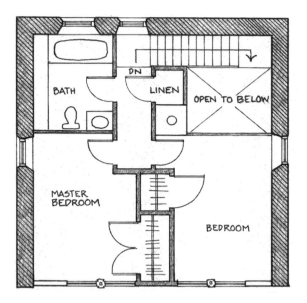

UPPER FLOOR

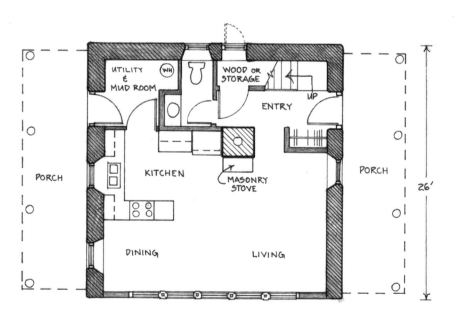

MAIN FLOOR

APPENDIX

RESOURCES FOR STRAW BALE CONSTRUCTION

* All of Arizona's area codes, except in the Phoenix area, will be changed from 602 to 520 after March 19, 1995.

The Canelo Project
Athena and Bill Steen
HC1 Box 324
Elgin, Arizona 85611
*(602) 455-5548
A nonprofit organization offering comprehensive straw bale workshops that cover bale-wall options, carpentry for straw bale structures, and alternative plasters and floors. Work-tours in Mexico focus on low-cost housing solutions using local resources and recycled materials. The uses of natural materials including earth, bamboo, and natural fibers are emphasized as well as designing and shaping spaces that enhance well-being, family, and community.

Center for Maximum Potential Building Systems
Pliny Fisk III
8604 FM 969
Austin, Texas 78724
Alternative building and design center; normally works on large projects. Specializing in regional resource use. Has been retained to rewrite the alternative building codes for the state of Texas.

DeHavillan Workshops
1039 E. Linden St.
Tucson, Arizona 85719
Specializes in straw bale construction workshops nationally. Has a pool of architects, builders, and individuals experienced in straw bale construction, including straw bale builder Jon Ruez, David Eisenberg, Jill Lorenzini, and Joanne DeHavillan.

Design and Building Consultants, Inc.
Paul Weiner
19 E. Fifteenth Street
Tucson, Arizona 85701
*(602) 792-0873
Design, building, and consultation services for straw bale buildings for both residential and commercial applications. Long-term experience with straw bale building as well as adobe, rammed earth, and native stone. Emphasizes straw bale designs which respect both the architectural and regional dictates of where they are placed.

The Development Center for Appropriate Technology
David Eisenberg
P.O. Box 41144
Tucson, Arizona 85717
Straw bale construction workshops focusing on affordable and sustainable techniques; consulting on straw bale design; code development and related issues; research and testing projects. Extensive experience both teaching and working with straw bales. Other construction experience includes rammed earth and adobe, structural steel, concrete, and wood-frame.

EOS Institute
Lynn Bayless
580 Broadway, Suite 200
Laguna Beach, California 94702
(714) 497-1896
Nonprofit education and resource center for ecological building design. Regional straw bale resources.

Genius Loci
Jan Wisinewski and JoAn Churchman
248 Anita Place
Santa Fe, New Mexico 87501
(505) 820-1134
A small group of individuals dedicated to designing and building alternative structures including ones built from straw bales. Their designs include a prototype small two-story home.

Rick Green
2130 County Road S
Willows, CA 95988
(916) 934-7225
Rice-straw bales available. Contractor with straw bale building experience.

Robert Laporte
Natural House Building Center
RR 1, Box 115F
Fairfield, Iowa 52556
(515) 472-7775
Workshops and publications on straw/light-clay construction with timber frames.

Tom Luecke
3785 Moorhead Avenue
Boulder, Colorado 80303
Straw bale construction with an emphasis on load-bearing structures utilizing strapping for roof-plate tie-downs.

Out On Bale - By Mail
1037 E. Linden Street
Tucson, Arizona 85719
A general resource, education, and information center for straw bale, with written material and videos available on straw bale construction.

Straw Bale Construction Association
Attn: Beverley Spears, Secretary
1334 Pacheco Street
Santa Fe, New Mexico 87501
A national association of architects, designers, engineers, general contractors, and subcontractors interested in straw bale testing, and the method's inclusion into code. Forum for sharing technical information.

Straw Bale Construction Management Inc.
Tony Perry
31 Old Arroyo Chamiso
Santa Fe, New Mexico 87505
(505) 989-4400
Consultant specializing in affordable housing; workshops and seminars. Distributor for "Quick Spray," a stucco spray machine.

Bob Theis and Dan Smith
Daniel Smith and Associates Architecture
1107 Virginia Street
Berkeley, California 94702
*(510) 526-1935
Coordinating the creation of a network of regional representatives to ensure that efficient, nonduplicative straw bale testing is performed under common research directives, regional perspectives, and the best use of engineering resources.

Sustainable Systems Support
Carol Escott and Steve Kemble
P.O. Box 318
Bisbee, Arizona 85603
*(602) 432-4292
Consultation, design, workshops, publications, and videos.

INTERNATIONAL RESOURCES

ArchiBio
François Tanguay, Michel Bergeron, Clode
    DeGuise
1267 Chemin Lac Deliguy, Ouest
Mandeville, Quebec, Canada JOK 1L0
Written materials, consultation, design, and
building of ecological housing including straw bale
construction.

Biotique Habitat
John L. F. Daglish
122 Avenue Saint Exupery
92160 Antony, France
A group promoting and developing vegetal
building materials, particularly straw bale construction, in France. Offers consultation for eco-biological
design.

Tapani Marjamaa
Sinikontie 3
c/o Keijo Marjamaa
74300 Sonkajarvi, Finland
Leading testing and research effort for national
code for straw bale homes in Finland.

Jorg and Helen Ostrowski
1909 10th Avenue, SW
Calgary, Alberta, Canada T3C OK3
Ecological design and building, planning,
consulting, research and development. Straw bale
construction.

PUBLICATIONS AND VIDEOS ON STRAW BALE BUILDING

*Building with Straw, Vol. I: A Straw Bale Work
    shop* (video)
by Catherine Wanek of Black Range Films.
The subject is the building of a two-story post-
and-beam straw bale greenhouse. Covered are solar
design, straw bale wall construction, and plastering. A
slide presentation is included which showcases a
variety of straw bale structures, and a printed insert
details cost factors. Available from: Black Range Films,
Star Rt. 2, Box 119, Kingston, New Mexico 88042;
or Out On Bale - By Mail, 1037 E. Linden Street,
Tucson, Arizona 85719. Approximately $29 plus
shipping and handling.

Building with Straw, Vol. *II: A Straw Bale Home
    Tour* (video)
by Catherine Wanek of Black Range Films
A tour of the interiors and exteriors of ten diverse
straw bale homes with owner/builder interviews.
Houses included in the video range from a simple
owner-built home to custom-built, bank-financed
houses costing over $100 a square foot. Introduction
by Matts Myhrman. Sixty minutes. Available from:
Black Range Films, Star Rt. 2, Box 119, Kingston,
New Mexico 88042; or Out On Bale - By Mail, 1037
E. Linden Street, Tucson, Arizona 85719. Approximately $29 plus postage and handling.

*Build It With Bales: A Step by Step guide to Straw
    Bale Construction*
by S.O. McDonald, Matts Myhrman, and
    illustrations by Orion McDonald.
An excellent and thorough how-to manual on
straw bale construction. Available from: Out-On-Bale
- By Mail, 1037 E. Linden Street, Tucson, Arizona
85719.

*Farm Buildings Using Rectangular or Round
    Baled Roughage*
by Dexter W. Johnson.
ASAE Paper #904550 1990, American Society of
Agricultural Engineers. Johnson has spearheaded the
use of bales for agricultural buildings. The paper
includes a nice review of history on the Great Plains.
Available from: ASAE, St. Joseph, Michigan 49085-
9659.

"Guidelines to Straw Bale Construction for the Owner/Builder"
by Steve Kemble of Sustainable Systems Support

A comprehensive booklet of design guidelines for the owner/builder, covering a range of sustainable building practices in combination with straw bale construction. The booklet contains information on creating an optimized, sustainable passive-solar straw bale home that is appropriate to the individual. References and suggested reading are included. Available from: Sustainable Systems Support, P.O. Box 318, Bisbee, Arizona 85603. $10.

Hay and Forage Harvesting
by the John Deere Company

The definitive book on hay and straw harvesting. Available from: John Deere Service Training Department, John Deere, Moline, Illinois. 1983.

How to Build Your Elegant Home with Straw Bales (video)
by Sustainable Systems Support

A comprehensive how-to video clearly covering all the steps in building a plastered straw bale structure. Contains clear footage, abundant illustrations, and discussion of various construction options. The video is divided into the different phases of construction which include design, foundation, bale wall raising, roof construction, and finishing. Approximately 70 minutes. Available from: Sustainable Systems Support, P.O. Box 318, Bisbee, Arizona 85603.

Straw Bale Construction (video)
by Kim Thompson

A 23-minute video detailing the Ship Harbor Project construction of a two-story, load-bearing straw bale home. The video also includes a brief history of baled construction, philosophy, as well as step-by-step technical details. Available from: Kim Thompson, RR1 Ship Harbor, Nova Scotia, Canada B0J 1Y0; (902) 845-2750. Approximately $34 Canadian.

The Last Straw
by Out on Bale

An excellent, comprehensive newsletter published quarterly. The newsletter is geared toward up-to-date information and resources for straw bale construction. Donated articles and photographs are sincerely welcomed. Available from: Out on Bale - By Mail, 1037 East Linden Street, Tucson, Arizona 85719.

"New Mexico Test Results of the Small Scale E-119 Fire Test on Uncoated Straw Bale Wall Panels and Stucco Coated Straw Bale Wall Panels and The Transverse Load Test"

Available from: Straw Bale Construction Association, P.O. Box 149, 227 Otero Street, Santa Fe, New Mexico 87504-0149. $25.

Straw Bale Building: An Introduction
by The Canelo Project

A thorough and concise booklet giving an overview of straw bale construction, its uses, construction options, and available resources. Available in French and Spanish. Available from: The Canelo Project, HC1 Box 324, Elgin, Arizona 85611. $5.

Straw Bale Construction: The Elegant Solution (video)
by Sustainable Systems Support

A 30-minute broadcast-quality production, intended to introduce, educate, and inspire people to this alternative building method. The video contains a historic overview and footage of several wall-raisings and modern-day structures, as well as interviews with owners, builders, designers, architects, and workshop participants. Available from: Sustainable Systems Support, P.O. Box 318, Bisbee, Arizona 85603. Approximately $33.

"Straw Bale Home Design Plans"
Offered through Sustainable Systems Support

Scale plans, $1/4$ inch to 1 foot, of several appropriate designs using straw bale construction. Designs include rectangular and T-shaped load-bearing (Nebraska-style) structures, and rectangular, square, U-shaped, octagonal and clerestory post-and-beam structures with bale in-fill walls. Packages include three complete sets of blueprints for the building shell, along with a materials list. Each set includes a sample floor plan, foundation, plan, elevations showing bale, window and door locations, roof framing plan, wall sections, and details. All packages available with a registered engineer's stamp, for building-code approval. Available from: Sustainable Systems Support, P.O. Box 318, Bisbee, Arizona 85603. Prices vary per packet: $200 to $400.

Straw Bale House Plans
Offered by architect Bob Lanning of Design and Building Consultants, 19 E. 15th Street, Tucson, Arizona 85701; *(602) 792-0873.

A Straw Bales/Mortar House Demonstration Project
by Louis Gagné, published by the Canada Mortgage and Housing Corporation, 1986.
A useful review of the mortared-bale method. Includes fire safety, humidity and strength testing which helped make early approval possible in some areas. Available from: Housing Technology Incentives Program, Canada Mortgage and Housing Corporation, Ottawa, Ontario, Canada K1A OP7.

"Summary of Results of a Structural Straw Bale Testing Program"
based on a master's thesis by Ghailene Bou-Ali.
Summary written and illustrated by David Eisenberg with Matts Myhrman and Judy Knox. This comprehensive, illustrated report is published by the nonprofit Community Information Resource Center (CIRC), and is available from: Out On Bale - By Mail, 1037 E. Linden, Tucson, Arizona 85719. All profits go to the Straw Bale Testing and Research Fund. $15.

MANUFACTURERS, RETAILERS, AND SERVICES RELATED TO STRAW BALE CONSTRUCTION

Bamboo Gardens
Retail and wholesale nursery selling bamboo plants, poles, fencing, garden fixtures and books. No mail-order of plants. 5016 192nd Place N.E., Redmond, Washington 98053-4602; (206) 868-5166.

Brother Sun
2907 Agua Fria, Santa Fe, New Mexico 87501; (505) 471-5157.

Central Fiber Corporation
"Woolex." Wellsville, Kansas 66092; (800) 638-0027.

Eastern Star Trading Co.
Bamboo stakes. (800) 522-0085.

Eco-Design Group
"Bioshield." 1365 Rufina Circle, Santa Fe, New Mexico 87501; (505) 438-3448.

E.M. Leonard
Bamboo stakes, burlap, plastic fence. P.O. Box 816, Piqua, Ohio 45356; (800) 543-8955.

Euro-American Trading Co.
Supplier of "Nature's Paints by Van Wyse." 400 S. 6th Street, Fairfield, Iowa 52556; (515) 472-0910.

Maine Wood Heat Co.
Construction of masonry heating and cooking stoves. RFD 1, Box 640, Norridgewock, Maine 04957; (207) 696-5442.

Midwest Faswall
Manufacturer of Faswall blocks. 404 N. Forrest Avenue, Ottumwa, Iowa 52501; (515) 682-1212.

New England Bamboo
Specializing in cold-hardy bamboos. Will ship worldwide. P.O. Box 358, Rockport, Massachusetts 01966; (503) 255-9275.

Northern Groves Bamboo - Rick Valley
Supplier of numerous varieties of bamboo including timber types. Will ship worldwide. 5629 SE Harney Drive, Portland, Oregon 97206; (503) 774-6353.

Real Goods
Nation's leading supplier of products for energy independence and sustainable living. 966 Mazzoni Street, Ukiah, California 95482-3471; (800) 762-7235; foreign orders: (707) 468-9214; FAX orders: (707) 468-0301.

Rodriguez, Anita
Consulting on earth floors, plasters and design. P.O. Box 1057, Ranchos de Taos, New Mexico 87557.

RoLanka
Supplier of coir netting made from coconut fiber. Different sizes available. Morrow, Georgia; (404) 961-0331.

Southwest Wetlands Group
Design and engineering for wetland waste water treatment systems. 1590 San Mateo Lane, Santa Fe, New Mexico 87502-6447; (505) 986-8225.

Tradewinds
Supplier of bamboo plants and books. Will ship worldwide. 28446 Hunter Creek Loop, Gold Beach, Oregon 97444; (503) 247-0835.

US&G (United States Gypsum Company)
Information booklets containing specifications related to US&G plaster products. 125 S. Franklin Street, P.O. Box 806278, Chicago, Illinois 60680-4124.

Warshall and Associates
Biological waste-water systems, watershed planning, environmental impact analysis, natural resource management. 4500 W. Speedway, Suite 7, Tucson, Arizona 85745; *(602) 624-5406.

ORGANIZATIONS OF RELATED INTEREST

American Institute of Architects
"Environmental Resource Guide" and videos. AIA, 1735 New York Ave NW, Washington, DC 20006; (202) 626 7331.

American Solar Energy Society
Excellent source of information and professional contacts. 2400 Central Avenue, G-1, Boulder, Colorado 80301; (303) 443-3130.

California Earth Art and Architecture Institute
   (CalEarth)
Founded by Iranian architect Nader Khalili to pursue research with the development of sustainable human shelter principally through earthen materials, domes and vaulted structures, and sandbags. 10177 Baldy Lane, Hesperia, California 92345; (619) 956-7533.

International Institute for Bau-Biologie and
   Ecology Inc.
Workshops and publications. P.O. Box 387, Clearwater, Florida 34615.

New Mexico Community Foundation
Bulletins and information on traditional and earth-based construction methods. P.O. Box 149, Santa Fe, New Mexico 87504; (505) 982-9521.

Rocky Mountain Institute
Information on energy efficiency, environmental design. 1739 Snowmass Creek Road, Snowmass, Colorado 81654-9199; (303) 927-3851.

ANNOTATED BIBLIOGRAPHY

ALTERNATIVE MATERIALS AND METHODS

Dadd, D.L. *Non-toxic, Natural and Earthwise*. Earthwise Consumer Guide, 1993. Dadd has helped uncover problems with building-induced sickness, and provides strategies to avoid it.

Grandjean, E. *Ergonomics of the Home*. New York, New York: Halstead Press, 1974. Very good information and research on building design, with people in mind.

Harland, Edward. *Eco-Renovation*. White River Junction, Vermont: Chelsea Green Publishing Company, 1994. Renovating homes in a ecological manner. An excellent resource for those considering a retrofit to an existing building.

Janssen, Jules J.A. *Building with Bamboo*. London, England: Intermediate Technology Publications, 1988. Basic guidelines to building with bamboo.

Khalili, Nader. *Ceramic Houses and Earth Architecture*. San Francisco, California: Harper & Row, Publishers, 1990. This work covers the basic principles of dome and vault construction in addition to ceramic and earth structures.

Laporte, Robert. *Mooseprint*. Natural House Building Center, 1992. A simple but thorough guide to cob (straw-clay) construction.

Lewis, Daphne. *Bamboo on the Farm*. Bamboo Gardens, 1993. An excellent guide to planting and propagating bamboo.

Oliver, Paul. *Dwellings: The House Across the World*. Austin, Texas: University of Texas Press, 1988. A definitive book on vernacular architecture.

Real Goods Solar Living Sourcebook: The Complete Guide to Renewable Energy Technologies and Sustainable Living. White River Junction, Vermont: Chelsea Green Publishing Company, 1994. Product guide and reference book on all aspects of independent living.

Stulz, R. *Appropriate Building Materials*. London, England: Intermediate Technology Publications, 1981. A global review of appropriate building materials; enough for the adventurous to get started.

Tibbets, Joseph M. *The Earthbuilder's Encyclopedia*. Southwest Solaradobe School, 1989. The master alphabetical reference for adobe and rammed earth.

Vale, Brenda and Robert. *Green Architecture*. Boston, Massachusetts: Little, Brown and Company, 1991.

BUILDING

Alexander, Christopher; Sara Ishikawa, and Murray Silverstein. *A Pattern Language*. New York, New York: Oxford University Press, 1977. An excellent guide for the professional as well as the owner-builder. Provides a language for building and planning by describing detailed patterns for towns and neighborhoods, houses, gardens, and rooms.

Fine Homebuilding. *Foundations and Masonry*. Newton, Connecticut: Taunton Press, 1990. An excellent and comprehensive guide to an assortment of topics.

Fine Homebuilding. *Frame Carpentry*. Newton, Connecticut: Taunton Press, 1990. Includes articles on roof framing and other carpentry subjects.

Kern, Ken. *The Owner Built Home*. New York, New York: Charles Scribner's Sons, 1975.

Roskind, R. *Before You Build*. Berkeley, California: Ten Speed Press, 1983. A thorough guide to site preparation and mental preparations for building. Highly recommended.

Seddon, Leigh. *Practical Pole Construction*. Charlotte, Vermont: Williamson Publishing Co., 1985.

Wing, C. and J. Cole. *From the Ground Up*. Cornerstone Builders, 1976. A favorite book on the basics of building and foundations.

Wolfe, Ralph. *Low-Cost Pole Building Construction*. A Garden Way Publication, 1993.

SOLAR/CLIMATICALLY ADAPTED DESIGN

Fanger, P.O. *Thermal Comfort*. New York, New York: McGraw Hill, 1972. This book may be a bit technical for some, but it provides a good introduction to understanding what helps make us comfortable.

Gipe, Paul. *Wind Power for Home and Business: Renewable Energy for the 1990s and Beyond*. White River Junction, Vermont: Chelsea Green Publishing Company, 1993. A complete reference on modern wind energy machines for homes as well as larger installations.

Mazzaria, Edward. *The Passive Solar Energy Book*. Emmaus, Pennsylvania: Rodale Press, 1979. A primer, source book, and workbook on designing an effective passive-solar-heated building.

Neubauer, L.W. "Optimum Alleviation of Solar Stress on Model Buildings." *Transactions*, American Society of Agricultural Engineers 15 (1):129-132, 1972. Some elegant work on solar/climatic design.

Olgyay, V. *Design with Climate*. Princeton, New Jersey: Princeton University Press, 1992, 1963. This is a delightful pioneering work.

Passive Solar Industries Council. *Passive Solar Design Strategies: Guidelines for Home Builders*. PSIC, 1511 K Street, NW, Suite 600, Washington, DC 20005; (202) 628-7400. One of the best resources for passive-solar design, containing guidelines for 228 different climatic regions in the United States.

Potts, Michael. *The Independent Home: Living Well with Power from the Sun, Wind, and Water*. White River Junction, Vermont: Chelsea Green Publishing Company. Detailed discussion of photovoltaics and other home energy systems.

Bainbridge, D., J. Hofacre, and J. Corbett. *Village Homes Solar House Designs*. Emmaus, Pennsylvania: Rodale Press, 1978. This 200-unit solar development in Davis, California, shows that eco-friendly neighborhoods work.

PAINTS AND WALL FINISHES

Gwynn, Kate, and Annie Sloan. *Classic Paints and Faux Finishes*. Pleasantville, New York: Readers Digest, 1993. An excellent reference on using natural materials to create paints and wall finishes.

Innes, Jocasta. *The New Paint Magic*. New York, New York: Pantheon Books, 1992. A complete guide to finishing everything from walls to floors, woodwork, and furniture.

PERIODICALS

Earthword: The Journal of Environmental and Social Responsibility. EOS Institute, 580 Broadway, Suite 200, Laguna Beach, California 92651. Particularly notable is issue no. 5 of this journal, which features sustainable and indigenous architecture.

EcoBuilding Times. NW EcoBuilding Guild, 217 Ninth Avenue North, Seattle, Washington 98109.

Environmental Building News. RR 1, Box 161, Brattleboro, Vermont 05301. A bimonthly newsletter on environmentally sustainable design and construction.

Fine Homebuilding. Excellent articles on construction; well-indexed. Often high-end costs, but reviews and in-depth reports are excellent.

Home Power Magazine. For independent home power systems and eco-technology.

The Journal of Light Construction. P.O. Box 869, Mt. Morris, Illinois 61054. Geared to everyday design issues. Very useful, perhaps best for people with some building experience.

An Invitation for Reader Response

In writing this book we have tried to present it as a broad and representative collection of what others have done in the process of creating bale buildings in a variety of conditions and climates. At the same time we have tried to present our own biases as directly and honestly as possible while attempting to allow our readers sufficient room to differ with them. We have made an effort to give this book a spirit of open dialogue and communication.

We would like to encourage further communication in response to this book or any other subject that is pertinent to, or compatible with, bale construction. We are interested in:

— Comments you have about this book pertaining to omissions, mistakes, clarifications needed, and opinions with which you disagree.

— Bale design and building ideas you have that might improve or add to what has been outlined in this book.

— Bale building projects that you have been involved with or know about that you think might be of interest to us.

— Natural-design strategies, techniques, and materials you feel would be compatible with bale construction.

Please reply to the authors through:

The Canelo Project
HC1 Box 324
Elgin, Arizona 85611

In that we are a small organization and have little idea of how much response will result from this request, we might not find it possible to respond to all the correspondence we receive. We will, however, do our best. If you would like to be included on our mailing list and remain informed of our activities and projects, please let us know.

INDEX

The Straw Bale House was designed by Ann Aspell, and set in ITC Galliard and Baker Signet. The floor plans and other illustrations were done by Athena Swentzell Steen. The text pages were printed on 70-pound Finch Opaque vellum; the color section was printed on Ikonorex Gloss; and the cover was printed on Champion Kromekote. All of the papers in this book are acid-free, and the cover and inserts are made with recycled fibers. The cover and color sections were printed by Whitman Communications Group and the text pages were printed by Capital City Press.